The Middle East in Soviet Policy

R.D. McLaurin
The American Institutes
for Research

Lexington Books
D.C. Heath and Company
Lexington, Massachusetts
Toronto   London

Library of Congress Cataloging in Publication Data

McLaurin, Ronald D., 1944-
The Middle East in Soviet policy.

Bibliography: p.
Includes index.
1. Russia—Foreign relations—Near East. 2. Near East—
Foreign relations—Russia. I. Title.
DS63.2.R9M33   327.47'056   74-31715
ISBN 0-669-98285-7

Copyright © 1975 by D.C. Heath and Company

Reproduction in whole or in part permitted for any purpose of the United States Government.

Published simultaneously in Canada

Printed in the United States of America

International Standard Book Number: 0-669-98285-7

Library of Congress Catalog Card Number: 74-31715

To all my parents

Contents

List of Tables

Preface

Since the Soviet Union figuratively hurdled the Northern Tier through arms agreements with Egypt and Syria, many observers in the West (and, indeed, in the Middle East) have expressed alarm over the Soviet Middle East presence. Yet, too few studies have considered the broad range of regional activities undertaken by the Soviet Union, while too many have employed polemics or ideology to arrive at their conclusions. The present study, then, is an attempt to analyze in as disinterested a fashion as possible Soviet interests, objectives, and policies across the whole breadth of Soviet actions in the Middle East.

This work owes much in conceptual origin to Mr. Robert Allen, at one time with the Department of Defense and presently with the Gulf Oil Corporation, and Paul A. Jureidini who served as project director. Its focus was refined in discussions with Thomas Donahue, Robert Kubal, and James Timberlake, all of whom served with the Office of the Assistant Secretary of Defense (International Security Affairs). To all of these individuals, the author wishes to express his gratitude. Ultimate design of the study was the responsibility of the project director, the author, and Mohammed Mughisuddin.

Throughout preparation of this study, the author benefitted from the assistance and counsel of a number of persons, only a few of whom can be acknowledged here. I would particularly like to express my appreciation to my colleagues, Paul Jureidini, M. Mughisuddin, William Hazen, Susan Haseltine, and Sally Skillings of the American Institutes for Research; and to Edward Azar, University of North Carolina; Larry L. Fabian, The Brookings Institution; Peter Gubser, Ford Foundation; Robert Kubal, Alfred B. Prados, James Timberlake, all in the Office of the Assistant Secretary of Defense (International Security Affairs); William B. Quandt, University of Pennslyvania, and Abdul Aziz Said, American University; Edward Schaefer, Department of State; Samuel Sharp, American University; and Leo Tansky, Central Intelligence Agency. I should also like to express my thanks to Arnold Horelick for permission to quote material from his *Soviet Middle East Policy: Origins and Prospects*. Although each of these individuals has aided in one or more sections of this study, the author is of course solely responsible for all errors of fact or judgment appearing herein.

A draft of the study on which this book is based was originally completed in March 1973. Developments since that date have been incorporated where possible. The research leading to the writing of this book was originally sponsored by the Office of the Assistant Secretary of Defense

(International Security Affairs) under contract DAHC-15-C-72-0280. The conclusions of this study are those of the author and should not be construed to represent the policies of the United States Government or the views of the American Institutes for Research.

**Part I
Soviet Policy in the
Middle East**

1 Soviet Foreign Objectives: Framework for a Middle East Policy

Introduction

In the study of foreign policy, one assumption is always made—at least until more dependable data provide a safer explanation—and that is the assumption of rationality. This study is necessarily subject to error introduced by the same assumption. That rationality must be presumed for the purpose of analysis is clear: irrational policy formulation precludes rational analysis (though not necessarily rational description).

At the same time, it should be recognized that an assumption of rationality is ipso facto fallacious. Decision makers, qua people, are not automatons. People are not capable of constant and "objective" analysis before the initiation of every policy or action. (Indeed, if we were, the numbers of actions taken in our daily lives would be very few.) Moreover, our knowledge of the circumstances within which or in response to which we must act is often imperfect. More important yet, from the analyst's point of view, the ingredients of the policy process are usually far too complex for a non-participant to reconstruct, much less describe. Even when the writer is identical with the decisive voice in the policy system, that process is dependent on other perceptions, on cultural forces conducing to or conditioning those perceptions, and on acts perhaps unperceived by those in the system, so that perfect verisimilitude remains elusive.

As if these limitations on policy analysis were not enough, the study of Soviet foreign policy has been encumbered with a struggle unique unto itself.[1] In place of the traditional quarrel between macro-analysis (the anarchic international system as a whole determines the foreign policy of its constituent elements, i.e., individual states) and micro-analysis (the internal forces and resources of a state determine its foreign policy), a debate between micro-analysts has characterized Soviet studies since World War II. Is Soviet foreign policy determined by communism? By the totalitarian nature of the Soviet state? Or, by the resolution of conflict among competing elements in the Soviet Union? This is not the forum in which to resolve such a debate. For our purposes, it is only important to recognize that the "The Sources of Soviet Conduct," as George Kennan phrased it in his famous "X" article a quarter century ago,[2] are still disputed. It will become evident that recent developments in the literature of foreign policy analysis[3] have great relevance to the particular subject of this study, for we believe the role and perceptions of several major interest groups to be important, perhaps decisive in the development of Soviet policy in the Middle East.

Soviet global policy is important in the context of this study, because—assuming reason governs policy to some degree—regional interests must be perceived and policies developed and implemented in such a way that they support the attainment of higher priority objectives. Since the Soviet Union is not a Middle East state, one would not expect the most important Soviet global objectives to be oriented toward Middle East matters. Yet, at the same time, since the USSR is a great power, its major interests and objectives, influencing as they do Soviet actions in world politics, have often had some long- or short-term effects on the Middle East. Many writers have pointed to what they identify as historical Russian interests in the Middle East.[4] Without denying that geographical and other more or less rigid constraints have resulted in intermittent Russian activism in the area, the sharp—and, some would argue, brief—discontinuity of policy after the establishment of Bolshevik power suggests this date is substantially distinct and, therefore, appropriate as at least one of the proverbial watersheds of Soviet policy.

The First Two Decades of the Soviet State, 1919–1939

The first priority of any state at any time is self-preservation. For the Russian regime newly installed after the overthrow of the Czarist government, security was a particularly complex requirement. Large areas of territory previously under Russian dominion or domination were no longer subject to Russian administrative control. Some areas were under the sway of Russian forces hostile to the Bolsheviks; some seceded from Russia; and, later, some Russian lands were under military occupation as a result of half-hearted and ill-fated foreign invasions. Large portions of the country still nominally under Russian control were in fact totally isolated from the national administration.

The Soviet Union moved to establish control over its far-flung territory as soon as possible. Although this was an essentially domestic effort, Soviet security policy had several important external manifestations. The first priority in this context was the establishment of good—or, at least, stable—relations with foreign powers, particularly bordering countries. Good relations were necessary both to preclude further intervention and to support economic rehabilitation.

The Middle East was generally outside primary Soviet interests in the early years. Nevertheless, even while insurgent armies threatened Moscow, the Soviet government, endeavoring to secure the southern flank from foreign presence, renounced the sphere of interest (established under the Czars) in the northern half of Iran (then Persia) and later concluded treaties with Riza Shah and Mustapha Kemal Pasha (Ataturk). These tactical moves towards traditional rulers hardly supported communism: they were intended to backstop Soviet security through an alliance with potential Western enemies. Indeed, while Soviet–Persian relations stagnated on all but the commercial front, Soviet–Turkish relations were close throughout much of this period.[5] Politically, then, borders were to be secured while the Soviet government reached a point of complete internal control. Economically, good relations were even more essential. Stability in foreign relations conduced to rebuilding the war- and revolution-shattered economy. Moreover, foreign expertise and capital were in vital need—both for reconstruction and for the industrial development to which the communist regime was dedicated.

At the same time, the USSR made agreements with a number of "capitalist" states after World War I by forswearing intervention in their domestic affairs, but at no time promising to halt "private" revolutionary movements since these were theoretically outside Soviet control. Meanwhile, an effort was launched to "compartmentalize" millenarian communism—that is, to organize it and bring it under the control of the Soviet state. The technique was the Comintern, established to oversee, support, and coordinate fledgling communist parties abroad. The Comintern initially consisted of groups existing largely on paper, but later, real communist parties grew in every area of the world. From the beginning, and through various doctrinal and policy changes, Moscow—the world's self-proclaimed leader of Marxism—subordinated international communist policy to Soviet interests.[6]

Throughout the pre-World War II years, the United Kingdom was considered the primary threat to Soviet interests. Therefore, the USSR endeavored to establish relations with those who opposed the British. This led to cooperative relations not only with neighbors to the immediate south, but even with such backwaters of traditional social order and political conservatism as Yemen and Saudi Arabia. In both countries in the 1920s, the Soviet Union made an effort to support rulers struggling against the British.[7]

Similarly, Lenin recognized the potential diversion of enemy resources that might result if colonial unrest could be enlisted to support Soviet anti–British policy. Therefore, he committed the Comintern and, to some extent Soviet policy itself, to the support of anticolonial movements in the underdeveloped world.

Several decades later, Soviet support took on a characteristic material face. In those early years of the new regime, however, when resources were inadequate even to meet the crushing internal needs of the Soviet Union, verbal support was of necessity as far as the USSR could go towards helping budding nationalist forces.

Thus, although Soviet objectives from 1919 to 1939 dealt with immediate security requirements such as those in Turkey and Persia, they did not eschew a small degree of foreign affairs involvement in colonial areas such as the Arab Middle East.

Postwar Soviet Foreign Policy Objectives, 1945–1953

For the purposes of this study we have omitted discussion of Soviet objectives during World War II. In spite of much speculation concerning Nazi–Soviet plans for mapping out the areas of possible Soviet expansion, these talks were undertaken at German initiative and with a view to discouraging known primary Soviet interest in the West. Such discussions, particularly under the sui generis conditions prevailing in 1940, are an insufficient foundation on which to assess Soviet objectives at a later date. Instead, it is to the Soviet strategic position in the immediate aftermath of World War II and during the onset of the cold war years that attention should be drawn.

Once again, in 1945 the Soviet Union found itself rebuilding from a costly war that would have left a lesser country effete. Much of the Second World War had been fought on Russian soil, and the USSR had suffered far greater casualties than any other combatant. Yet, from this holocaust, the Soviet Union emerged as indisputably the second most powerful country on earth. As a result of the war, the Soviet economy required reconstruction in order to return to its path of development. As a result of the war, too, however, the Soviet Union came to dominate most of Eastern Europe.

The foreign policy of the USSR after the war continued to be determined by immediate security considerations. However, the world conflagration had fundamentally altered the nature of these concerns. Apart from reconstruction needs, Soviet security was influenced in 1945 and 1946 by rapidly deteriorating relations with its wartime allies and by the effort to consolidate gains in Eastern Europe. As the United States increasingly took the lead among the Western nations in opposing the Soviet Union, the need to develop nuclear weaponry became evident. Russian war doctrine during the early postwar years assumed general war with the United States and other major countries of Western Europe. There was no planning for limited war. Within four years, the USSR had developed an atomic bomb and within eight, the hydrogen bomb. These developments must have been considered vital to Stalin and his military establishment.

The above is not to indicate that Moscow's foreign relations exemplified fear before its development of nuclear weapons. Indeed, the immediate postwar period was the era in which Soviet control over nearby areas enjoyed its greatest growth: most of Eastern Europe, northern Korea, and large areas of China and Vietnam came under the domination of Soviet-controlled or Soviet-influenced regimes. The Baltic states, Tannu Tuva, Bessarabia, and parts of Germany, Finland, Poland, Czechoslovakia, and Japan were integrated into the USSR. So far as the Middle East is concerned, Moscow's actions in Iran and Turkey bespoke temerity more than trepidation. However, when confronted by Western opposition at a level likely to rekindle general war, the Soviets backed down.[a] The consistency of Soviet modus operandi in this respect suggests that the policy of expansion and increasing Russian influence was married in an eminently rational way to the "sound propaganda line of minimizing the importance of the new weapon."[8]

From Soviet actions, then, it can be deduced that the overriding objectives of Soviet foreign policy from 1945 until about the time of Stalin's death in 1953 were (1) rebuilding the Soviet economy and (2) safeguarding Soviet security through (a) consolidation in Eastern Europe, (b) development of conventional[b] and nuclear strategic power, (c) establishment of Soviet influence in border areas not under Moscow's control, and (d) above all, prevention of the outbreak of a general war with the United States. In addition, Soviet relations with the United States and Western Europe during this period indicate a concerted effort to secure recognition as a great power, and, even more, as one of the two dominant powers in the world with all the perquisites such status implies.

The postwar world was characterized by a growing number of new actors in international politics. The 1947 speech by Zhdanov, often referred to as evidence that the Soviets believed only two camps could exist in the world, was important in party activities, particularly outside the USSR. But the speech itself does not reject collaboration with all African and Asian regimes, as allusions to it generally imply. Indeed, Zhdanov named specific pro–Soviet regimes and others "sympathizing with" the socialist countries.[9] (The latter included Egypt and Syria.) Continued

---

[a]Unofficial pressure, however, did not respond in a similar manner. Soviet propaganda has always shown an ability to diverge from the official policy line where such a divergence supports Soviet interests. Even in the 1920s, when relations with Iran and Turkey were sometimes warm, if it was clear propaganda media would not disturb this warmth, the attacks on the "reactionary" regimes of Ataturk and Riza Shah were numerous. Moreover, the facile assumption in the West after 1946 that opposition movements closely associated with or subservient to local communist parties acted only on orders from Moscow is now recognized to have been simplistic even at that time, which explains another segment of the divergence from solidarity with Soviet policy.

[b]It should be pointed out, however, that Soviet military manpower *declined* from 1945 to 1948.

emphasis was placed on support of anti–Western groups, particularly liberation movements in colonial areas, and local communist parties. Due to the economic situation, however, the support continued to be verbal only. Given the date of the Zhdanov address, it is hardly surprising so few overseas regimes were seen as sympathetic, for the speech antedated the fruits of the decolonization movement by some time. While several new countries had been granted independence, nationalism was just gathering momentum in most of the developing areas. Communist party and front organizations were probably the optimum investments at this moment.

Stalin to Khrushchev, 1953–1962

By the time of Stalin's death, several major changes were already underway in Soviet politics. Potential successors had been jockeying for position over some time. Concurrently and associated with this struggle, rival politico-military philosophies confronted each other more or less openly (at least for Soviet society).[10]

The political world outside the USSR had also gone through a considerable transformation. First, most of the important countries of Western Europe had established the North Atlantic Treaty Organization (NATO), which after an initial period of dormancy had developed into a genuine military alliance, and this was not the only alliance aimed at the Soviet Union. Indeed, the United States, as Western leader in the "cold war," was in the process of establishing a series of alliance systems along the periphery of the USSR. Second, since the war, the number of newly independent countries had continued to grow. More important, perhaps, the effectiveness of nationalist groups within the remaining colonies—which were still numerous—had increased markedly. Third, in the same year that Stalin died, the Soviet Union exploded its first hydrogen bomb. Fourth, military aid to China included support for the development of Chinese nuclear technology. Fifth, the Soviet economy, rebuilt after the war, was expanding to such a degree that economic resources would soon cease to represent the major impediment to constrain foreign affairs activities.

From 1953 to 1962, then, foreign policy focused upon ensuring Soviet security through (1) maintenance of the international status quo in Eastern Europe, (2) the prevention of war (synonymous with nuclear war in Soviet doctrine) with the United States, and (3) the undermining of Western alliances. Another major goal derived from the rapidly evolving colonial situation—that is, attracting support from the developing areas. A third objective was to move from world recognition of the Soviet Union as a great power, now clearly achieved, to recognition of the *legitimacy* of the Soviet Union as a great power.

Ensuring Soviet Security

Only one threat to Soviet security existed in 1953: a conflict with the United States. In the case of such a conflict, the very survival of the Soviet state would be in doubt. The USSR had tested a hydrogen bomb in 1953, only one year after the United States had. Both countries were working on early stages of missile delivery systems. In the context of its alliance systems and individual agreements, the United States had begun to expand its base system ringing Soviet territory. From these bases, virtually all important centers of the Soviet Union were vulnerable to attack from American aircraft.

Clearly, then, a major Soviet objective was to undermine the U.S. alliance system without, however, resorting to acts that might result in war with the United States. As before, Soviet doctrine indicated general nuclear war to be the only form hostilities with America could take. Since the USSR now had "the bomb," however, a greater appreciation of its power was evident in public statements. Indeed, whereas earlier the USSR had minified the importance of nuclear weapons, during the 1953–1962 period the Kremlin threatened—or implied the possibility of—their use in several cases. (The most noteworthy in the context of this study was the 1956 Suez crisis.) This era roughly coincides with a period of concentration on global (strategic) rather than local military force. Naval matters were not generally discussed in Soviet statements.

Soon after Stalin's death, the competing would-be successors became associated with several varied strategic alternatives. The victorious group, headed by Nikita Khrushchev, supported the most militant policy option: neither temporary appeasement nor acceptance of the status quo, but, instead, a political offensive in the developing areas combined with a temporary armistice in the industrialized northern hemisphere while the USSR moved toward nuclear superiority.[11]

Third World Support

The southern hemisphere, or the "Third World," appeared the most likely area for Soviet inroads. The significant anti–Western element in which many nationalist movements resulted; the determination of the elites in these areas to develop their societies as rapidly as possible; and the desire not to take sides in the East–West conflict, or, if sides had to be chosen, to choose the winner—all of these circumstances propelled the Kremlin toward greater involvement.

What, on the other hand, could the USSR expect from the new countries? Even if many of them had become allies, it would not have altered the strategic situation vis-à-vis the United States very much. We believe that support for any movement that would weaken the West in any way—that might erode the unity of Europe to any degree—was the original objective. Certainly, support for anticolonial countries and movements had this capability. After the first few years, this policy may have gathered a momentum of its own much as its counterpart did in U.S. thinking. For although gains were registered in specific areas—and most prominently in the Middle East—the USSR continued to support the almost unqualified pursuit of this policy in all developing areas until about 1967 or 1968.

The prime sub-objectives of the goal of attracting support from developing areas were (1) identification of the Soviet Union with the anticolonial movement; (2) identification of Western alliances and powers, especially the United States, with colonialism; (3) establishment of cooperative relations with all but the most pro–Western regimes; and (4) widespread perception of the USSR as a friend of developing countries.

Soviet Legitimacy

One positive result of better relations with the emerging states—a result that contributed to the attainment of a discrete but related objective—was the increased legitimacy of the Soviet Union as a great power. For over a decade after 1945, the USSR was recognized as one of the two superpowers, but it was also an outcast. Close ties between a number of the countries granted independence soon after World War II and their previous suzerains prolonged this isolation. Indeed, almost any initiative dealing with otherwise apolitical matters in the United Nations was condemned to a premature death if the USSR proposed it or, often, even supported it. As a result of this image, friendly, cooperative relations with countries outside Eastern Europe and the communist regimes in East and Southeast Asia were virtually impossible to maintain. Regimes that dealt with the Soviet Union were in danger of being overthrown, by virtue of either their own instability or external machination. In any event, the countries in which such regimes acceded to power tended to be of only marginal importance in the international political order.

Not until after the Suez and Hungarian crises of 1956 did dealing with the Soviet Union become respectable. Thus, by the early 1960s the Soviets had achieved their objective of legitimacy. Similarly, the modest short-term goals of Soviet Third World activity had been accomplished: Most of the new countries proclaimed themselves neutral in the cold war, and most accepted Soviet offers of diplomatic relations at face value.

Khrushchev and After, 1962–1972

Although the ascendancy of Nikita Khrushchev as Soviet premier and CPSU chairman was to last until 1964, the seeds of his political destruction were sowed earlier. After a number of Soviet–American confrontations at various points around the world, the Cuban crisis of October 1962 marked a pronounced turning point. It contributed to the alteration of the Kremlin's military priorities for the next decade. It reduced the Soviet vulnerability to missiles on the Turkish front. It resulted in a greater degree of security for the Castro regime. But above all, the Cuban missile crisis was widely perceived as a clearcut defeat for the Soviet Union. This event, rapidly deteriorating Russian relations with China, and recurrent agricultural failures led to Khrushchev's demise.

In general, Soviet strategy envisaged achieving strategic parity with (or then superiority over)[c] the United States in the 1960s and 1970s. The missile crisis preceded the rapid development of the navy as a means of increasing Soviet local power. The Cuban crisis had shown that strategic power sufficient to create a stand-off left the decisive power in the hands of the country most able to bring local force to bear at a moment of crisis. The Soviet Union had already begun a program to develop its navy. The importance of this decision as well as the fact that non-nuclear confrontations between the superpowers were more likely than nuclear war were both underscored by the Cuban crisis. (In the mid-1960s, the imminent development of the Polaris A2, which would be able to target major Soviet cities from the Mediterranean, was probably seminal in the decision to deploy a Soviet naval squadron in the Mediterranean Sea.[12])

A second objective of this era concerned the Western alliances. No longer was a short-term goal merely to reduce their effectiveness. Rather, by the mid-1960s, the Soviet Union could aspire to breaking up these blocs, at least for all practical military purposes. France's disenchantment with NATO was increasingly evident long before its withdrawal from the organization. Turkey and Greece clearly had doubts (for some years) as to the relevance of NATO to their own interests after the British left Cyprus. The Baghdad Pact, by now CENTO, was never able to attract Arab countries to membership. The single exception, Iraq, which gave its capital's name to the alliance, left precipitously after the 1958 coup that ended the Hashemite Kingdom in Iraq and brought to power a vociferously anti–Western regime. (Indeed, many incorrectly attribute the presence of the USSR in the Middle East to the Baghdad Pact.) SEATO, characterized by temporization and reluctance from the start, had never really got off the ground; after 1965, it was moribund. (Post-facto invocations of SEATO obligations by the United States in terms of its involvement in Vietnam had a distinctly hollow ring.) Each of these alliances, because of its multilateral nature, had countries more and less susceptible to détente with the USSR.

Another "alliance" was breaking up in 1962, for it was not until the 1960s that signs of friction between China and the USSR began to receive

---

[c]The debate over Soviet naval objectives continues; see Chapters 2 and 6 of this volume.

attention. In fact, the uneasiness was sensed in the late 1950s by Peking and Moscow. But so deeply ingrained in Western observers was the concept of monolithic communism[d] that the few early signals of tension went largely unnoticed. Nationalism had struck blows against an unpopular regime, for example, in 1956—Hungary. Nationalism, in fact, was a force throughout Eastern Europe. The Chinese, too, took their own path by following Chinese interests as they saw them. As a result, the 1960s witnessed increasing verbal and in some cases even small-scale military conflicts between China and the Soviet Union. No longer was China Moscow's ally; indeed, a significant Soviet military force was stationed around or designated for defense against China. Thus, an important objective of foreign policy was the containment of China. In this goal, the Soviet Union had the intermittent help of the Chinese leadership, which was far from consistent in its overseas interests and involvements.

Containment of China did not, however, supersede competition with the West, as we have pointed out. On the other hand, by greatly increasing the ends in the pursuit of which Soviet foreign resources might be expended, the emergence of the Sino–Soviet dispute probably contributed to the articulation of more modest goals as regards the West and to a conclusion that a modus vivendi should be reached in areas of high conflict potential and in areas of lowest priority to Soviet interests. The important point is that containment of China must go hand in hand with containment of the United States, not take its place.

In view of the great dissimilarities between China and the United States, the Soviet containment approach to each is essentially different. Containment of the United States means stabilizing the politico-military situation in areas of competition where the United States stands to advance (relative to the USSR); consolidating Soviet influence to exclude, as far as practicable, U.S. interests and influence in areas where the USSR has become or is becoming the predominant external power; and gently harrassing the United States in those areas where neither country wishes to extend itself or where the United States is the predominant influence but is vulnerable. Containment of China involves the more systematic and reactive policy (similar to that employed by the United States towards the Soviet Union from 1948 to about 1960s) of excluding foreign intercourse with China and all forms of Chinese influence everywhere outside the Chinese mainland except southeast Asia.

---

[d]Yugoslavia was always an anomaly. Once again, though, its marginal importance conduced to simplistic, if accurate, situational explanations that evaded the principal implications for Soviet imperialism.

Summary

From 1917 when the Bolsheviks seized power in Russia and commenced a somewhat isolationist period in Soviet foreign policy until about 1962 when many of the Soviet Union's initial post–World War II objectives had been attained, the USSR was a revolutionary regime. It sought to safeguard its own security through promoting unrest against hostile regimes in their own countries and in their overseas possessions, protectorates, and spheres of influence. Its pronouncements and involvements were directed against the status quo and were driven by interest both in revolution and in establishing Soviet security. Resources, however, were devoted almost exclusively to "socialism in one country"—that is, to Soviet development. By the 1960s when the Soviet Union had a zone of exclusive influence in Eastern Europe, was recognized and accepted as a legitimate superpower throughout the world, and perceived politico-military threats from communist and other revolutionary regimes at least as great as those posed by the West, a noticeable status quo element made itself felt in Soviet foreign policy.

These currents in the global policy of the USSR could not but ramify on Soviet policy in the Middle East.

2

Soviet Regional Objectives in the Middle East

Introduction: Importance of the Middle East

In the context of our examination of Soviet foreign policy worldwide, Soviet interest in the international political evolution of the so-called Third World (i.e., the developing areas) was indicated. However, Moscow's policy has long manifested a greater willingness to become involved in the Middle East than elsewhere. Why?

The most obvious reason for Soviet interest in the Middle East is geographical. Although the West has been loath to accept this principle, it is a fact of geography that the Soviet Union is a Middle East power in a way that the United States is not. The borders of the USSR are very close to the Mediterranean; the Black Sea coast of the USSR is vulnerable to naval operations from the Mediterranean; more graphically, the oilfields of Baku are closer to Iraq's, the Persian Gulf's, and far closer to Iran's oilfields than Cairo is; and Cairo is closer to Soviet territory than it is to the capitals of Sudan, Saudi Arabia, either Yemen, Oman, the Union of Arab Emirates, Qatar, Bahrain, or Iran, not to mention Libya or the rest of the Maghreb. Thus, while the Soviet Union is "external" to the area by the judgments of scholars and Western diplomats alike, the proximity of the Middle East and therefore its relevance to the defense of the USSR cannot help influencing Soviet decision making.[a]

A second feature of the Middle East in Russian policy is geographic location with respect to the rest of the world. While the USSR is not as affected by this consideration as are, for example, Italy, Yugoslavia, or Turkey, nevertheless the eastern Mediterranean is a major outlet for Soviet activities in the rest of the world. This is true not only from the point of view of commerce, but also in terms of cultural and non-governmental relations.

The value of the Middle East is considerably enhanced as well by the economic resources of the region. Although oil is the most prominent of these resources, there are several others also found in abundance in the Middle East. Of particular interest to the Soviet Union, even in the face of

---

[a]Indeed, one can only be impressed with the rather relaxed attitude taken by Moscow in the years when the Mediterranean was an exclusively Western military preserve, and a highly fortified one at that.

plentiful Soviet resources of both, are the two energy sources—oil and natural gas.

Finally, the political importance of the Middle East among the nonaligned countries is noteworthy. Middle East states have enjoyed a level of prestige far greater than that of much of the Third World. If swaying the opinion of the developing areas is important—and both superpowers, whether justified or not, have acted as if it is—the prominence of the Middle East states in these circles cannot be overlooked.

Of course, the single greatest element of importance in the Middle East for the Soviet Union may well be the denial of the economic and geographical resources of the area to the West. Without Middle East oil, for example, the long-term military effectiveness of many of the countries hostile to the USSR would be seriously undermined. Without bases in the Mediterranean and overflight rights in adjacent countries, military and naval operations inimical to Soviet interests and Soviet security would be made significantly more difficult.

In spite of all of the above, a dispassionate analysis must conclude that, at least for the present, the Middle East is not vital to the USSR. For all its undeniable importance, the Middle East was generally inhospitable to Soviet activities from 1948 to 1955 while the Soviet Union went through a period of rapid consolidation and growth in economic, political, and military power. Technological developments notwithstanding (see Chapter 6), the relevance of the Middle East to Soviet strategic defense seems marginal in view of the circumstances in which a nuclear war would take place. Most probably, Moscow's bureaucracy, not noticeably immune to the ills of decision making that plague other capitals, evaluates the Middle East as "vital" now that Soviet presence in the area is established. However, when the chips are down, operational evaluation would probably indicate that although the Middle East is among the most important foreign regions for Soviet activities, it is not vital.

Political Objectives

Soviet Goals in the Middle East

As we have pointed out above, many writers attempt to link current Soviet activities in the Middle East with centuries-old aspirations in that direction, the "search for warm-water ports," and the like. In fact, the reasons for Soviet interest have varied, but expansion of Russian influence in the region has often held potential rewards because of the geographical proximity of the Middle East to Russia. Thus, while interest in the region may have remained more or less high, the reasons for that interest have altered as economic, political, and military developments dictated.

Soviet Objectives, 1919–1939. The most important goal sought in the Middle East after the 1917 revolution was the reestablishment of an area of security to the south. To this end, treaties were signed with the governments of Afghanistan and Persia, and friendly relations were established with Turkey. Particularly in the case of Persia, the concessions made by the USSR[1] illustrate the weight placed upon what might be called the "Soviet Good Neighbor" policy in the area during this period. While the support by Moscow of Ataturk and Riza Shah in their foreign relations[b] was unstinting in the early 1920s, at the same time efforts to move the two dictators even further from the West were conditioned by the necessity to reconstruct and preserve good relations with the West.[2] One important part of the secure southern frontier Moscow sought was control over the Black Sea. Both the Soviet Union and Turkey were dissatisfied with the provisions of the Treaty of Lausanne (1923) governing the Straits. Eventually, in 1936, the Montreux Convention established a new set of conditions that recognized Turkish control, Russian right of egress with few (but important) restrictions, and, in effect, Soviet naval dominance in the Black Sea. At the same time, the changes introduced to the provisions concerning the Straits brought to an end important mutual interests of Turkey and the USSR.

The second regional political objective—encouragement of anti–Western, especially, anti–British, regimes—coincided, then, with the first. To the immediate south, it entailed promotion of good relations with the Kemalist and Riza Shah regimes in Turkey and Persia, respectively, at least as far as their opposition to the West was concerned. In the other countries of the Middle East it meant backing similar governments (e.g., those of King Saud and Imam Yahya in the Arabian peninsula) and promoting "every national revolutionary movement against imperialism."[3] Communist parties were also founded in many areas of the Middle East in the 1920s, but most had little or no popular support throughout the interwar years (see below). The low level of Soviet commitment to the area is a proper reflection of its significance to Russian diplomacy during this period.

Soviet Objectives, 1945–1955. Once again, after World War II the Soviet Union sought security to the south. This policy entailed three initiatives:

---

[b]Soviet support in foreign affairs does not always immunize the subject against Soviet criticism in domestic matters. For example, revolutionary groups inside Turkey were given propaganda support on a low level by Moscow even as Kemalist foreign policy in its anti-Western orientation was warmly applauded. See Jane Degras, ed., *The Communist International, 1919–1943: Documents* (London: Oxford University Press, 1956), p. 109.

(1) territorial concessions in Iran and Turkey, (2) a buffer state near the former, and (3) another revision of the Straits regime.

Soviet troops were in occupation of northern Iran as a result of a wartime accord with London. However, when British and American forces left Iran, their Soviet counterparts did not. Meanwhile, within the territory of Iran occupied by Russia, an autonomous Azerbaijani regime was set up; its head was the same individual who had established a communist Azerbaijani regime after World War I. In addition, the Mahabad Republic, a Kurdish polity, was also founded. If the latter was less a creature of Soviet interests, still no efforts were made to discourage the leaders; indeed, Soviet troops prevented Iranian forces from entering both areas. Eventually, after Western protests and support for Teheran, the USSR withdrew its troops on the understanding that an oil company with 51 percent Soviet ownership would be instituted and communists admitted to membership in the Iranian government. (Although these demands were acceded to, the Iranian Majlis refused to implement them.) The Iranian Army eradicated the Azerbaijan and Mahabad governments.[4]

In Turkey, the USSR attempted to realize several objectives concurrently. Demands were made that Turkey cede the provinces of Kars and Ardahan to the Soviet Union and border areas near Thrace to Bulgaria. More important, Moscow wanted major revisions in its favor of the Montreux Convention and military bases in the Bosphorus. Turkey refused to acquiesce in the Russian demands, and eventually Turkey became one of the first beneficiaries of the Truman Doctrine. The demands on Turkey and Iran, in retrospect, can be seen as among the first steps toward the containment policy. Because maintaining friendly regimes in power in Iran and Turkey had been an immanent part of Soviet strategy since the Bolsheviks took power, it must have been with considerable distress that the Kremlin saw both its southern neighbors move towards the United States, and move, after all, as a result of Soviet tactics. As a ring of hostile bases was being constructed around the USSR over the next decade, Soviet decision makers could not but have reflected bitterly on these two important contributions to the process.

Apart from (1) establishing secure zones to the south of the USSR and (2) obtaining Soviet control over the Dardanelles, the other major postwar objective in the Middle East could also be traced to prewar years; namely, the uprooting of Western (i.e., British and French) influence and power around the Mediterranean. The most effective anti–British nationalist forces in the early postwar years in the Middle East were the Zionist underground and terrorist groups in Palestine. Although traditionally hostile to Zionism itself, the USSR supported the Zionists' efforts to set up a Jewish state in Palestine and even provided arms (through Czechoslovakia). Indeed, the Soviet Union was the first state to recognize Israel *de jure*.[c]

We have pointed out that the Kremlin did not in reality view the world with quite the Manichean glasses usually attributed to it until Stalin's death. There were several regimes in the Middle East that seemed to hold out promise of better relations, the most important being Syria and Egypt,[d] which was taking a number of strong stands against the British. Still, given the isolation of and the opprobrium attached to the Soviet Union in this period, Moscow could do little more than observe events with interest and growing hope.[e]

After 1950, with the "containment policy" advanced and well on the path to implementation by the United States, the USSR sought to break through the barriers erected on its periphery by undertaking productive relations with friendly states in the Middle East—of which there were few. Unlike the West, however, the Soviet Union did not request *commitment* in the East–West cold war. In 1950, there would have been little to gain.for Arab states from closer relations with Moscow, but events were already in motion that altered that situation. Among them, the Tripartite Agreement on arms supply to the Middle East is noteworthy. It established a policy of coordination in the Western arms monopoly in the area. By this means, it was sought to balance arms shipments to the Arab states, on the one hand, and to Israel, on the other, at least to the extent that no side would have a clearcut quantitative or qualitative edge so great as to encourage the recurrence of hostilities.

Another important change took place when the United States led a movement to formalize "containment" by the establishment of multilateral military alliances along the lines of—or supplementary to—the North Atlantic Treaty Organization (to which Turkey was admitted as a member in 1951).

From 1945 to 1955, then, the USSR was isolated to the south by a combination of the effects of its own diplomacy toward two neighboring

---

[c]The United States was first to grant de facto recognition.

[d]Recently, it has been almost forgotten that Faruq's last years in power in Egypt were characterized by a pronounced nationalism in the Egyptian government; that the Soviet Union was displeased when the Nasser-Naguib–led coup overthrew the King in 1952; and that several of the early foreign policy moves and foreign and domestic statements of the coup leaders reinforced Moscow's regrets.

[e]Soviet willingness to support Israel "shows how little impressed Moscow was there with the anti-imperialist potential of Arab nationalism." Arnold L. Horelick, *Soviet Middle East Policy: Origins and Prospects* (Santa Monica: Rand Corporation, 1971), reprinted in U.S. Congress, House of Representatives, Committee on Foreign Affairs, *Soviet Involvement in the Middle East and the Western Response*, Joint Hearings before the Subcommittee on Europe and the Subcommittee on the Near East, 92nd Cong., 1st sess., October 19–21, November 2–3, 1971, p. 190.

states in which it sought to strengthen its security, and the regional effects of the diplomatic quarantine to which the Soviet Union was subjected throughout the world.

Soviet Objectives, 1955–1962. Throughout the postwar years until about the time of the major arms agreement with Egypt, the USSR concentrated on supporting regimes hostile to the West in the Arab Middle East. Although the primordial objectives of the Soviet Union in the area—in Iran, Turkey, and the Black Sea—had been rendered unrealistic by postwar events, the economic and political situation within Russia had improved considerably. By 1955, it was clear that the Arab Middle East offered more opportunities than Iran and Turkey for the attainment of Soviet regional goals in the short term.

The movement to incorporate the Middle Eastern countries in a collective defense arrangement was well underway in 1953. By the end of 1954, rumors concerning the announcement of such a pact—embracing Iraq and Turkey and, eventually, other states—were circulating freely in the Middle East. For a number of reasons, Gamal Abdul Nasser, who had by this time established himself as the undisputed leader in Cairo, was firmly opposed to such a pact; other Arab leaders, including King Saud, were equally opposed to it. Even more firmly against the alliance was the Soviet Union, for it was no secret that the organization was to be founded in opposition to aggression from that quarter.

It is difficult to determine the immediate cause of the Soviet–Egyptian arms deal of 1955. Its story has been told on numerous occasions—each time somewhat differently.[5] In any event, certainly the formation of a bloc of Arab states committed against the USSR was a major ingredient, and the inclusion of Iraq, Egypt's primary Arab rival, was no less crucial. Nasser had already approached the Soviet Union for arms in the past but had been unable to negotiate an agreement. Now, however, the incentive to break up the incipient alliance, to upset the Western arms monopoly, and to undermine Western influence in the Middle East was shared in almost identical terms by the leadership of both the USSR and Egypt. In September 1955, it was revealed that Egypt and Czechoslovakia had already begun transferring materiel under a recent major arms agreement. This was the first of several Soviet (and Soviet-sponsored) military assistance accords.

The objectives inherited from the postwar period had not changed very much in 1955. The USSR still sought to undermine Western influence in the area. In view of the consolidation of the containment barriers to the immediate south (i.e., Iran and Turkey), Moscow wanted to politically leapfrog its southern neighbors and establish its presence in the Middle East. Eventually, an arrangement might be arrived at to resurrect the era of good relations with Iran and Turkey. For the present, that was clearly too much to anticipate.

Even after the 1956 Suez War, which increased the salience of the Arab–Israeli dispute significantly, the immediate goals of scuttling the Baghdad Pact and eliminating foreign military installations and personnel from the area were more important to the Soviet Union than the manifest political gains that might accrue from a policy of support for the Arab states against Israel. As late as 1957, Moscow proposed to replace the Tripartite Declaration with an agreement with Britain, France, and the United States that none of the parties would deliver military arms to the Middle East, that all foreign bases and foreign military troops would be withdrawn, and that no military alignments would be established.[6] The defensive nature of Soviet foreign policy in the area is evident in this construction of priorities.

The heightened salience of the Arab–Israeli conflict was merely one opportunity susceptible of exploitation, but it was the major one. Until the mid-1950s, the USSR had remained "non-aligned" with respect to this dispute. As we have discussed, the first relations of the Soviet Union with Israel were highly cooperative. It did not take long, however, for the lustre to tarnish. Nevertheless, even while Moscow's relations with Israel from 1949 were not much better than correct, there was no Soviet movement toward the encouragement of Israel's perceived enemies. About 1954, however, Soviet delegates began to support the Arab position in an increasing number of UN debates. After the arms deal, this tendency was even more marked.

At the same time, it is probably true that no policy of commitment was reached until about the time of the overthrow of the Hashemite monarchy in Iraq (1958). Suddenly, there were *three* Arab states whose political position in both domestic and international politics afforded hope of long-term cooperation with the Soviet Union.[f] In a sense, this is probably the biggest single turning point in Soviet policy toward the Middle East, or certainly toward the Arab Middle East. From 1958 to the present, the Soviet Union has pursued positive regional goals directed toward the growth of its influence in the Middle East rather than the basic defensive objectives that characterized its policy theretofore (establishing a security zone to the immediate south; support of forces that might lead to the diminution of influence of states hostile to the USSR).

In pursuance of this more activist perception of its interests, the Soviet Union has exploited the two most salient conflicts internal to the Middle East—neutralist/reformist Arab regimes against pro–Western/traditionalist regimes (until 1967) and especially Arab states as a group against Israel.

The encouragement of inter–Arab quarrels was never an unqualified

---

[f]We do not mean to suggest that a relaxed attitude toward communist parties was a factor in this decisional process: quite the contrary is the case. By "domestic" politics we refer, rather, to the espousal of major reformist, *soi-disant* socialist, philosophies. It is still true that international attitudes were the primary criterion by which Arab regimes were judged.

policy. Indeed, the paramountcy of the goal of undermining Western influence was consistent, so that traditional regimes such as those of Yemen and Saudi Arabia found themselves benefitting from strong Soviet support in their quarrels with the West (the United Kingdom, in the case of Riyadh and San'a).[7] Yet, to the extent the quarrels developed, there was a growing overlap between traditionalism and a Western orientation in the Arab East.[g] This overlap moved the USSR to promote the "progressive" regimes, and a variety of communist doctrinal innovations were introduced to rationalize support for these Arab nationalist governments, most of which were inclined to subject their domestic communist parties to the strictest controls—that is, outlawing the parties and often imprisoning leaders and even members.

By far the area's most important problem—much more salient after the 1956 war—was the Arab–Israeli conflict. In this arena, the Soviets increasingly became the primary backers of the Arabs by providing arms and economic and political support to Egypt, Iraq, and Syria. Almost overnight, following the important 1955 arms accord with Egypt (where Czechoslovakia acted on behalf of Moscow), the USSR had undertaken a major role in the Arab world with the pledge to support the Aswan Dam after an agreement with the West fell through.

From 1955 to 1962, the Soviet Union definitively broke through the barriers of containment in the Middle East and became a major political actor in the region. This change in roles left behind the days when the USSR looked at the Middle East only in terms of how it affected the global political conflict between the superpowers.

Soviet Objectives, 1962–1967. From 1962 to 1967, the Soviet Union was still engaged in the effort to minimize Western threats to Soviet security. In effect, this goal translated into undermining the effectiveness of and eventually eliminating CENTO; reestablishing good relations—or at least better relations than Russia's enemies enjoyed—with Iran and Turkey; and bringing about a political situation in which the United States was unwelcome in the Middle East and the Sixth Fleet unwelcome in the Mediterranean; and avoiding military confrontation with the United States.

Because the area was no longer merely instrumental in Soviet policy, regional objectives also included some aspirations pursued purely for Soviet regional benefits. These included the development of ties with the progressive Arab states and consolidation of the Soviet position in Egypt; promotion of the "non-capitalist path" of development; and preclusion of the establishment of Chinese influence in the area.

While the threat posed by CENTO diminished as United States–USSR

---

[g]This was to be an even more pronounced phenomenon after 1962.

relations improved after 1962 and while the southern front was certainly of less immediate importance than, say, its European counterpart, Soviet leaders could still not have relished the existence of a hostile alliance including their two southern neighbors, in which the mobility of the Soviet Black Sea Fleet beyond its waters could be subject to enemy control. It is hardly a revolutionary precept in politics that a state tries to undermine a hostile alliance.

Iran and Turkey, as members of that alliance, were the most pressing concern. However, political alignments were in flux by the 1962–1967 period: U.S. equivocation on the Cyprus dispute proved a great disappointment to the Turkish government (which would have viewed *anything* less than complete support with disappointment); and the Shah, in increasingly firm control of Iranian politics, engaged in periodic conflicts with the West (over petroleum and security matters) in which greater political flexibility would increase his bargaining power. The Soviet Union renounced its claims in both countries.

After a turbulent period (1959–60), both Iran and the USSR sought a détente. In 1962, it was announced that Iran would permit no foreign nuclear missiles on its soil. This step was among the first towards reconciliation. Throughout the 1960s, a number of important agreements were negotiated and signed between Iran and the Soviet Union and between Iran and eastern Europe. The Soviet Union's role in the Iranian economy grew only slightly from 1962 to 1967 but the path was paved for a major share in the late 1960s and beyond.

In Turkey, too, a major improvement in relations took place in the early 1960s. As was the case with Iran, the Soviet "threat" to Turkey had receded by 1962. Later, and more important, the major international conflict in which Ankara was embroiled in these years was no longer the Straits or Turkish territorial integrity vis-à-vis threats from the north, but, rather, with the Greek and Makarios governments over Cyprus. The USSR, while "neutral" in the dispute, upheld the Turkish viewpoint in several respects in its official position from early 1965. Both countries made an evident effort to improve their relations.

Undermining Western interests in the Middle East—especially those of the United States as the British and French regional roles declined—was more difficult. Jordan, Saudi Arabia, Iran, the Persian Gulf states, Libya, and Morocco remained monarchies and continued to look to the West for aid, support, and military and economic relations. Only Jordan among these states was actively involved in the Arab–Israeli conflict. Turkey, Lebanon, and Tunisia also had close and cooperative Western ties. The Sudan entered a period of instability, but its government throughout this period was nationalist and had relatively good relations with the West. Only Iraq, Syria, the U.A.R. (Egypt), Yemen—in which a civil war broke out that lasted for the entire period from 1962 to 1967—and occasionally the Sudan fell among the "progressive" states to which the Soviet Union gave its political support and attached its political hopes. However, the instability characterizing the regimes in these countries—every one except the U.A.R. underwent at least one coup between 1962 and 1967—added to the difficulty in consolidating Soviet influence. Moreover, a movement to normalize relations with the socialist states did not necessarily militate against continued good relations with the West. Rather, it was hoped that the exacerbation of the Middle East "cold war," to use Malcolm Kerr's phrase[8], and the Arab–Israeli conflict would together further the Soviet cause in pushing at least several key Middle East states—especially Egypt, but also possibly Iraq or Syria—into greater and greater reliance on Soviet political support.

Another aspect of this objective was the promotion of anti–Western movements and ideologies on the non-governmental level. In the Middle East, the Soviet Union attempted to increase the identification of the United States with Israel. The Soviet communications apparatus gave this effort its constant attention—just as Western propaganda machines continued to propagate anti–Sovietism—and local youth, labor, and other groups controlled by the Soviet government furnished the nucleus around which others, motivated by any of the numerous issues of the day, demonstrated against, struck, or boycotted Western interests. The much greater involvement of the United States in world affairs since World War II provided the circumstances, and U.S. interests and policies the means by which this great power, largely untarnished before 1939, joined the "fallen angels." Now, so broad was the scope of American involvement that whenever Washington acted—or failed to act—one or another group was offended.[h] In a decade it would be called "overcommitment"; in a decade it would be the foundation for self-criticism and a cause of profound malaise within the American body politic. In the early and mid-1960s, however, it was seen to be the fault of "radicals," "Soviet-supported agitators," "anarchists," or of "irresponsible governments." Whatever the cause, it is certain that the USSR gave public support to anti–Western movements and groups and joined in decrying the effects of "aggressive alliances" such as NATO and CENTO on the countries of the Middle East and the Mediterranean generally. The constant irritant of the Arab–Israeli conflict was instrumental in achieving Moscow's ends, since Soviet mili-

[h]The participation of the United States in a number of particularly unpopular developments between 1962 and 1967 materially abetted groups critical of U.S. policy. Among these situations must be mentioned U.S. actions in the Dominican Republic, the Congo, and Vietnam, and U.S. policy on the Rhodesia problem and, in the Middle East, the Arab–Israeli conflict. At the same time, violence in racial relations within the United States and the assassination of President Kennedy presented the international image of American society in crisis.

tary supply (increasingly monopolistic) of the Arab regimes most vociferous in their anti–Israel fulminations forced the West—to the extent it desired to "balance" such military deliveries—to supply Israel, thereby (1) alienating Arab governments and peoples as well as (2) supporting the Soviet claim that Israel was an imperialist wedge or dagger—an agent of Western imperialism—in Arab lands.

Further development of the links between the "progressive" Arab regimes and the USSR was also pursued in a variety of ways (see Part II). By 1962, Soviet economic assistance and, to a lesser extent, trade with the Third World were well established. Economic exchange—aid and trade— provided a vehicle for the Soviet involvement in societies previously penetrated only by the West.[i] Soviet economic assistance and trade were of especial importance to Egypt and Syria.[j] The relations of these states with the Soviet Union grew closer—if not always happier—as the economies and societies of the former and latter developed greater interaction and mutual dependence. (Recognizing the relative sizes involved, however, "real" dependence could only occur on one side of the relationship, an observation of which the Middle Eastern partners of the Soviet Union were very conscious.)

Along the same line, encouragement by Moscow of Middle East states' pursuit of the "non-capitalist path" to development was consistent. The objective of this approach, similar to the last one, was to reduce the remaining links with the West and Western commerce and strengthen ties to the Soviet Union and the other socialist states (except China). This was a particularly important goal in Egypt, where a certain movement away from private ownership had, in any case, been intermittently pushed by the government, especially after about 1961.

A final objective in the 1962–1967 period was the extrusion from the Middle East of the People's Republic of China, which had extended limited amounts of economic and military aid to both the Middle East and North Africa and which had utilized its contacts in Egypt to exert influence upon various African groups and movements.

The period of 1962 to 1967 featured a major departure, then, in Soviet policy. However, as "the Soviet Union ceased to regard its position in the Arab Middle East exclusively in instrumental terms . . . [and] began to concern itself more directly with political objectives in the Middle East *per se*,"[9] the opportunity to overlook the question of long-term benefits was born. For example, while the effort to swing the Middle East states to stronger ties with the Union of Soviet Socialist Republics might provide

---

[i]We are not considering here the substantial inter-penetration of Arab societies, since this phenomenon is conceptually discrete from external penetration.

[j]The significant aid to Iraq was of less importance to that country's economy than was Soviet aid to Egypt and Syria.

some important political benefits to Moscow (if the effort succeeded), the costs and economic and military ramifications of the policy might be far greater than intended. Only when regional policy is subjected to constant review and critical analysis is there a reasonable probability that the policy retains its "instrumental" value—which is, after all, its fundamental merit. Once regional policy is found at odds with global policy, its contribution to state interests is outlived.

Soviet Objectives, After 1967. The June 1967 Arab–Israeli war constituted another turning point in Soviet policy. Although several of the objectives sought before 1967 were still viable goals—namely, undermining CENTO, improving relations with Iran and Turkey, reducing Western influence in the Middle East, and avoiding conflict with the United States over regional crises—changes affected others.

Soviet relations with Turkey and Iran after 1967 continued to improve and cultural contacts increased substantially. Short of acts (e.g., neutralization) symbolizing the complete triumph of the new policy, the relations prevailing between the USSR and its southern neighbors after 1967 could probably be described as short-run successes of Soviet diplomacy.

The effect of this success was the further erosion of the importance of CENTO. Since the organization was directed at Soviet expansion, the evolution of friendly and economically productive relations between the Soviet Union and Turkey and Iran seemed to signify the end of the usefulness of the organization. However, for political reasons, none of the governments associated in CENTO wanted to see its existence terminated. As a result, CENTO survives; but its political meaningfulness is open to serious question. This, too, can hardly be seen as a defeat for Soviet policy.

The objective of reducing Western influence in the Middle East and U.S. interests in the Mediterranean was given a considerable assist by the West and the United States, respectively. The consistent attempt to view the Middle East in cold war terms had been a costly case of myopia from 1955 on and one the West could certainly have avoided. However, most Western governments are answerable in some measure to domestic political pressures. At the same time, the Americo–European cultural identification with Israel and the absence of a large Arab constituency resulted in the subjection of most Western governments after 1967 to pro–Israeli pressures despite a much greater economic stake in Arab lands. Thus, the position on the Arab–Israeli question of Western governments, excepting France but including especially the United States, was extremely unpopular among the Arab states of the Middle East, and given the saliency of the 1967 conflict, this heightened unpopularity predictably affected Western governmental and non-governmental relations and presence.

Moreover, for a number of reasons (some discussed earlier), the United States presence in the eastern Mediterranean—in Greece as well as Turkey and the Arab states—became the rallying point for individuals and groups aligned against American policy in the Far East, Middle East, or elsewhere. Even a routine visit of U.S. military or naval personnel might result in demonstrations or riots. In spite of U.S. efforts to play down these episodes, host governments were increasingly reluctant to discuss—or eventually even to permit—such visits. (This problem was true of some countries—e.g., Turkey—but the general terms used here should by no means be taken as an indication that it was true everywhere or even in most countries. The importance of the phenomenon is discussed in Chapter 6.)

The June war had another effect. From the outbreak of hostilities it was clear that no mere skirmish was involved. Therefore, the military confrontation Moscow sought to avoid between the Soviet Union and the United States seemed a possibility sufficiently real to employ the Moscow–Washington "hotline." In fact, no confrontation took place; neither did one seem imminent during the six-day war. More important, however, while this Soviet objective remained unchanged, the importance of reducing the potential for a superpower confrontation was underlined. Since neither power was likely to withdraw from the Middle East, only a few alternatives remained to reduce the conflict possibilities. The most realistic—if elusive—of these alternatives was a peace settlement. However, a peace settlement might seem to meet Western needs more than Soviet objectives unless a number of other criteria were met as a function of the settlement. This objective, then, was surrounded by important conditions. These conditions argue against the feasibility of the goal, since they are unlikely to accord with Israeli and Western conditions. To the USSR, a détente is only desirable (1) if it promises to continue or heighten the current dependence of several Arab regimes on the Soviet Union or (2) if it takes place under such conditions that Egypt, Iraq, and Syria are strongly in favor of it (to the extent that the USSR would be criticized by those governments for impeding it). Certainly, destruction of Israel would be as unwelcome as (but no more than) a settlement from which political benefits did not accrue to the USSR. Similarly, while the restoration of Arab lands lost to Israel in 1967 is of no particular relevance to Soviet interests, it *is* central to the policy of Moscow's Arab friends, and therefore has become an objective of Soviet policy. Only a settlement that perpetuates or increases Arab indebtedness to the Soviet Union is desirable to Moscow. Yet, even less desirable than a settlement that did not result in that end—indeed a situation to be avoided at all costs—would be a turning of the Arabs to the United States.[10]

We have already noted that from 1962 to 1967 Soviet diplomacy concentrated on improving relations with the "progressive" Arab regimes. Indeed, one of the means chosen to achieve close ties was the aggravation of the "Arab cold war." After 1967, however, Soviet objectives broadened to include the Arab world as a whole or, at least, all of it save Tunisia. Greater emphasis was placed on Arab unity,[k] and Soviet offers of political, military, and economic support embraced almost every Arab state. (Only in the case of Saudi Arabia was no great effort exerted toward the improvement of relations.) The goal of identifying the United States as the main support of Israel having in large measure been achieved, domestic pressures existed in many Arab countries—pressures aided where possible by the Soviet Union—to move towards the one apparently consistent friend of the Arabs, Moscow.[1]

The reformist Arab states were augmented during this period also. Soon after the June war, the British left Aden where the People's Republic of South Yemen (later, the People's Democratic Republic of Yemen—PDRY) was proclaimed amid civil war and near anarchy; in May 1969, a left-wing coup resulted in the overthrow of the Mahgoub government in the Sudan; in September of the same year, Idris I of Libya was deposed. (On the other hand, a more conservative regime came to power in the Yemen Arab Republic.) Though the Soviet Union was involved in various relationships with virtually every Arab state, the widest range of its dealings remained centered in Egypt, Iraq, Syria, Yemen, Algeria, and the Sudan. Of these positive commitments, Egypt continued to be the most important. Iraq and Syria were unstable, each having had a succession of coups. Algeria and Egypt, on the other hand, were both relatively stable with bureaucratized administration and a technocratic leadership.[11]

Egypt had long been considered the single most important Arab state and had presented, in any case, the greatest opportunity for the development of a Soviet political presence. The commitments made by the USSR over the years to Egypt cannot be presumed to have been undertaken without some agonizing consideration. And to have made such commitments indicates a rather high priority must have been placed on exploitation of the Egyptian opportunities. Such a priority argues against Egypt's having been viewed as merely one country among many or even as only

---

[k] "Arab unity" has always been a problematic concept for the USSR. Because of the idea's widespread appeal in the Middle East, the Soviet Union has endeavored to avoid public ridicule or condemnation of Arab unity. On the other hand, under Khrushchev and his successors as well, Arab communists and Arab politicians well-disposed to the USSR have been advised to look to class unity in the Middle East instead. In two celebrated cases—the Egypt–Syria merger of 1958 and the Egypt–Libya decision to unite thirteen years later—Moscow has preferred to acclaim these "concrete" steps to Arab unity though both cases are known to have been considered setbacks in the Kremlin.

[1] In the June war, a number of Arab states even broke diplomatic relations with the United States: Algeria, Egypt, Iraq, the Sudan, Syria, Yemen (A.R.), and Mauritania. As time went on, however, the lack of formal diplomatic relations did not seriously impede the development of productive relations when both parties were determined to resurrect and maintain them.

that country where the opportunities of the moment were greatest. On the contrary, it seems probable that Egypt held the primary interest of Soviet planning.

In 1972, Egyptian President Anwar Sadat ordered the departure of most of the Soviet military advisors and personnel in Egypt. This action probably facilitated the implementation of a change of policy that may well have antedated the action itself. Sadat had long displayed signs of pro–Western, and especially pro–American, inclinations; yet Soviet policy, as we have seen, presumed cooperation with any willing regime. Under the circumstances, Moscow decided to concentrate on the broadening of its relations with Iraq and Syria. The aftermath of the 1973 war—particularly the key role the United States played in the postwar peacemaking—has only underscored the new foci of Soviet interest.[m] Moreover, the realization that Egypt has only limited flexibility because of the intensity of its previous relationship with the USSR (read weapons situation) suggests Moscow can wait.

Examined in terms of the comparative advantages various Arab states could offer if in close cooperation with the Soviet Union, the shift of focus from Egypt is hardly surprising, for none of the Middle East states is of more than marginal importance in a global political sense, but the *concrete* advantages that Iraq, Syria, and the Gulf countries can offer—in even purely denial terms—are more important now that many of the early Soviet political objectives have been attained.

Currently, then, the Soviet Union is pursuing some of the goals it has sought before. At the same time, having realized some of its earlier objectives and having accepted certain fundamental changes resulting from the June 1967 war and other developments (e.g., the death of President Nasser), new objectives seem to have been established for the Middle East. These include the permeation of Iraqi and Syrian societies by Soviet personnel, state cooperation, subnational activities, the development of better and broader relationships with the countries of the Gulf, and the leveling off (in some cases, even the reduction) of the Soviet commitment to Egypt while consolidating and rationalizing the Soviet position there and bringing Egypt to higher level of societal integration with the USSR.

Economic Objectives

Soviet economic objectives have not played a major role in the Middle East except as supportive of other strategic political or military goals. In view of

---

[m]What the 1973 war also showed, however, was the reservoir of good will still enjoyed by the United States in the region, which reservoir can be drawn upon when the United States makes the necessary commitments.

the fact that the Soviet economy is overwhelmingly inward-looking (i.e., a very small portion of the economy is affected by or geared for international trade) and the land relatively self-sufficient, subordination of economic objectives to other strategic needs is hardly surprising.

Yet, the Middle East *is* important to the Soviet Union, and much of its importance is economic, even if the reasons *for* this importance are political or military. Eighty percent of European NATO's military and economy depend on Middle East oil, and certain patterns of economic relations with Europe are often significant desiderata in the foreign policy decisions of Middle East states. Thus, the denial value of the area is high.[12]

That military conquest and subjugation are less common and accepted approaches to political dominance today is clear. As a result, the role of economic means in domination has grown (in prominence if not in effectiveness). In that connection, the USSR since Stalin's death has used economic aid and trade to create ties between the economies of certain Middle East countries and the Soviet economy. This apparently remains a major goal of Soviet policy in the area. It is, however, tempered by the desire to avoid an overcommitment of resources.[13] As a matter of fact, Moscow has remained one of the few external trading partners with the Middle East to maintain a positive balance of trade with the area.[14]

In spite of these self-imposed restraints, the policy of creating economic dependence—or at least intimate economic relations—has succeeded to a degree in Egypt. As a result, some of the advanced techniques associated with this objective are being implemented in Egypt as well (see Chapter 5). Most probably, the new leadership of the Soviet Union recognizes and places greater stress on the potential political implications and pay-off of strong technocratic links between the USSR on the one hand, and high-priority Middle East countries, on the other.[15]

Thus, the major "economic" goals in the Middle East have a pronounced politico-military flavor. At the same time, however, the Soviet Union does have some identifiable economic objectives per se. Clearly, Soviet trade with the area has been profitable to Moscow, and there is no reason to expect this situation to change. The energy with which commercial relations have been pursued suggests in fact a desire to see this intercourse increase in importance.

Too, the Middle East constitutes the most economical means of transportation between the European and Far Eastern sectors of the Soviet Union itself, being about 50 percent cheaper than the overland route when the Suez Canal is open.[16] (The Black Sea–Mediterranean–Red Sea–Indian Ocean route is also less vulnerable than the overland alternative, which consists, essentially, of one major road and the Trans-Siberia Railroad.)[17]

Because the Suez Canal influences the importance of the Black Sea outlet for Russian trade with the rest of the world, another goal of Soviet policy is the reopening of the Suez.[n] More generally, in fact, the stability of the entire Mediterranean basin is advisable insofar as it contributes to the growth of profitable and productive commercial relations worldwide and regionally as well.

In sum, Soviet economic objectives in the Middle East do not appear to have played a major role in the development of Soviet policy towards the area; nor does it appear that they will be more crucial in the future in this regard. The single exception to this general observation is—oil.

Economic Objectives: Oil

Background. One of the major reasons for the importance of the Middle East is its role as a major supplier of energy for the rest of the world. This wealth in certain energy resources—primarily oil, but also natural gas—has increased the contribution of the area to industrialized countries as those countries have shifted to the use of oil and gas. Today, the developed countries are overwhelmingly dependent upon these sources of energy. The major factors in the importance of Middle East oil to the world— indeed, the essential tests of any fuel—are quantity, quality, and cost. The growing weight of the oil factor in Soviet decision making for the Middle East is a function of the above and a number of other interrelated but diverse considerations. Essentially, the relationship connects the Soviet energy situation, oil reserves and production in the Middle East, and the energy requirements of the rest of the world.

Soviet Domestic Oil Situation. The USSR has never opened all information to the public concerning its oil reserves. However, it is characteristic of countries where oil exists in some quantity *not* to carry out exacting surveys of the proven reserves.[o] What is clear is that the Soviet Union has long been an oil-exporting country. Its production has increased enormously even in recent years (14 percent from 1960 to 1970), but oil consumption has risen even further.[18] Currently, the Baku and Volga–Urals areas

---

[n]In this regard, Soviet economic policy and politico-military policies collide. There is no inherent Soviet interest in maintaining the closure of the Canal, but the political costs of a closed Suez may be far less than what might be required to re-open the Canal. Thus, while the USSR stands to benefit from opening the Canal, and therefore favors re-opening it, Soviet policy subordinates this objective to other political goals.

[o]"Proven reserves" means the amount of oil recoverable under present technology at current costs without economic loss. In an industrialized country where internal demand for oil exceeds supply, exploration will be intensive and extensive and thus proven reserves may be taken as fairly accurate (particularly as regards known fields). In countries with a ratio of reserves to production weighted heavily on the side of reserves, the reserves figure tends to be quite conservative. Thomas C. Barger, "Middle East Oil Since the Second World War," *Annals*, vol. 401 (May 1972), p. 34.

are the major sources of Soviet oil production. However, they are expected to decline rapidly in importance over the next decade.

The vast size of the Soviet Union means that exploration, drilling, and production costs may be less important than transportation costs if the USSR maintains its self-sufficiency in oil. This has been Soviet policy in the past, since the development of dependence on external sources was considered unwise from a strategic point of view. (Moreover, the importation of oil in large quantities could have played havoc with economic planning.)[19] However, the next major domestic source of oil is in the Far Eastern USSR, and its cost will be about double the price of Middle East oil.[20]

If cost were the only problem, there is no doubt that the USSR would continue its autarchic policy in petroleum. However, quantity, too, is emerging as a factor in the future. That the USSR has consciously attempted to rely upon its own oil reserves should not be understood to mean that it has restricted consumption of its petroleum to itself. On the contrary, the Soviet Union was for most of the postwar years virtually the exclusive foreign supplier of oil to Eastern Europe. This was a highly profitable enterprise, since Moscow charged its allies inflated prices. Still it is evident that there were controlling political—rather than solely economic—reasons for this commerce. Nor has Eastern Europe been Russia's only petroleum customer. The best-known consumer of Soviet petroleum, after all, was Cuba. In recent years, as the cold war has dissipated, the USSR has placed a high priority on the negotiation of commercial agreements to supply oil to Western Europe. Even apart from the political pay-offs of long-range trade with the West, the opportunity to obtain convertible currency was particularly attractive. Similarly, from a purely economic standpoint, it would clearly be in the interest of the USSR to arrange the sale of Soviet Far Eastern oil to Japan and import Middle Eastern oil for Soviet requirements.[p]

[p]A quasi-precedent has already been established in Moscow's agreement to allow Britain to fill Soviet oil commitments to Ceylon and Japan in exchange for Russian shipments to Europe to meet BP and Shell commitments there—all because of Suez. See C. Powell Hutton, "Changing Soviet Oil Interests: Implications for the Middle East," *Naval War College Review*, vol. 24, no. 2 (October 1971), p. 83. The reason economic needs are more efficiently met through the exchange addressed in the text is the relative cost and dependability factors of Middle East and Siberian oil to the industrial centers of the respective countries. There is, however, some question as to the feasibility of a large-scale agreement along these lines due to Japanese minimum requirements for quality (see below). Other major considerations are (1) the possibility of Sino-Japanese agreements on the development and use of Chinese oil and (2) the importance to the USSR of precluding such agreements. For a number of other factors, see David I. Hitchcock, Jr., "Joint Developments of Siberia: Decision-Making in Japanese–Soviet Relations," *Asian Survey*, vol. 11, no. 3 (March 1971), pp. 279–300; and Richard Ellingworth, "Japanese Economic Policies and Security," *Adelphi Papers*, no. 90 (October 1972).

In the face of growing external possibilities for the sale of Soviet oil, the rapidly increasing domestic consumption is diminishing the exportable oil surplus. Indeed, while the USSR remains a net exporter of petroleum, it has been importing greater quantities each year to cover the difference between Soviet consumption *and* exports, on the one hand, and production, on the other.[q] Oil experts have not reached a consensus regarding when or to what extent the Soviet Union may become a net oil importer, but most—and, significantly, this does not include Soviet authorities who foresee self-sufficiency through 1980[r]—believe the USSR will be at the net importation point sometime between 1975 and 1980.[21] Soviet petroleum policy has consistently been determined by political considerations, and it is unlikely that this situation will change. However, in the face of pressures to export oil to Eastern Europe, Western Europe, the Third World, and Japan—all for political leverage—and at the same time dramatically increase the quantities of energy resources available at home, it is difficult to see how the USSR can avoid augmenting its petroleum imports considerably over the next decade. The only alternatives are to shift to natural gas, oil shale, or nuclear energy as power sources. The massive investment such a conversion would entail; the inadequate technology in, for example, the case of oil shale; and the great distance between the location of the resource and the site where it would be used—these and other problems make conversion economically less feasible than the importation of oil.[s]

Already the USSR has informed its Eastern European allies that they will be expected to procure their oil elsewhere. Given the state of political upheaval at the time this initiative was taken and the loss in profit to the USSR (because of the inflated prices charged its allies), it is clear that this decision must have been agonized over for some time.[t]

Oil Situation in the Middle East. The three important factors to consider in relation to petroleum, as we have indicated, are quantity, quality, and cost.

---

[q]The Soviet Union is a marginal importer of Middle East oil, having taken 1 percent of the area's petroleum in 1971.

[r]The Soviet representatives at the 1971 World Petroleum Conference indicated that recent discoveries would enable the USSR to maintain this status. See "Soviet Treaties should Boost Middle East Trade," *Middle East Economic Digest*, vol. 16, no. 29 (July 21, 1972), p. 812.

[s]The Soviet Union has immense resources of natural gas but has so far followed a policy diametrically opposed to its traditional oil policy; instead of striving for self-sufficiency in natural gas production, the USSR is importing the product from Iran. The Middle East has great natural gas reserves as well as petroleum reserves. See Hanson W. Baldwin, "The Stakes Are Oil," *Army*, vol. 21, no. 8 (August 1971), pp. 11–12.

[t]It has been suggested to the eastern European countries that they invest in Soviet Far Eastern oil development. See John A. Berry, "Oil and Soviet Policy in the Middle East," *Middle East Journal*, vol. 26, no. 2 (Spring 1972), p. 153.

The word "oil" has become synonymous with the Middle East. The reasons are:

1. Quantity—about two-thirds of the world's proven resources of oil are located in the Middle East;
2. Quality—the sulphur content of most Middle East oil is very low, and that of some of the oil of the area is remarkably so;
3. Cost—the extraction cost of Middle East oil is extremely low.

While it is the abundance of Middle East oil that has received greatest attention, the other factors are of singular importance. Japan, for example, has exacting pollution laws that require petroleum of very low sulphur content, and Iranian oil, because of its extraordinarily high quality, is actively sought to meet this need. Fully 90 percent of Japanese oil is imported from the Middle East.

Meanwhile, the oil situation in the Middle East is changing. The June 1967 hostilities resulted in the closing of the Suez Canal, and since that time supertankers have come into their own.[u] Also coming into its own in the mid-1960s was the oil production of North Africa, particularly Algeria and Libya, both of which are now major producers (7th and 4th greatest in the region in 1971; see Table 2–1). However, as the proven reserves of the Middle East increased over the decade, so did those of some other areas. We have noted the development of Soviet deposits in Siberia. In North America and the North Sea, too, new oil deposits were identified. Major oil production began in the Bight of Biafra as intensive exploration continued. Nevertheless, these discoveries will scarcely cover consuming countries' growth in demand. The Middle East's resources represent two-thirds of the world's total proven reserves,[22] and it is on these reserves that the developed world must rely for some time.

The significance of the abundance of Middle Eastern oil is that it is needed, and while some writers have suggested that Middle East oil is of declining importance to Europe in view of the discovery of oil in Canada, Alaska, Nigeria, and elsewhere and in view of the development of other power sources,[23] the simple fact is that the Middle East is for the present and the foreseeable future the major Western power source. The same constraints apply to American, European, and Japanese power conversion

---

[u]The canal would have been expanded to handle the first generation of supertankers by now, probably, had political problems not ordained it to remain closed. Even now, in spite of the comments often heard that Suez is unimportant, its reopening would be rapid if it were not for the continuing political difficulties. Most European countries, not merely those in the Mediterranean, suffer marked economic hardships as a result of the closure of the canal. See Jean-Jacques Berreby, "Le Pétrole: enjeu stratégique autour de la Méditerranée," *Politique étrangère*, vol. 36, nos. 5–6 (1971), pp. 523–4.

Table 2-1

Crude Oil Production in the Middle East, 1961–1971

(Million tons)

Middle East	1950	1955	1960	1965	1970	1971	% Change 1950–71	% Change 1960–71
Abu Dhabi	—	—	—	13.6	33.3	44.5	∞	∞
Bahrain	1.5	1.5	2.2	2.8	3.8	3.8	153 %	73 %
Dubai	—	—	—	—	4.3	6.5	∞	∞
Egypt	2.4	1.8	3.5	6.4	20.9[a]	21.0[a]	775 %	500 %
Iran	32.9	16.4	52.3	93.8	191.7	227.0	590 %	334 %
Iraq	6.7	33.8	47.5	64.4	76.6	83.0	1139 %	75 %
Israel	—	—	0.1	0.2	0.08	0.07	∞	−30 %
Kuwait	17.3	54.9	81.8	108.7	137.4	145.0	738 %	77 %
Neutral Zone	—	1.3	7.3	19.0	26.7	26.4	∞	262 %
Oman	—	—	—	—	17.2	14.7	∞	∞
Qatar	1.6	5.4	8.2	10.9	17.3	20.0	1150 %	144 %
Saudi Arabia	27.3	48.1	62.3	101.0	176.9	222.0	713 %	256 %
Syria	—	—	—	—	4.4	6.5	∞	∞
Turkey	0.02	0.2	0.4	1.5	3.5	3.3	16,400 %	725 %
Maghreb								
Algeria	0.003	0.06	8.8	26.5	47.3	36.5	1,216,567 %	315 %
Libya	—	—	—	58.5	159.2	132.0	∞	∞
Morocco	0.04	0.1	0.09	0.1	0.05	0.02	−50 %	−78 %
Tunisia	—	—	—	—	4.1	4.2	∞	∞

[a]Includes production of Israeli-occupied Sinai.

Source: *The Middle East and North Africa 1972-1973* (London: Europa Publications, Ltd., 1972), p. 34; American Petroleum Institute, *Petroleum Facts and Figures: 1971 Edition*, pp. 552, 556, 589.

that apply to the Soviet Union. Indeed, even Japan, heavily engaged in research on the extraction of oil from oil shale, recognizes its dependence on oil for some time.[24]

Probably the most significant change in the Middle Eastern oil situation, however, is the terms upon which this resource is available to the rest of the world. For years, it had been pointed out by political scientists that natural resources should not necessarily be considered as contributing to the national power of the state in which they were found; it is to the state in which control over these resources is vested that one must consider them as contributing. The best example of this phenomenon was the Middle East, where the oil was under Arab soil but under Western control. The ill-fated nationalization attempt of the Mossadigh government in Iran in 1951 only proved the validity of this point.

Yet, as early as 1933, the terms of the oil concessions in Iran had been revised—a process taking place in the Arab states only in the 1950s. Later in that decade, concessions began to be replaced by government/producer partnerships with terms increasingly favorable to producing countries.[v]

In the 1960s, dissatisfied with the return they were receiving on the exploitation of their own natural resources, the Middle East governments, brought together in 1960 under the Organization of Petroleum Exporting Countries (OPEC), moved individually towards the greater use of service contracts. OPEC bore few apparent results in its first decade, but in 1971 it began to take on greater importance in coordinating and furthering member interests. The future appears to hold the greatest possibility of foreign companies' restriction to downstream operations. The movement is clearly towards complete ownership and production of oil by host governments. Meanwhile, as the coordinated action of Arab oil producers showed, the governments of oil producers have been given through market conditions a tool for influence that they know how—and have the will—to use.[w]

Political Ramifications of Middle East Oil. Reliance upon a single source for a vital energy product is undesirable in any event, but it is particularly so when that source is subject to highly volatile and unpredictable political

---

[v]The changes to the benefit of the producing countries derived from the willingness of smaller U.S. companies and European government-owned companies to be more forthcoming than the large, private corporations such as BP, Esso, and Gulf, in order to break into the Middle East oil picture.

[w]The major financial issues arising from the oil situation after the large price increases in 1972 and 1973 are not directly germane to this study. It suffices to recognize the magnitude of these problems to understand the threat of a major restructuring of the international economy. The political impact of these developments will not be understood for some time, but it is clear that some oil producers will have vastly increased influence in international monetary matters.

pressures. Three times since the end of World War II the Middle East has seen war; yet even this fact understates the political instability in a region where coups d'état, revolutions, insurrections, civil wars, assassinations, and other major acts of political violence over a quarter of a century have been legion. It is, nevertheless, incontestable that Western Europe is dependent upon the Middle East for oil.

As a function of this dependence, Arab states have occasionally attempted to exert pressure on Europe and the United States through the use of an oil boycott. This technique until the early 1970s had failed of success, largely because cutbacks in the oil from some states were compensated for by increasing its importation from others. Iran has been noticeably reticent to join others in a boycott, and indeed Iran and several other states profited considerably from the brief boycott instituted after the June 1967 war. That Europe—and eventually all industrialized Western countries individually—remains vulnerable to such action is an irrefragable argument, however. Short of increasing storage capacity[x] or converting to other energy sources (see above), the only alternative to dependence on Middle Eastern oil is diversification of source. To some extent, this process is underway, but we have already seen that only the Middle East contains sufficient oil reserves to meet Europe's current and future petroleum needs.

Soviet Policy on Middle East Oil. The Soviet perspective on Middle East oil has undergone a metamorphosis more or less concurrent with the evolution of the Middle Eastern oil situation discussed above. In view of the traditionalism prevalent in the major oil-producing areas, Soviet analysts seem to have given little thought, much less support, to the idea that Middle East governments might seek better terms from the oil companies. Not until 1960, the year OPEC was formed, did concerted action on the part of the oil-producing states merit attention.[y] Soon, recognizing the potential reunification of the birth of joint action, Soviet analysts favored the development of a movement toward nationalization of Western oil holdings.[25] In support of this objective, Soviet technical assistance and advice were extended to Egypt, Iraq, and Syria. Soviet propaganda supported OPEC

[x]This is an unfeasible solution. Oil is difficult and expensive to store. Nor can one type be stored more than others: "All the products of the refinery must be moved continuously to enable the refinery to run. If the gasoline tankage is empty, but the fuel oil tanks are full, the refinery shuts down, as it cannot make one product without making the others simultaneously." See Barger, "Middle Eastern Oil since the War," p. 32.

[y]The attention, however, was not initially directed toward OPEC, but, rather, to the Jidda Conference that had taken place in 1959 and had established the need of and support for revisions—the concession areas and terms among other issues. See R.N. Andreasyan, "Middle Eastern Oil: Present and Future," *International Affairs* (Moscow), July 1960, pp. 26–29.

and its individual members when occasional disputes arose between host governments and the oil companies.[z] As time went on, however, the call for nationalization was silenced, probably in appreciation of the insuperable obstacles to such a course at that time,[26] and it has not been sounded again in any forceful way, even at obviously opportune moments.[aa] On the other hand, specific and limited measures of pressure on the West's oil supply to secure specific and limited political objectives *have* been supported. The Arab oil embargo following the June 1967 war was endorsed, even as was the decision of the Conference to end the embargo.[27]

Soviet policy in this arena supports the producers and will probably continue to take this tack in bringing pressure to bear on Western interests but does not appear to contemplate going beyond the initiatives of the Middle East states themselves (nor would such external leadership be welcomed by the producing states).

We have already pointed out the likelihood of the emergence of the Soviet Union as a net oil importer by the early 1980s and the fact of growing imports of Middle East oil even at the present time. It is partly in view of this growing role of the USSR in Middle East oil affairs that we believe Soviet policy will continue to be less than radical. As the countries of Eastern Europe and the Soviet Union itself become more dependent on Middle East petroleum, they too are captive to the inherent explosiveness of the political situation in the Middle East, while enjoying far less influence over it than Western Europe.[bb] Whatever the USSR chooses to contribute in such a situation might understandably be more supportive of stability than turbulence.[28] Yet another compelling reason to suggest the Soviet Union has a significant interest in the stabilization of the Middle East oil situation—contrary to the recent past, when USSR oil dumping negatively affected oil revenues[cc]—is the total debt of the area to the USSR

[z]Soviet observers were even sent to OPEC meetings.

[aa]For example, the USSR did not propose such a step at the time of Khartoum Conference, which was convoked in August 1967, when measures to force Israeli withdrawal from territories occupied in the June war were under discussion. See, however, text following this note.

[bb]The slight influence is a function of the Soviet and Eastern European demand for Middle East oil—growing, but small relative to Western European and Japanese demand. The Soviets and Eastern Europeans "have neither markets for buying oil nor wares to sell which are better than those currently available." Barger, "Middle Eastern Oil Since the Second World War," p. 43.

[cc]In the early 1960s, the Soviet Union practiced oil dumping in an effort to break into the European market, thus driving down the price paid for Middle East oil (and provoking several Arab countries into condemnation of Soviet oil policy). More recently, Soviet efforts have included the proposed extension of the Friendship Pipeline (which sends oil to Eastern Europe) into West Germany. See Joseph J. Malone, *Dynamics of Military Balance: Middle East/Mediterranean—Final Report* (research study prepared for the Advanced Research Projects Agency, Office of the Secretary of Defense, U.S. Department of Defense, 1972), pp.

in loans, much of the repayment of which will depend upon regional oil income.[29]

In conclusion, we believe Soviet economic and political objectives regarding oil in the Middle East to be in flux. Although it is sought on the one hand to reduce the role and importance of Western oil companies and to reduce the political collaboration for which oil cooperation creates strong incentives to some rulers, it is, on the other hand, no longer Soviet policy to create economic dislocation and instability in the Middle East nor to bring about xenophobic or nationalistic pressures that might give rise to a situation in which the growth of Soviet and Eastern European oil investment in the area might be impeded. The conflicting interests of the Soviet Union in this regard have probably not been adjusted, but it is evident that modest support for action against Western oil companies—particularly in regard to the old concessions and some of the partnership provisions—will continue at the same time socialist countries undertake purchase and technical assistance agreements with Middle East oil producing governments. The increasing involvement of the socialist states in exploration, drilling, and other ventures leaves the future open to doubt, but Soviet policy may embrace a long-term objective of greater control than the West over regional oil disposition. This is unlikely to be projected and even less likely to be realized, since Middle East governments now prefer to diversify their oil production and marketing[30] and would derive far less economic benefit from dealing with the USSR and its allies than with the West and Japan (see above).

Military Objectives

Like its economic and cultural ends, Soviet military objectives in the Middle East carry both a derivative and an inherent character—that is, they support political objectives as well as reflect military needs.

Politically Derived Military Objectives

In one sense, all military goals must support political goals—that is, the raison d'être of a military establishment is national security. From national

24–25; Stephen Page, *The USSR and Arabia: The Development of Soviet Policies and Attitudes towards the Countries of the Arabian Peninsula 1955–1970* (London: Central Asian Research Centre in association with the Canadian Institute of International Affairs, 1971), p. 56; Benjamin Schwadran, "Middle East Oil in 1960," *Middle Eastern Affairs*, vol. 12, no. 6 (June–July 1961), p. 167; and Schwadran, "Middle Eastern Oil 1961," ibid., vol. 13, no. 8 (October 1962), p. 228.

security policy and in line with its priorities flows the determination of military requirements to support that policy. In order to ascertain the specific regional military objectives that find their direct provenance in foreign policy, for the area, it is necessary to first consider the latter (see the section on political objectives).

The undermining of CENTO involved the interweaving of tools on the military as well as the political, economic, and cultural fronts. From a military point of view, it was not considered practical to *support* Iran and Turkey, as, for example, with military equipment or training—at a time both were still hostile to the USSR. The need was evidently to defuse this hostility in order to build more cordial military relations and at the same time show the futility of alliance with the West in case of military conflict. A détente with both Iran and Turkey—a détente led in spirit by the Soviet Union—culminated in a military sales agreement with Iran. The growth of the Soviet Mediterranean squadron and the development of close, cooperative relations with Iraq and Syria effectively brought about the encirclement and, to a lesser extent, sense of political isolation of the Northern Tier states.

A second politico-military objective was the reduction of Western influence in the Middle East. To this goal Soviet military policy contributed in general ways. First, the introduction and growth of the Mediterranean squadron served to reinforce states and revolutionary movements pursuing anti–Western policies by creating the impression that Western intervention was now unlikely. Second, where Soviet naval or military forces were present in Middle East countries, military action against those countries either by Israel or the West was in large measure deterred because of the danger of involving the Soviet forces and therefore the USSR. (This function was not essentially different from the role of American forces in Europe.) Third, the growth of local Soviet military power increased Soviet prestige and probably, to some degree, influence, which automatically served the cause of reducing Western prestige and influence since these are by nature *relative*.

The need to avoid military conflict with the United States, either locally or globally, was also served by the pursuance of military objectives. The Soviet Union sought to utilize its military assistance personnel to supervise, where possible, Arab military units in order to prevent the outbreak of another round of hostilities in the Middle East.

Soviet support for progressive Arab regimes was also aided by the growth of the naval squadron as well as by the increasing number of Soviet military personnel in certain Arab countries. Thus, one function of the increasing naval operations was to establish close links with the riparian states of the Mediterranean and Red Seas. Financial and technical assistance was provided in some cases, and a number of ports along the

Mediterranean and along the Red Sea—some ports regularly visited, or assisted in development, by the Soviet Union—were no longer considered open to United States vessels. This face of the objective of Soviet presence and involvement was also concentrated on airfields, civilian and military, where major Soviet assistance efforts were launched.

Solely Military Objectives

The military objectives of the Soviet Union in the Middle East are several. Although, as we have indicated, the Middle East is not vital to national security, the proximity of the USSR and the Middle East ensures that the latter is and will remain *relevant* to Soviet security.

Thus, the first priority among regional military objectives is to reduce Soviet vulnerability to hostile military operations that might be conducted against the USSR from Mediterranean-based forces. From this goal, in turn, flow several related objectives.

First, the military security of the Black Sea must be established. This has been a strategic requirement for centuries,[dd] and it must be recognized that the Soviet Union has largely succeeded in creating the impression that the Black Sea is a Russian *Mare Nostrum*.[31]

Second, the USSR has sought to counter the strategic nuclear forces employed in the Mediterranean by the United States. These forces included importantly attack carriers with long-range aircraft and several generations of Polaris missiles. While the Polaris AI could not hit major industrial targets, later versions of Polaris missiles were able to target such areas and were therefore probably the primary cause of the entry of the new Soviet squadron into the Mediterranean in 1964. Consequently, it is probable that the Soviet Black Sea Fleet and its Mediterranean squadron were given the mission of sinking as many carriers and Polaris submarines as possible in the case of war between the U.S. and the Soviet Union.[32]

The Western debate over Soviet naval policy is a continuing one that embraces a range of questions of only tangential relevance to the Middle East. We believe, however, that a reasonable means of ascertaining Soviet intentions must include review of naval construction, changes in naval construction plans, deployments, and changes in deployments. So far as the construction-deployments interaction for the Mediterranean is concerned, Soviet policy has seemed to retain its strategic defensive character mixed with flag-showing or other political duties.[33]

[dd]Arnold L. Horelick points out that the traditional Russian pressure to control the straits was not an attempt to challenge European predominance in the Mediterranean, but, rather, was aimed at limiting the passage of European ships of war into the Black Sea. See Horelick, *Soviet Middle East Policy*, p. 189.

Third, the Soviet Union has tried to reduce the U.S. Sixth Fleet's threat by subjecting its presence in the Eastern Mediterranean—and even the Mediterranean as a whole[34]—to political and public pressures to withdraw.[35]

Fourth, and more generally, the two major anti-Soviet alliances of the Mediterranean are targets of sabotage. The regional effectiveness of NATO, encompassing both Greece and Turkey, has been reduced by the withdrawal of France from the organization and the continued rivalry between Athens and Ankara, as well as the reduction in British involvement in the area. Britain's reduced commitment level has had an even greater impact on CENTO, but the new era of good relations between the Soviet Union, on the one hand, and Iran and Turkey, on the other, has already relegated CENTO to a somewhat marginal role.[ee]

Other Military Objectives

Given the continued pressure of the U.S. Sixth Fleet in the Mediterranean, a further objective is the improvement of the Soviet tactical position in the area. The Mediterranean squadron gives the Soviet Union a limited intervention capability that could serve to support friendly regimes or deter Western military action.

Additionally, the USSR seeks overflight and visiting rights in the area. These are less important for current military objectives than for potential operations and for political goals, since they serve the purpose of making more visible the Soviet presence.

As we have already pointed out, the Black Sea–Mediterranean–Red Sea–Indian Ocean–Pacific route is the fastest and most economical means of transportation and communication between European Russia and East Asia, in general, or the Far Eastern USSR, in particular. It is also the safest route with respect to possible Chinese interference. This route is moreover the preferred route for the reinforcement of the Soviet Pacific Fleet.[36] For all of these reasons, obtaining the reopening of the Suez Canal and establishing close, cooperative relations with the states of the Red Sea littoral are also objectives of Soviet policy. Although they are subordinate to several of the political and military goals already advanced, it is still clear that Moscow supports the opening of the Suez—so long as it does not prejudice more important interests.[37]

Whether or not the canal is reopened, the provision of military assistance to various Middle East countries may serve to implant Soviet outposts throughout the area, which outposts may support tactical or strategic

---

[ee]This statement refers to CENTO's military efficacy, not to its political significance, which is only partially a reflection of military needs.

military objectives.[38] Important during these support missions may be the collection of intelligence.[39]

Soviet military objectives in the Middle East, both instrumental and independent, strategic and tactical, are an important motive force for continued involvement in the area.[ff]

Cultural Objectives

Because the Soviet Union's primary interests in the Middle East are all political and military, other objectives are essentially derivative of—that is, their realization is designed to support—the political or military ends. That cultural aims relate more closely to political than to military interests is clear.

In particular, two political purposes are served by Soviet cultural diplomacy: the reduction of the Western involvement in the Middle East and its replacement by Soviet influence. To undermine and reduce the dominant Western cultural presence and to supplant it with a sense of identification on the part of the peoples of the Middle East between their own culture and that of the Soviet Union are the resulting cultural objectives. However, the ease with which they are formulated is indicative of their generality, and such generality, in turn, is indicative of the fact that they represent only the beginnings of Soviet movements in this realm.

All this is not to say that Moscow has neglected the cultural front in its political efforts; it is simply to demonstrate that in no endeavor must the Soviet Union overcome greater odds in the realization of its purposes. In virtually every aspect of culture, the Middle East, while by no means overwhelmingly occidental, is by *all* means overwhelmingly more inclined towards Western culture than towards other alien cultures. Indeed, Western Europe has been so intimately and intensely involved in Middle Eastern cultural development for so long that no analysis of the regional culture could overlook the interaction.[40] The truth is that while more specific goals might be developed, any opportunity for the demonstration of Soviet culture is exploited even now.

In two areas of popular culture and one of more restricted relevance, there have been some positive results from Soviet initiatives. With regard to the former, interest in Soviet athletic techniques has grown, as has the number of students of the Russian language. Indeed, educational exchange—primarily the dispatch of Arab students to the Soviet Union[gg]—has been heavily used for some years. With respect to the more

---

[ff]See Chapter 3, however, for some military interests leading to *reduction* of Soviet presence or involvement.

[gg]But also the secondment of Russian teachers—see Part II.

restricted area, the scientific and technological accomplishments of the USSR have occasioned considerable popular interest in high-visibility exploits and more sophisticated attention and cooperation on the part of a much more limited audience.

Generally, however, the attempt to exploit areas of Soviet achievement has not reduced regard for Western culture. Even in the limited areas of substantial interaction and demonstrable Soviet progress, Middle Eastern interest has been eclectic, anxious to make use of all the resources available from the West and the East to the extent these resources can be mobilized for the development of the Third World. To the extent they cannot, interest may not have more than a short-run impact on the consciousness of the peoples of the area. While this may be all that is desired—such seems to constitute the approach—it is unlikely that displays of high visibility but little practical import will support the objective of reducing Western cultural influence in the Middle East.

Ideological Objectives

To what extent do Soviet political objectives envisage the development of Middle Eastern regimes espousing Marxism–Leninism? That is the fundamental question of ideology. How important is communist ideology in Soviet Middle Eastern policy?

Manifestly, communism is not the criterion of good relations with the governments of the area, for there have never been any Middle Eastern communist regimes and yet Moscow has enjoyed unusually close relations with a number of Arab countries. Indeed, relations with some of these countries have been more productive when indigenous communist parties were most strictly—at times, brutally—suppressed.

Can it be concluded, then, that communism is utterly irrelevant in Soviet foreign relations? It cannot. Simply put, we do not believe the Soviet Union is greatly concerned about the welfare of communists in Arab countries, nor even about the welfare of communism there. However, for several reasons, the ideological question *is* pertinent.

First, the mantle of leadership of communism is presently Moscow's. It is in the vocabulary and frame of reference of communism that the Soviet Union speaks and acts, not only to the international community but to its own citizens as well. Loss of its legitimacy as leader of much of the international communist movement would arouse problems both doctrinal and actual that are better avoided. The question of the passing of this leadership role from the Soviet Union to China would not and has not been a matter of inconsequence to Moscow.

Second, the communist movement, led by the Soviet Union, posits goals that further the interests of its leader. So long as this is the case—that is, so long as the movement retains its role as a supporter of Soviet interests—the USSR usually perceives more benefits than costs—and there are costs—arising from the growth and development of local communist parties.

Third, and similarly, recognizing Moscow's leadership, local communists are more likely to be favorably disposed to the USSR than are non-communists, and they are far more likely to be anti–Western. Therefore, the goals of local communists generally reflect the Soviet objective of a reduction of Western influence in the Middle East.

In view of the above, the fate of local communists and local communist movements is evidently not irrelevant to the USSR, nor is it important, however. Even in the very unlikely event that a communist party or group acceded to power in one of the countries of the Middle East, past experience has suggested that it would almost certainly pursue a policy independent of the Soviet Union.[hh]

Therefore, the USSR will support communist parties and individuals in the Middle East only when the cost of this support will not detract from other Soviet objectives. This approach has been a constant of Soviet foreign policy,[ii] and there is no indication that the relative priorities in this regard will change.

Soviet Objectives in the Middle East: An Overview

A review of several categories of Soviet aims in the Middle East establishes the definite primacy of political objectives, and particularly the reduction of Western presence and influence in favor of Soviet influence. Soviet policy also aspires to the exclusion of U.S. military or naval presence from the eastern Mediterranean or, to the greatest practicable extent, reduction

---

[hh]In cases where communist regimes have not been imposed or assisted by a Soviet military presence, they have without exception acted rather independently of Moscow's lead. Yet, these regimes are all neighbors of the USSR, while Arab countries obviously are not.

[ii]Many writers (e.g., Aaron S. Klieman, *Soviet Russia and the Middle East* [Baltimore: Johns Hopkins Press, 1970], p. 12; Thomas W. Wolfe, *The USSR and the Arab East* [Santa Monica: Rand Corporation, 1969], p. 3) suggest that Moscow *shifted* in emphasis from ideological—backing local communist groups—to strategic—stressing good relations with all but the most fanatic anti-communists. We believe this to be a misreading of history. It is true that emphasis was early—indeed well into the cold war era—placed upon communist parties, movements, and activity in the Middle East as opposed to state relations. However, this emphasis evolved in the *absence* of, rather than instead of, state relations—that is, it was felt that no real opportunity existed for the development of cooperative and fruitful intergovernmental relations. When such an opportunity *was* perceived, the Soviet Union moved with alacrity to exploit it in even the most backward and conservative countries.

of the threat to the USSR posed by U.S. strategic forces located in Mediterranean and Indian Ocean waters. The growing involvement of the USSR in the Middle East has led to specific regional political goals independent of global strategy. Preeminent among these goals is the consolidation of the considerable Soviet influence in Iraq and Syria, the continued construction of tight relations (especially in economic matters for the time being) with Egypt, and the development of friendly and cooperative state relations in other countries of the Middle East, especially those in the Gulf area.

For political reasons, the USSR seeks to establish a degree of economic dependency that (1) will allow its political influence to be if not decisive at least important, (2) will reduce Western influence, and yet (3) will not create too great a drain on Soviet resources. However, the projected requirement for importation of oil, most probably to come from the Middle East, has resulted in a conservative approach to the problem of foreign oil companies. Indeed, the economic importance of the Middle East for the Soviet Union, currently minimal, may be much more significant in the 1980s as a consequence of Soviet oil needs.

Military objectives focus on the security of the Black Sea, reduction—either by arms limitations or by countering forces—of the strategic threat to the USSR posed by the U.S. Sixth Fleet in the Mediterranean, and the exploitation of Middle East countries' military interests for the political purposes of the Soviet Union.

The regional cultural and ideological objectives of the USSR are wholly derivative of political goals: exploitation of all available resources to effect the reduction of Western influence and to replace it by Soviet influence. In this context, local communist parties play a marginal role at best.

3 Constraints on Soviet Policy in the Middle East

Soviet foreign policy is shaped by plethoric influences—some systemic, others non-systemic. This chapter seeks to identify and describe the major influences on the formulation of Soviet policy in the Middle East.

Domestic Political Constraints

Interest Groups

The role of interest groups in Soviet political life is considerably more elusive than their role in Western democracies. Because they receive no better than quasi-official recognition—and usually do not even benefit from that—interest or "pressure" groups in the USSR often take on an almost conspiratorial image. This appearance is accentuated by "the historical tendency of the Soviet system . . . to try to suppress the emergence of autonomous interest groups of any kind that might develop a life of their own."[1] Nevertheless, they play a major role in most areas of decision making, and in some areas, their influence can be decisive. Even within a single group—that is, a number of individuals unified by interest, affection, vocation, ethnographic background, or other bonds—views may differ widely. As in other polities, changes in the nature of the issues or in the circumstances surrounding the formulation of policy or simply the passage of time may occasion the dissolution or coalescence of new alliances within and between groups.

With respect to the Middle East issue the number of interest groups is particularly diverse. These include the "nationalities," especially the Jewish community but also Muslim groups; the party; the military establishment; the industrial sector, particularly defense industries; and sectors of the government involved because of the wide range of Soviet activities in the Middle East.

"Nationalities." The "nationalities" have traditionally played an intriguing and unusually marked role in Soviet foreign policy. Concern about the ultimate loyalties of the hundreds of national groups within the USSR and about the designs of states along its periphery have clearly been decisive in several cases.[a] In the early years of the communist government, religious and ethnic differences were officially attacked—the unifying principles of communism were to submerge bourgeois differences. After some time, however, certain unique characteristics of various groups were allowed to "exist." Among these was, to a limited degree, religion.

In a population of 242 million, there are about 2 million Jews and perhaps 15 times that many Muslims.[2] Yet, this in no way gives an accurate portrait of the role of the Jewish population in the USSR, for a very substantial portion of the scientific and technical elite—particularly in the field of nuclear physics—is Jewish.[3] Moreover, there is a definite identification on the part of many Soviet Jews with Israel, an identification to which a few historic occasions have clearly attested.[b]

On the other hand, even apart from intermittent outbursts of anti–Semitism, there are countervailing pressures, such as those from the approximately 30 million Soviet Muslims. There have been efforts—largely unsuccessful—to Sovietize the Asian USSR Muslims. Nevertheless, while their feelings about the rest of the Muslim world may be accorded somewhat greater weight because this very large group has long been contemned, its views do not carry the weight numbers might suggest.[4]

This, then, is the dichotomous influence of the ethnic groups: Soviet Jewry generally unhappy with policy in the Middle East, and Soviet Muslims generally pleased at least with the alignment of the USSR and the Arab states.[5]

The Party. The extent to which the Communist Party of the Soviet Union (CPSU) may in fact be a unified group pursuing agreed ideological or other objectives of its own is probably only a very small fraction of that image. Although it is true that the most powerful ideologues tend to be in the party rather than the government, it does not follow from that fact that the party is composed entirely or even predominantly of ideologues, nor that the most powerful voices within the party are ideologically tuned. Indeed, quite the contrary seems to be the case.

So far as its interests may be differentiated from the government's *and* from those involving leadership of the international communist movements following Moscow, the CPSU does unite individuals whose official in-

[a] For example, the question of a pan–Turanian movement potentially sponsored or supported by the Turkish government was an important element in Soviet policy considerations at the end of World War I and for some time thereafter.

[b] Most notably, the initial trip of Golda Meir, then the first Israeli ambassador to the USSR, to a synagogue in Moscow. Indeed, this identification is one of the major reasons the Soviet Union has been consistently anti–Zionist. Its opposition to Zionism antedated the birth of Israel and persisted even throughout the brief period of good relations between Israel and the USSR.

terests are, at least for the time being, more ideological than those of the government. For bureaucratic reasons, the results of the influence of the ideological constituency in the Soviet Union have more to do with the form than with the substance of foreign policy.

Industrial and Defense Industry Groups. As in the United States, industrial interest groups in the Soviet Union are not of one mind on matters international. Their interests are affected in diverse ways by overseas engagements. In the USSR the dichotomy may be usefully drawn between heavy industries, whose interests most often lie with those of the defense establishment, and light industry, whose interests are more clearly related to the consumer sector.[6] While more or less overt lobbying carried out in some Western states has no place in the USSR, that function is replaced to some extent by the government-industry relationship required for the rationalization and supervision of economic planning and the integration of military and other government needs into the planned economic system. Eight government ministries produce the great majority of military materiel.[7]

The defense industries' key role in the Soviet governmental hierarchy is evident in the assignment of individuals representing defense-related ministries and defense industries in disproportionately large numbers to central decision-making bodies, for example, in the Central Committee.[8] Thus, the process of allocating state resources and determining priorities is heavily influenced by the defense industries.

Military Establishment. Much more significant than any of the preceding interest groups is the Soviet military. Elements of the government bureaucracy have very important vested interests in the extensive and varied Soviet military presence in the Middle East. The policy of Soviet military presence and growth in the Middle East has increased the prestige of the military and, as a result, increased the interest of at least important elements of the military establishment in securing the success of the policy. It appears that Soviet theater forces have been dominant over strategic forces, sometimes winning and sometimes losing the support of military intelligence.[9]

Moreover, "the Soviet military has extraordinary channels of access to decision and policy making organs"[10] In addition to institutional leverage, the opportunities for individual military officers to bring informal—or, if in the appropriate place, formal—pressure to bear is very great. The party and government are both heavy with military representation.[11]

Therefore, the Soviet military has been an active participant in the policy debate on the Middle East. Military journals give prominent play to Middle Eastern affairs. Once again, this is not to say that all military opinion is of a mind. On the contrary, there have been sharp differences in the past and these have probably increased in number and significance with the growth in the Soviet presence and the new options and international constraints such a development has entailed. On the whole, however, while the military has been reluctant to effect certain *specific* acts and activities, the evidence is that a forward position in the Mediterranean and in the Indian Ocean has enjoyed the support of the defense sector (see below, "Military Constraints").

Middle East Government Bureaucracy. While we shall discuss Soviet bureaucratic interplay over Middle East issues in the following section, it should be noted that it is particularly over the last decade that

factional groupings have spilled out of the central organs of the Communist party, sub-institutional groupings have developed within various Soviet institutions, and associational and socio-functional groups have become increasingly characterized by subgroup activity. As a consequence "interests" have aggregated on the basis of *issues* cutting across institutional and functional lines . . . .[12]

With the growth of the bureaucracies concerned with Middle Eastern affairs as a result of Soviet cultural, economic, political, and military activities in the area, the importance of this interested interdepartmental bureaucracy has probably grown considerably. Its combined weight—in evidence only when an issue arises that unites the interested bureaucracy against *other* interests—is, however, probably brought to bear on a Middle Eastern question relatively seldom, since it must be assumed that most regional questions of real moment would fragment the Soviet Middle East constituency.

Bureaucratic Politics

While little is known (relative to open societies) about the competition within the Soviet establishment between the groups described above as well as between their constituent elements, it is clear that much greater interests are involved in the process than heretofore.

The enlarged Soviet role and presence in the Middle East since the June war means in the first instance that there are now powerful vested interests in Soviet Middle East policy operating at various levels in the Soviet policymaking structure. With 10,000–14,000 "instructor" and "adviser" personnel on the ground, 40 to 60 ships at sea nearby, Soviet pilots flying regular reconnaissance missions from Egyptian bases, others ready to scramble in MIG–21–J jets from UAR airfields, units manning SAM–3 missile sites, a huge (by Soviet standards) foreign aid program, etc., it is clear that there has been an expansion and proliferation of key bureaucracies whose fortunes are directly connected with course and outcome of Soviet policy in that area.[13]

Below the national leadership level, however, typical bureaucratic rules of the game can be presumed to come into play in Soviet decision making. For example, evident success of Soviet policy from 1955 to 1962 and even more clearly thereafter undoubtedly created pressures to continue or even increase Soviet activities in the Middle East. The momentum of involvement, evident during the 1960s in U.S. decisions relating to Southeast Asia, must inexorably take its toll, like the laws of physics, on the USSR. Equally predictable was the outcome: involvement of the Soviet Union in regional crises over which it could exert little or no influence.

Even our limited knowledge of Soviet bureaucratic politics has indicated a number of sharp disagreements on various Soviet Middle East policies,[14] although some of these struggles have been placed in the context of larger strategic debates.[15] Notwithstanding the often professional nature of these differences, it is clear that in the Soviet establishment as in other societies the personal costs of error can be high.[c] It is therefore clear that a determined leader, well-placed in the Soviet hierarchy, can effectively preempt the institutionally sanctioned policymaking channels. So long as the Middle East remains an important area of Soviet activities, key policy decisions will continue to be made at a high level. Thus, it can be presumed that policy *discontinuities*, by way of either innovation or reaction, have been reviewed and considered at the highest level in the USSR.

That this assumption of high-level review does *not* include the routine operations of the foreign affairs apparatus is suggestive once again of the limitations on the ability of an outside observer to force Soviet actions into the rational mold. It is easier to continue activities already underway than to change them; it is easier to change them less than to change them more; it is easier to change them in a manner suitable to all involved decisional elements than in a way ideal to some but unacceptable to others. Such principles derivative of the theory of complex organizations have an important effect on major governmental decisional outputs; it must be clear that their effect on day-to-day operations is even greater, and probably decisive.[16]

Public Opinion

The absence of a pressure of public opinion in closed societies has often been identified as one of the elements conducing to more efficient policy formation. By the terms of this model, the public is informed only through

---

[c]For example, there were reports of considerable acrimony and large-scale accusations of incompetence following the 1967 war. See the *Sunday Telegraph* (London), June 25, 1967; *As-Sayad* (Beirut) June 15, 1967; *Jeune Afrique*, June 25, 1967.

government or government-sponsored communications media, is informed of the truth only as the government wants it to be perceived, and as a result, is capable of no audience interest in or influence on government processes. The paradigm is inadequate.

Control of the Media. Although it is quite true that media in the USSR perform a role very different from media in open societies, it is incorrect to assume that messages are received and accepted at face value by the Soviet public as intended. The audience in such cases develops—and in the USSR has developed—highly sensitive "filters" used on messages transmitted by the mass media.[17] Thus, even if control over mass communications were complete, the Soviet audience could not be considered to be as passive as the model suggests. In fact, however, the control is far from complete.

Permeability of Soviet Society to Non-Governmental Communicators. It has been pointed out that in the modern age, even with the greater technology available to national governments, no country's boundaries can be effectively sealed from external communications.[18] This is particularly true of the Soviet Union, which is subject to concerted communications efforts from external sources.[19]

External communications apart, there develops within the totalitarian state a series of means to communicate information and views that do not accord with those dispersed by the government.[d]

Salience of the Middle East. It is in spite of—not due to the lack of—the availability of information on the Middle East that public pressure on the Soviet government regarding Middle East policy or interest is very limited.[20] This is due to two factors: the danger of publicizing differences with the government and the low salience of the Middle East to most of those outside government. The effect on the nationalities of various Soviet policies is probably at least marginally taken into account, but it is manifestly true that there is no public opinion mobilized or readily mobilizable to put potentially decisive pressure upon the government in policy deliberations relating to the Middle East.

Soviet Perceptions of the Outside World

Of vital importance in decision making are the perceptions held by those involved in the decisional process of foreign relations. The significance of

---

[d]The development of *samizdat* exemplifies this phenomenon within the USSR. See Bohdan R. Bociurkiu, "Political Dissent in the Soviet Union," *Studies in Comparative Communism*, vol. 3, no. 2 (April 1970), pp. 74–148.

this element—so great that it usually passes without comment as understood—is especially relevant for the activities of other states. In other words, from the Soviet side, the United States–Soviet interaction—to the extent decisions are rational reactions to or anticipations of the external environment—is based upon what Soviet leaders *believe* they observe and know about U.S. policy, about the Middle East as the *champs de bataille*, and about the other factors affecting U.S. policy. Similarly, international opinion is only important to the extent their perceptions of its potential ramifications influence the actions of Soviet leaders.

For other governments. the role of Soviet perception means that initiatives taken to influence local actors (e.g., the Jordanian government or elements of the Palestinian resistance) may be perceived by third parties as actions taken to support other interests associated with the initiator. It is likely, for example, that the objectives of the United States and those attributed to Washington by the Kremlin with regard to the eastern Mediterranean for the first decade after World War II bore only slight resemblance. Yet, whatever importance U.S. objectives had in Soviet decision making, it was on the basis of Moscow's *perceptions* of these objectives that Soviet policy was formed.

Ideology

A non-analytical reading of Soviet statements at any single point in time conduces to the assumption that ideology is a major constraint in Soviet policy. However, even the most cursory analytical review of Soviet policy indicates clearly that this is not the case. Indeed, we find ideology itself has not operated at all as a constraint in Soviet Middle Eastern policy. Rather, ideological justification for policy has gone through numerous metamorphoses to explicate Soviet policy in Marxist–Leninist terms.[21] This ideological flexibility was particularly evident in the development of concepts to explain the support of the socialist states for the nationalist governments of developing countries. From the Zhdanov two-camp theory propounded in 1947 until about 1965 or 1966, a series of concepts and terms—including (1) "association" and "sympathy" with the socialist states, (2) national democracy, and (3) revolutionary democracy—was suggested to rationalize this alliance for communist theory.[22] The unexpected collapse of a number of the most important of these regimes—Ben Bella in Algeria, Nkrumah in Ghana, and Sukarno in Indonesia—probably served notice on the USSR that no attempt to rationalize the Soviet relationships with Arab regimes would be meaningful in unstable circumstances. Thus, since the end of the June 1967 war, there has been less emphasis to justify Moscow's varying support for individual regimes in the Third World on ideological grounds and a more open recognition of the marriage of political desiderata and ideological forms.[23]

Domestic Economic Constraints

Economic constraints on policy are fewer than their political counterparts but have at times been decisive in the elaboration of Soviet foreign policy in the Middle East. Until the mid-1950s the economic reconstruction of the USSR had not progressed far enough to allow for major political initiatives requiring large-scale economic support.[24] This was certainly a major consideration as regards economic and military assistance but also affected other programs, since most active politico-military policies require substantial economic support.

The USSR's great economic resources have been tapped much more effectively since the mid-50s, but demands for those resources have never ceased to exceed supply. In a full-employment economy, foreign aid requires domestic cutbacks. Since there is a tremendous demand for, and very high return on, capital for internal Soviet investment, "the economically rational procedure is to eliminate those projects which use the most capital, take the longest time to 'pay off,' have the lowest rate of return, and are in nonessential sectors of the economy. Soviet loans to the LDCs [lesser developed countries] fit to a T this description of undesirable projects."[25]

Thus, Soviet assistance programs have a greater "real cost" for the USSR than do programs at the same funding level implemented by countries without over-full-employment economies.[26]

One constraint with which Soviet foreign policy planners have not been burdened—unlike most of their great power counterparts—is the specific problem of natural resources found in the Middle East, especially petroleum. As we have already pointed out, however, the Soviet domestic oil situation is undergoing marked changes, and its future is open to speculation. At the least, it is clear that even optimum domestic oil production under foreseeable changed circumstances would result in considerably increased cost for petroleum products. As a result of these changes, Soviet energy needs may become a major policy constraint soon.

A key economic consideration, already adverted to in the context of bureaucratic politics, is the product of the continued deemphasis of consumer priorities ever since the establishment of the Soviet Union, but especially since postwar economic recovery made the Soviet Union the second greatest industrial power of the world. This pent-up demand often unites the consumer, agricultural, and public service sectors of the Soviet economy,[27] including light industry, consumer goods, trade, housing, agriculture, services, and welfare. When these interests coalesce and are opposed only by vacillating or uncertain representatives of the Soviet military-industrial group, they can be decisive in directing allocation of resources useful in international affairs to domestic purposes.

Domestic Military Constraints

The last major category of internal parameters on Soviet foreign policy involves military considerations. Essentially, military constraints concern less the military resources available to the USSR than the attitudes and perceptions of the Soviet military establishment. That the resources themselves should not be a constraint results from the fact that the Soviet Union is a superpower and from political decisions to exercise a certain degree of restraint in the exercise of the symbols and reality of this power in the outside world.

We have already indicated that the military establishment is a highly effective interest group within the Soviet decision-making hierarchy. This effectiveness should not be misconstrued to equal adventurism, however. On the contrary, while the Soviet military leaders have pushed for the allocation of greater resources to security needs, and while they have at times advocated a "hard line" vis-à-vis the West, they have at other times constituted a voice for caution, reluctant to overextend Soviet military commitments.[28] This factor has been particularly conspicuous with reference to the Middle East where advanced Soviet equipment in the hands of the Arab military forces, in whose proficiency the Soviet military hierarchy has not had cause for great confidence, would be observed and possibly even captured, and weapons technology thereby compromised.

Domestic Cultural Constraints

Cultural parameters are not important in the delineation of Soviet foreign policy. Indeed, the most significant cultural contribution is the most invisible: the decision makers' cultural attitudes and culturally influenced thought processes.

International Constraints

The constraints within which policy is formulated and implemented are often external. In the case of Middle East policy, these factors are both worldwide and local—that is, they derive from international considerations both outside and within the Middle East.

Worldwide

Global limitations on Middle Eastern policy need be addressed only very cursorily, since most are operative on all Soviet foreign policy, not merely the policy on this or another particular region. These constraints are political, economic, and military in nature, though political considerations substantially overlap in practice, as they often override in planning, the other areas.

International Political Constraints. Among the most important political constraints is U.S. foreign policy. The priorities, flexibility (and rigidities), commitments, and understandings implicit in American overseas operations are major inputs to Soviet policymaking. We believe that few have given sufficient emphasis to this area of implicit cooperation, for given the worldwide involvement and the scope of activities of the two superpowers and given the pressure within each to avoid appeasing the other, the fact of having avoided military hostilities for over a quarter of a century suggests a high degree of sensitivity to each other's interests, expectations, and decisions. This area of psychological cooperation[e] has probably been as important as any other single factor in the avoidance of nuclear war. Preventing the outbreak of such a conflict with the United States as an objective of Soviet foreign policy (see Chapter 1) is also a restraint in its formulation and execution. In fact, all primary objectives serve as constraints in that they are important criteria by which decisions are made on tactics and on resource allocation.

Apart from the policies of other powers (primarily the United States) external to the Middle East, and Soviet policy objectives viewed as constraints, major changes in the international environment have played a significant part in influencing policy parameters. These changes include (1) the increasing saliency of differences among the Western allies and between them and neutral states, (2) internal developments in countries and regions of interest to the USSR that might make greater Soviet involvement more feasible than formerly, and (3) developments relating to the Sino–Soviet relationship.

Problems within the NATO alliance grew in importance as the immediacy of what Western Europe had perceived as the "Soviet threat" receded. These differences were exacerbated by the diverging interests of NATO members—disagreements over colonial matters, defense priorities, and nuclear strategy. When the alliance began to diminish in importance as its members perceived their interests differently, the USSR attempted to

---

[e]Viewed from the optic of a great power seeking to overturn the status quo and achieve superpower status, this "psychological cooperation" greatly resembles the Soviet–American "conspiracy" to which Chinese leaders have often referred.

accelerate the process by improving relations with France,[f] Turkey, and with each of the other members individually. No development was more painful for NATO than the process of decolonization as a result of which the ties of Belgium, France, Portugal, and the United Kingdom with the other members of the alliance (and with each other to a surprising extent) and with the Third World were strained almost to the breaking point.[29] These stresses considerably abetted the Soviet attempts to reduce the alliance's cohesion and to establish itself as a legitimate friend of the emerging countries of Africa and Asia.

Throughout much of the postwar era, China and the Soviet Union stood together on most international issues. The strong American reaction to the Korean conflict had included the decision to defend Nationalist China on Taiwan. This determination, together with the vehement U.S. anti-communist Chinese feelings that defeat of the Nationalists had occasioned and the hostile attitude of the Chinese regime itself, contributed to the embittered relations between the United States and China that endured for two decades. When Soviet–Chinese interaction became increasingly hostile, the USSR's leaders still enjoyed the luxury of knowing Sino–American collusion was unlikely. Even then, such a *rapprochement* could not have been viewed with equanimity in Moscow. Since the improvement in Sino–American relations after 1970, a major concern of the Soviet Union in the Middle East as elsewhere must be to avoid any initiative that carries the potential of significantly enhancing the new relationship of the Soviet Union's two primary protagonists.

International Economic and Military Constraints. Less often considered in studies of the "Soviet" presence in the Middle East are international constraints. While this is undoubtedly because the Soviet decisions in question are overtly political in nature, the USSR, like the United States, does not arrive at political determinations in a vacuum. The demands on Soviet resources are as many and varied as those on American resources, even if the form of the demands and the process of allocating the resources are different. In 1971, economic grants and credits extended to developing countries by Moscow equalled more than $850 million. And from 1954 to 1971, the figure was $7,615 million.[30] Even if there were no other external expenditures beyond the standard diplomatic activities, the magnitude of the amount shows that inexhaustible supplies of excess resources are not lying idle for use in the Middle East. In fact, however, the Soviet military assistance and technical assistance programs are also extensive. Moreover, as we have already indicated, the dollar terms are not a good equivalency because the "real cost" of Soviet assistance is considerably

---

[f]France withdrew from NATO, but has continued to cooperate in a number of areas.

higher than its counterpart in economies that are not centrally planned. In fact, an additional problem the Soviet Union has faced results from the use of "credits" in its overseas assistance programs. These credits sometimes go unused and, in the case of large grants, are seldom drawn in the same year they are granted. Thus, when years of credits are outstanding to large numbers of countries, their use can be a perturbing factor to the Soviet economic plan.

Military constraints have generally been a major influence in the elaboration of foreign policy. Cohesion of the containment barriers until 1955 was a military as well as a political limitation within and toward which plans had to be prepared. During the period before friendly relations with certain of the developing countries evolved, this military constraint also reinforced the need to concentrate on the development of strategic defensive weapons systems against the Western bloc, thereby reducing, once again, the resources available for other purposes. In another context, military assistance, which became a major tool of Soviet diplomacy in the Middle East, labored under constraints analogous to those relating to economic aid, especially the great demand factor.

Regional

The particularities of any region comprise important considerations limiting policy freedom for the attainment of regional objectives by a government external to that region. That this generalization applies to the Middle East, where intraregional differences have attracted international—and often tragic—attention, is self-evident. Because the area has both unusually strong unifying factors and uniquely potent differences—each entailing noteworthy ramifications on cultural and ideological matters—Middle East regional limitations on Soviet policy will be considered in several domains—cultural and ideological as well as political, economic, and military.

The primary constraint on the efficacy of Soviet policy in the Middle East is regional autonomy. Historically, and presently, great powers have been unable—even with a significant land presence—to shape local events.[31] Middle East autonomy has been remarkable in the past; with Soviet and American forces at a stand-off in non-general-war conditions, local autonomy is likely to be even further enhanced.

Regional Political Constraints. The presence and activities of powers external to the region have consistently been of capital importance in the development of Soviet policy. While this is most clearly the case in regard to U.S. operations (since, as we have already pointed out, it is a priority of the first order to avoid a military conflict with the United States), reaction to the presence and activities of other states is also reflected in Soviet policy. Before political conditions paved the way for the Egyptian arms agreement, the success of the West in isolating the USSR from the Middle East was obviously a decisive constraint, since few options existed.[32] In the contemporary context, the need to maintain peaceful even if competitive relations with the United States often acts as a brake on Soviet undertakings in the Middle East.[33] At the same time, the United States–Soviet implicit partnership in maintenance of Middle East peace cannot be allowed to manifest itself in such a way that the USSR appears to collaborate in the subversion of Arab objectives.[34]

A second consideration, potentially (but not necessarily) related to outside influence as well, is the possibility of nuclear proliferation in the Middle East[35] and the impact such a development would have upon Soviet–American relations there.

Third, proximity to the Middle East imposes certain requirements on Soviet foreign policy. So long as direct control over the Dardanelles is not in Soviet hands, a premium will be placed on good relations with Turkey.[36] Even apart from Turko–Soviet relations, however, the geographical propinquity of the Middle East and the USSR must substantially influence the latter's politics *because* of economic, cultural, and military—as well as political—needs.

Probably the most important, and certainly the most complex, category of policy constraints derives from developments within the Middle East itself. These include decolonization, the internal socio-political evolution of the local states, relations between Arab countries, the Arab–Israeli conflict, and the Palestinian movement.

Decolonization has been important for a number of reasons. Colonialism had been a major irritant in regional politics and provided another complaint on which to base anti–Western propaganda. Decolonization has also brought to power regimes with an interest in demonstrating their independence. One means to realize this interest has been to undertake formal or better than formal relations with the USSR. Soviet support of liberation movements has also resulted in a certain mutuality of interest during preindependence and, sometimes, postindependence periods. Too, the effects of the anticolonial movement have been perturbing to regional political development; this environmental instability has often assisted in advancing Soviet interests.[37] However, decolonization has also brought about a situation as a result of which most of the Middle East is grouped into sovereign states. Thus, while the Soviet Union could cooperate with antiregime elements in colonial days without repercussions on its relations with regimes it sought to support, today support for opposition elements entails the consequence of a deterioration of relations with the regime in power. Indeed, any attempt to advance Soviet interests that is perceived by local governments as a threat to their sovereignty or freedom of action is unwelcome.

Inter–Arab relations are a potentially major constraint on Soviet policy. Indeed, the kaleidoscopic nature of Arab interaction, varying greatly from one country to another and changing rapidly over time, has already operated to set parameters for Moscow's activities in the region. During the period of little Soviet presence, the major policy problem of *choice* was virtually nonexistent. As the USSR became more deeply involved in the Middle East, however, and the magnitude and nature of relations with Arab regimes grew, the problems of choosing between regimes, movements, and individuals became increasingly pronounced. In North Africa, for example, Moscow was faced with Algerian–Moroccan enmity in 1963. The saliency of the Arab–Israeli conflict has tended to reduce the significance of the dilemma of choice to the extent that the importance of other issues has been reduced in comparison with the Arab–Israeli issue. Nevertheless, the conflicts between Arab governments and within Arab countries are so numerous without reference to the Arab–Israeli dispute that choice is increasingly necessary and seldom easy. The withdrawal of the United Kingdom from the Gulf brings many of the disputants together in their confrontations, which can only make more difficult the task of maintaining cooperative relations with both. Two examples will suffice. In the southern Arabian peninsula, the Democratic People's Republic of Yemen (DPRY), the only *soi-disant* Marxist Arab regime, was engaged in military conflict in 1972 with the Yemen Arab Republic (YAR), a more stable, and progressively less anti–Western regime, yet one in which much more Soviet assistance had been invested.[g] Similarly, Iraq, having entertained alternately close and hostile relations with the Soviet Union since 1958, and one of Iraq's major rivals, Iran, contested a number of issues, including a shared waterway, Iranian rights in the Gulf, and rights of Iranian nationals as minority residents in Iraq. The USSR was intent on maintaining good relations with both. Too often observers applaud the "diplomatic skill" of a state not directly involved in regional conflicts when it is in reality the involved states who have "the monopoly of committing mistakes."[38] The burden of choice was not obvious before 1967 while the Soviet Union was taking the part of the progressive Arab states in their rivalry with traditionalist regimes. This, however, was a relatively easy "choice" in some cases, for most traditionalist regimes did their best to avoid intercourse with the USSR during this period.[h] Perhaps because the

[g]During the winter of 1972–1973, in a development almost typical of Arab politics, both regimes announced "unification" of the two states at some time in the future.

[h]Most, in fact, dealt or had dealt with the Soviet Union for some reason, but none felt comfortable with such a relationship on other than a very ephemeral basis. Saudi Arabia and

progressive states were more outward looking, disputes between them seemed chronic. When Soviet objectives broadened to encompass all the Arab world, the problem of choice magnified.

Similarly, within many Arab states turmoil seems almost endemic. As the USSR became even more deeply involved, remaining aloof from the personal rivalries and vendettas of turbulent political environments was increasingly difficult. Localism, family ties, and minority problems are all pertinent here. More problematical yet was the dilemma of government-to-government relations. In a situation when coups have become a way of life in several countries, close Soviet–Arab intergovernmental relations with one regime were potentially a death knell for good relations with its successor. Personal relationships arduously established with certain individual leaders over a period of years sometimes laid a foundation of distrust for the construction of good relations with successor regimes.[39]

Economic and political development along the lines of Western or partly Western models has been the especial target of Soviet propaganda and political communications. Yet, for reasons discussed below,[i] most Arab elites are strongly influenced by their perceptions of Western development. Moreover, since political philosophy as well as trade and cultural patterns reflect experience, the heavy involvement of the West in the Mediterranean has brought extensive transmission of, as reactions to, Western political thought, tradition, and organization. These legacies of the past are impediments in the present to the linkage of Arab polities to the USSR, and although Western-influenced politico-economic structures are in flux in many Arab states, their reality is still a hindrance with which Soviet attempts at penetration of Arab societies must deal.

The most important political factor in the Middle East situation today is the conflict between Israel, on the one hand, and the Arab states, especially those bordering Israel, on the other. This confrontation has facilitated the growth of Soviet influence in the region, and U.S. reaction to the situation has considerably speeded this growth. As a result, the Arab–Israeli conflict is usually portrayed as an opportunity for the USSR and a problem for the United States. While we do not take issue with the verisimilitude of this portrait, it is still true that this most salient of regional problems has important negative ramifications on the effectiveness of Soviet policy as well. Once again, if the USSR were not involved directly,

Yemen enjoyed friendly relations as early as the mid-1920s, the latter's renewed three decades later. Saudi relations with Moscow have generally been poor except for brief periods such as 1955 when the King opposed the Baghdad Pact. The Kremlin had begun to look with sympathy toward pre-revolutionary Egypt as early as 1947, and particularly in the period before King Faruq's overthrow. The Cherifian Kingdom enjoyed a brief period of warm relations with the Soviet Union around 1960, but relations deteriorated as Algerian–Moroccan friction grew.

[i]See sections dealing with the situational economic and cultural restraints on Soviet policy.

these problems would be less important; since Moscow is now a major actor on the Middle East scene, however, they are key policy limitations. Since it is evident that the Soviet Union will avoid direct military involvement in hostilities•between Israel and the Arab countries, Soviet support must deliver benefits of almost equal value, such as the provision of decisive military equipment or a settlement favorable to Arab interests. However, none of these benefits is deliverable, because each must be considered in the context of the reactions to it that are likely—that is, "decisive" military equipment, for example, even if it were deliverable and effectively operable by Arab military officers, would be met by Israeli technological development or Israeli weapons acquisition from the West. Yet, what is the point of reliance on the Soviet Union if that reliance does not result in a net benefit to the Arabs? And if the United States should be able to secure concessions from Israel while the USSR cannot, is it not more reasonable to work with the former?[40] There are, then, weighty reasons for the Soviets to move toward the support of Arab objectives, even when they may conflict with Moscow's own short-term goals, in order to achieve more important long-range objectives. The traditional objective is to seek the support of the most powerful ally (so long as the objectives of the most powerful do not conflict with one's own). The Soviet Union, however, has moved to ally itself with the weaker party in the Arab–Israeli conflict.

From Moscow's point of view, this weakness may appear so profound that it debases the political value of the dependency relationship that arises from it. A political base is built so that it can be used to achieve some political end. But the Soviet Union's extensive political base in the Middle East has seemed so insecure that shoring it up has become the major Soviet policy preoccupation in the region.[41]

Similarly, the Soviet Union's stance with regard to the Palestinian movement has been characterized by ambivalence.[42] Although the immediate needs of the movement (financial and materiel support, for example) are more easily met than are those of Arab governments, the long-term meaning of the movement as a whole poses important problems and potential problems for the Soviet Union in its relations with Arab countries, particularly now that these relations have broadened to include more than only "progressive" states.

Regional Economic Constraints. Among the several economic considerations that limit the options open to Soviet policy is Arab awareness of the superiority of Western technology and organization.[43] This problem handicaps the Soviet Union in trade, and conditions the interest of elites in Soviet approaches to economic planning in several fields.

Also problematic in the past has been the failure to adapt Soviet economic tools and materials to the Middle East environment. Similarly, Soviet standards have not always reflected either Middle East requirements on the one hand, or the local absorption rates, on the other.[44]

These failures were due in large measure to the emphasis on the political objectives of economic assistance. In recent years, however, the USSR has become much more thorough in the pre-project evaluation and planning stages of economic development projects with a view to more accurately analyzing the feasibility and effects of proposed projects. The essential fact in this matter, however, is that the political sector in the Middle East (and, we suggest, other) countries is remarkably well insulated from economic incentives and punishments.[45] On matters of importance, Arab governments act in accordance with their own interests largely irrespective of exogenous economic considerations.

Regional Military Constraints. There are also constraints of a military character on Soviet policy in the Middle East. These flow in some cases from the nature of the Soviet interest in the area—that is, from its proximity[46] and from the importance of its lines of communication.[47]

Other factors imposing restraints on the substance of Moscow's regional policy in the past were the Western military alliances (the Baghdad Pact/CENTO, NATO). More important, apart from their role in regard to political and military objectives (see Chapter 2), today the foreign military forces in the area operate as a consideration primarily in the task of contingency planning. Forces external to the Middle East that may take a role in hostilities there include the U.S. Sixth Fleet, and the fleets of Italy, Spain, Yugoslavia and Greece, as well as units of the French fleet. Of these the most important in a non-nuclear context is the Italian fleet, which is larger than the Soviet Mediterranean squadron.

Because the U.S. Sixth Fleet poses a potent offensive threat to the physical security of the Soviet Union itself, we have already seen that intelligence and other defensive preparations relating directly to the Sixth Fleet are Soviet objectives in the Mediterranean. To the extent the Fleet's presence occasions the need for these specific programs, it can also be considered a constraint on Soviet policy, for these strategic needs divert resources from other purposes and may in some cases involve considerable political cost (when, for example, intelligence operations directed against the Sixth Fleet incur the resentment of local leaders who do not wish to play such a direct role in the Soviet–American confrontation). The lack of air support organic to the Mediterranean Squadron is a major reason the USSR needs use of nearby air bases for its strategic requirements vis-à-vis the Sixth Fleet.[48]

In terms of local politics, the growth of the Soviet military presence has entailed several major constraints as well as major benefits. First, the presence of large numbers of foreign military personnel can be an irritating phenomenon producing friction where good relations existed. The United States encountered this problem in Vietnam, in Japan, and in the Mediterranean *before* the Soviet squadron garnered a major role.[49]

Second, the absence of local Soviet military forces provided an excellent excuse for military non-intervention in local crises in 1956, 1958, and until about 1965 or 1966. The only feasible operations prior to the build-up of the Mediterranean squadron consisted in recourse to missiles or long-range bombers, and such threats were, in fact, resorted to on several occasions when the outcome was already known or the circumstances indicated no physical harm to the USSR would eventuate. After 1966, however, non-intervention was more difficult to explain, and, indeed, conflicting expectations arose in this regard.[50] Following the 1967 war, it was clear that only American participation would engender direct Soviet military intervention in renewed Arab–Israeli hostilities. This realization once again imposed a major constraint: how to communicate substantial support for the Arab side of the conflict to Arab governments without in fact being willing to take steps clearly within Soviet capabilities to realize Arab objectives.[51] At the same time, U.S. forces (the reason Soviet capabilities would not be maximally utilized) imposed even greater constraints on Soviet freedom of action. Since Soviet forces were now in a position to intervene, it was imperative in the event of hostilities—and preferable even in the case of a threat of hostilities—to communicate to the United States that Soviet forces would not participate. Indeed, this requirement was of higher priority than the preceding one, inasmuch as the prevention of a Soviet–American conflict was preeminent among Moscow's global aims.

Further, local constraints on Soviet policy devolved from the nature of the societies with which the USSR interacted. First, armed forces personnel were not highly educated, nor had they been socialized to an industrial society.[52] As a result, training was difficult, tedious work, and indigenous capabilities did not improve as rapidly as the Soviets had probably hoped. Despite the transfer of large numbers of modern weapons, relatively little of the weaponry could be effectively absorbed at a time.[53]Some of the equipment originally developed for the use of Soviet forces had little utility in the Middle East environment, but it was years before serious efforts were made toward the adaptation of materiel and training techniques to the local situation.[54]

The transfer of weapons and other military equipment to local armed forces sometimes had the desired effect of demonstrating Soviet interest in and support for, first (until the late 1950s) developing countries, then the Arabs, in particular. On the other hand, and especially when large numbers of advisory personnel accompanied the weapons transfers (which, however, was the only feasible approach to attempting to upgrade local absorption capability), relations between Arab military officers and the Soviet Union and its representatives sometimes deteriorated. Among the problems the USSR encountered was the usually anti-communist, often bourgeois, and sometimes pro—Western attitudes of the officer elites. These attitudes and the natural resentment at the presence within one country of representatives of a foreign power assisting indigenous military personnel—which suggests the local military are not as competent as their foreign counterparts and constitutes therefore an implicit affront to their dignity—were a major potential irritant in Soviet–Arab relations, and conditioned to some degree the effectiveness of the Soviet military assistance program.[j]

Regional Cultural Constraints. While the cultural objectives and interests of the Soviet Union are not of great significance to Soviet Middle East policy, the local constraints posed by cultural factors on the effectiveness of that policy are much more important. Communism is alien to the Middle East, and whether Soviet policy utilizes the "soft" or "hard" sell in this regard, the USSR is still identified with communism by many Arabs. Similarly, the Soviet campaign against organized religion (including Islam) still operates to some extent within the USSR even though the antireligious movement has been silenced internationally.[k] Atheism has little direct effect upon intergovernmental relations,[55] but it is associated with communist philosophy and with the USSR, and atheism remains repugnant to most Arab Muslims.[56]

Second, there is a widespread feeling in the Arab world that Western technology and organization are superior to their Soviet counterparts (see above). Similarly, there is a feeling of greater identity with the West than with the USSR as a result of the age-old intercourse among Mediterranean societies and the concentrated penetration by many states of Middle Eastern societies during the colonial period. This traditional interaction has been reinforced by the Western-oriented or Western-influenced education of the present-day elites of most Arab countries.[57]

Regional Ideological Constraints. Ideological objectives, like cultural objectives, are not important to Soviet Middle East policy. Like cultural

---

[j]Before 1967, the Soviet program does not seem to have emphasized effectiveness, anyway, since relatively little training, follow-on support, or the other concomitants of an effective assistance program (of any type) were provided. After 1967, however, a much greater interest seems to have been shown in upgrading Arab military capability—or, at the least, in the appearance of determination to upgrade that capability.

[k]The religious repression is much less pronounced now than it was in the early years of the USSR.

constraints on that policy, too, however, ideological limitations are more significant than the objectives.

If communism were an attractive philosophy to the populations of the Middle East or, more importantly, to the elites, then greater efforts might be exerted by the USSR in behalf of local communist parties. However, because the parties have been able to gain only relatively few adherents, they are not particularly significant actors in the domestic political environments of most Arab countries. The communist parties themselves constitute a constraint on the effectiveness of Soviet policy, because they are considered opposition elements by ruling circles. Thus, since the USSR provides external verbal support, its roles both as a foreign mouthpiece of a local opposition and as sponsor of an internal opposition are viewed as interference in domestic affairs.

As chief sponsor of the international communist movement, the USSR is identified with a philosophy alien to the beliefs and attitudes of the Arab Middle East, where nationalism and, outside the elites, religion are more compelling ideologies. As sponsor of an opposition element, espousing a revolutionary ideology,[58] the Soviet Union is associated by Arab elites with a threat to their dominance. Soviet behavior, in this regard, does not support this concern. Yet, Moscow's actions on behalf of local communist parties or leaders continue to arouse Arab governments' suspicions.

The Constraints on Soviet Policy:
A Summary

Too often the foreign policy of a great power is considered without reference to any but the most important limitations on the state's freedom of action; too seldom is the entirety of constraints within which the decision-making apparatus must operate scrutinized. In fact, we find this corresponds to the decisional process itself, where many or most of the parameters remain unstated but understood. The disadvantage of this silent communication is that different individuals perceive the same factors in a different light. The advantage is equally important: the human mind cannot grasp and assess such large numbers of variables simultaneously.

We have tried in this chapter to elaborate many of the most important constraints on the substantive formulation and on the effectiveness of Soviet foreign policy in the Middle East. Although international global considerations were briefly addressed, it is important to recognize that any activity (even deliberation on foreign policy questions) requires the allocation of resources that are limited. As a result of the already large and still growing Soviet involvement in international relations in virtually every region of the globe the major policy constraint will continue to be the relative importance of any single initiative in the Middle East in terms of the many competing demands for Soviet resources elsewhere.

**Part II
Soviet Activities in the
Middle East**

Introduction to
Part II

Since the early 1950s when only a few states in the Middle East maintained diplomatic or other relations with the USSR, Soviet involvement in the Middle East has grown across the entire spectrum of international and transnational relations. In Part II, we shall discuss the instruments of influence employed by Moscow and the techniques by which optimization of the effectiveness of these instruments is attempted.

The foreign actions of nation-states may be grouped in a number of ways; these actions include representation, cooperation (and conflict), communications, and penetration. Note that we employ a misrepresentation here: we are grouping actions together as if all activities executed by persons (individual or organizational) residing in foreign states are carried out on behalf of the persons' countries of origin. While this is clearly not the case, it is close to being a valid simplification in terms of the Soviet Union, whose nationals (other than permanent expatriates who should not, in any event be considered in this model) and overseas enterprises act responsively to, if not at the direction of, the government of the USSR.

By *representation*, we refer to the enduring symbol of one state in the territory of another and to the single body endowed with the right to represent the foreign country (indeed, to represent its chief of state), the "permanent diplomatic mission."

By *cooperation* is meant the entire spectrum of cooperative-conflictual relationships. This includes diplomatic negotiation, treaties and their implementation; many aspects of economic, military, and cultural assistance, both planning and effectuation; foreign trade; cultural and scientific exchange; joint *démarches* to third countries or international organizations; joint military or commercial operations; statements by one government supporting or opposing the policy of another and made with the intent of demonstrating to governmental actors a degree of cooperation or disagreement; and acts of war.

"Communication" refers to those activities that seek to establish or utilize a channel for the interchange of ideas between the government or peoples of one state and individuals, groups, or the society of another as an audience.

"Penetration" suggests a relationship directly between one state (or its peoples) and the peoples of another. In a sense, communication, as we have used it, is a specialized form of penetration. The ties of one government to youth groups, political parties, or communication media in another society are all forms of penetration. Cultural interchange, apart from its forms (i.e., cooperative elements), is another example of penetration.

These functions are carried out through political, economic, military, and cultural activities. Unfortunately, activities and functions do not fall into discrete categories, but they may be generally catalogued as shown in Table 1.

Table 1
Important International Governmental Activities

Functions	Activities			
	Political	Economic	Military	Cultural
Representation	X			
Cooperation	X	X	X	X
Communication	X			X
Penetration	X	X	X	X

Exemplary activities of each type are shown in Table 2.

Table 2, then, presents the typology of activities we propose as a framework within which to consider Soviet activities in the Middle East. The activities overlap functional categories in many cases, but that is reflective of reality: individual actions of states often serve several functions (e.g., military advisory teams serve cooperative, communications, and penetrative functions) and, though they may be typed as, say, political or military, they may in fact be both. Indeed, most of the relations of great powers with developing countries serve political ends, either for communication or penetration. (The ship visit, for example, is a military activity with cultural and economic ramifications, but undertaken for political purposes.)

As the instruments of Soviet policy are reviewed below they will be considered in terms of the *type* of activity—that is, political, economic, military, or cultural—irrespective of the several types of impacts, and irrespective of the function or functions the activity might have been initiated in order to serve.

Table 2
Typology of International Governmental Activities

	Political	Economic	Military	Cultural
Representation	Diplomatic mission	Economic experts	Military facility	Visits
Cooperation	Agreements, joint démarches, negotiations, threats, war, and so forth.	Aid, trade, government agreements on economic matters, foreign economic enterprises.	Military assistance, military agreements, joint overseas training, and so forth.	Cultural enterprises, scientific and educational exchange and agreements, and so forth.
Communication	Propaganda, visits, public statements, and so forth.	Propaganda, visits, and so forth.	Visits.	Propaganda, visits.
Penetration	Ties to and use of interest groups, political parties, and so forth.	Foreign economic enterprises, interest groups, training, advisors, exhibitions, visits, and so forth.	Advisors, training.	Educational and scientific exchange, books and other media, friendship societies, language and other interest groups, and so forth.

4

Political Activities

The political instruments of the Soviet Union in the Middle East are, apart from the local communist parties, not greater than those of other major powers.

Political Representation

The diplomatic missions of the Soviet Union in Middle East and North African countries are larger than those of most other states external to the region. However, unlike their Western counterparts, Soviet diplomatic missions, are generally not very involved in the community of the host country. Members of the diplomatic missions are intentionally isolated and tend to generate the impression of a formal barrier between representational interaction and their private lives. They usually live together and keep to themselves more than the American diplomatic community.

On the other hand, the Soviets have been able to utilize one resource not as plentiful in the West for representation—Soviet Muslims.[1] A number of Soviet Muslims from Central Asia have held ambassadorships or other high-level representational roles in the Arab world.[a]

Not surprisingly, the precise nature of the personal relationships between members of the diplomatic mission—especially the ambassador—and officials of the government to which he is accredited varies markedly from case to case. It is a function of circumstance as well as of personality, but personality clearly does play a key role in this regard. That this variable has a significant impact upon the overall quality of Soviet political relations with a regime is highly dubious except in the most unusual circumstances.

Soviet diplomatic missions seem to try to convey the impression of intimacy with certain regimes, namely, those regimes that are (1) popular or stable, (2) inclined to support the Soviet political line on international matters of low priority to the Middle East, and (3) not on particularly bad terms with other Arab governments.[2]

Political Cooperation

Instruments to operationalize the cooperative-conflictual dimension of

---

[a] Examples of the use of Soviet Central Asians as envoys to the Middle East are current Soviet Ambassador Azimov (Lebanon), Mohieddinov (Syria), and Rakhmatov (Yemen).

Soviet–Middle Eastern intergovernmental relations are diverse and of particular importance in supporting Soviet policy objectives in the area.

From the 1920s on, the USSR has been involved in the Middle East in one way or another, but until the mid-1950s, most of this Soviet activity centered on relations with Iran and Turkey. Relations with Yemen and Saudi Arabia were established in the 1920s in order to demonstrate and furnish support to those two governments in their conflicts with the British.

After World War II, continuing the prewar support for anti–British regimes, the USSR was the first state to extend recognition *de jure* to Israel and entered into discussions with several countries on weapons transfers in the early 1950s. Relations were skeletal with most of the states of the region but were improving except in the case of Israel. Soviet support, in the absence of close relations, was demonstrated primarily through communications media.

The deepening Arab–Israeli conflict and the growing rift between the reformist and traditionalist Arab regimes provided the opportunity for Soviet entry into the Middle East scene. While most observers justifiably stress Soviet exploitation of the two major political conflicts of the Middle East, we believe it is far from clear to what extent the Soviet Union intentionally exploited those conflicts. Although they were aggravated by a number of factors—mostly internal to the Middle East—the two conflicts acted to create for certain Arab states a circumstance in which a turn to the USSR was manifestly the best tactic.[3] Thus, rather than a conscious shift in strategy designed to destabilize a shaky situation, the movement toward closer and broader relationships with some Arab states seems to have taken place almost automatically. It was probably only after the process was well under way that trends were clearly enough drawn to enable Soviet policymakers to recognize the opportunities that confronted them. This recognition probably took place about the same time as the later stages of the Suez crisis.

The structuring of the political environment on which the Western powers had begun to establish postwar security institutions was in flux in the early 1950s, even though the results were not evident for several years thereafter. Shifts in this structure caused the interests of the centers of Arab nationalism and those of the Soviet Union to coalesce. The four principal trends of Arab nationalism—neutralism, anticolonialism, anti–Zionism, and development—were in large measure antithetical to the policies pursued by Western powers, especially the United States, at that time. They fitted in well with the interests of the Soviet Union, however, which asked not commitment in the cold war but even-handedness,[4] which opposed the colonial powers, inasmuch as they were the chief allies of the United States, which held long-standing objections to Zionism (though not to Israel), and which had supported revolutionary change as a tool for rapid socioeconomic and political development.

The Suez crisis, following on the Egyptian arms purchase, was a turning point in Soviet–Middle East relations. From 1956, when Moscow must have *determined* to exploit Arab–Israeli problems, the Arab countries could count on Soviet support against Israel in the United Nations, a relatively new phenomenon. A concentrated effort was made to establish the full range of relationships between the governments of the Arab Middle East and the Soviet Union.

As in any relationship between sovereign states, the objectives of the Soviet Union could best have been realized by influencing local states in such a way that they, too, sought the same (or similar) goals, even if for different reasons. This, in any event, is the essence of international relations: the use of promises, rewards, threats, or punishments to influence the actions of other states. In order to be in a position to employ these approaches effectively in the Middle East, where there had been few links between Moscow and the local states in the past, the Soviet Union pursued a strategy of building a degree of dependency into these relationships.

Yet, from the mid-1950s on, the USSR has increasingly abjured the use of "violence, threats, and intimidation even when irritations and difficulties developed."[5] This restraint has facilitated and probably accelerated rapprochement in a number of cases. Such behavior also fits well with the image of the USSR as a true friend of the Arab states, an image the Soviet Union is probably interested in propagating more outside government circles than within them (where it is unlikely to be accepted).

Along the same lines, the USSR was quick to come to the defense of Arab friends in 1956 when it implicitly threatened the use of nuclear weapons during the Suez crisis. Although the United States also supported Egypt in 1956, the effects of the U.S. position on the Arabs was dissipated as a result of (1) the stronger stance of the Soviet Union and (2) U.S. support for Israel on the question of rights in the Straits of Tiran. Again in 1957 and in 1958 Moscow acted as protector of Syria and Iraq, respectively, when threats to those regimes were said to exist.[6]

Cooperative relations between the Soviet Union and Arab states were emphasized by the signing of accords in various areas, and by numerous visits both to the Soviet Union by high levels of the Middle Eastern governments and to the Middle East by similar Soviet delegations and leaders. These visits often resulted in attention being given to the broad areas of policy agreement between the Soviet Union on the one hand and several Arab governments on the other.

So long as the USSR was not expected to participate in military operations in the Middle East, little restraint was counselled to those governments acquiring arms through Moscow. However, after the 1967 war and growth of the Soviet Mediterranean squadron, restraint was imposed through limitations on arms transfers by type (rather than by quantity). Permitting the continued quantitative arms increase served Soviet interests by forcing Israel to continue to look to the West for arms that were, after 1967, supplied almost exclusively by the United States, which was a shift in arms transfer patterns that also served Soviet interests. Limiting the type of weapons sent to Arab governments was an effective means of preventing any serious inclination to attack Israel to regain territories occupied by the latter in 1967.

After the 1967 war, the USSR turned in several areas to consolidate its position in the Middle East. But since the Israeli occupation of Arab territories led Arab governments toward either conquest of Israel or some form of settlement, and given the impossibility of the former, the lack of Soviet influence in negotiations with Israel led Moscow to support multilateral approaches on this issue.

Before and after the 1973 war, the Soviet Union attempted to dissuade the Arabs from large-scale violence, although it is not known whether or to what extent this may have been the case just prior to the October 1973 war.[b] Counseling against violence has not conflicted with consistent diplomatic support of the Arab cause, however. With those Middle East governments that took a "hard line" on the Israeli question, Moscow simply deemphasized that aspect of bilateral relations. To the degree differences have been public, Soviet statements have tended to a minimalist rather than an activist position in criticizing the positions of Arab governments.

After 1967 and again after 1973, the Soviet Union supported a settlement. However, a settlement, or the possibility of a settlement, that would exclude the USSR but return lost Arab territories would certainly *not* be in the Soviet interest; at the same time, even less in the Soviet interest— because of the importance of the possibility to local governments— would be the appearance that Moscow was blocking the return of the territories.

It is important to note that Soviet diplomacy in all matters in the Middle East is built upon bilateralism. The USSR does not publicly attack the idea of Arab unity, but Arabism, and therefore Arab unity, has some potentially significant disadvantages for Soviet policy. It would tend to stress the cultural ties of the Arab world, which are much more closely linked with the West than with the Soviet Union. Moreover, since World War II, the major efforts toward Arab unity have been made in those states in which the Soviet Union has had great political and economic investments, and these efforts might have been wasted. Once again, however, Soviet statements on the subject have been general (i.e., not country-oriented) and low key. Even in cases where Moscow's decision makers have been known to

---

[b]Since the USSR had come under mounting Arab criticism for not supplying more advanced weapons, it would not be surprising if the easier path—that of silence and non-interference in Arab decision making—were taken.

be disappointed, Soviet statements have generally *supported* the specific cases of Arab unity.

The single, most important symbol of agreement is a political treaty. Since a treaty of this type generally seeks to legitimize the status quo, it is not surprising that the USSR avoided treaty making in the Middle East for some time. Indeed, as we have already pointed out, the interests of the local regimes, and of the Soviet Union parallelled each other in abnegating commitment. Later, however, when the USSR enjoyed a more influential position in the Middle East, it was Moscow that sought the treaty commitment, even if the commitment was defensive in character,[c] in an effort to solidify its dominance in certain polities.

Political Communication

Communication with the peoples of the Middle East is accomplished through diverse means. These include public statements by Soviet officials; joint statements, communiques, and the like, issued with Arab governments; the printed media, and the broadcast and telecast media as well, of course, as face-to-face communications.

Persuasive communications do not always try to "persuade." Much of propaganda or psychological operations is designed merely to keep channels of communication open,[7] to build the credibility of the source. The Soviet Union has been particularly active in the communications effort in the Middle East, and its resources for this effort are greater than those of most other countries.

Overt radio broadcasts to the Middle East from the USSR feature programs in Arabic, Armenian, Azerbaijani, Hebrew, Kurdish, Persian, Tadzhik, and Uzbek, and originate from half a dozen different stations. In addition, clandestine radio stations have operated from Soviet and East European territory (e.g., Radio Iran Courier, Voice of the Iraqi People). The latter often propounded views slightly divergent from Soviet policy and more in line with the supposed views of their audiences inside the target states.[8] Resources also include books and journals published in the Soviet Union and Eastern Europe, and similar materials published in the Middle East by groups well disposed toward, or subsidized by, the Soviet Union.

Increasingly, local news media receive information from NOVOSTI, the Soviet press agency. Indeed, some government-sponsored news media in the Middle East today receive most of their foreign news from Soviet, East European, or Chinese press agencies. These agencies, which employ a much more interested stance in the presentation of news than even their

[c]For example, in Egypt and Iraq.

Western counterparts, may play a role of increasing effectiveness in the shaping of Middle Eastern perceptions and attitudes (see Chapter 7).

Political Penetration

As in political communication, the USSR disposes of unusually rich resources in other forms of political penetration. Most prominent are the local communist parties that for the most part adhere to Soviet policy. In addition to the parties, however, there exist in most Middle Eastern countries individuals whose Marxist, quasi–Marxist, or strongly reformist attitudes conduce to easier identification with the Soviet Union than with other governments, including, perhaps, their own. Moreover, apart from communist party members, ideologues, and radical reformists, Moscow, like other great powers, employs individuals indigenous to the Middle East to carry out or support its policies in the area, by helping in demonstrations, writing and circulating tracts on various subjects, supplying intelligence, engaging in espionage and sabotage and similar acts. Last, groups and associations, nominally considered constituted for other purposes, are utilized to support or spread the Soviet viewpoint on issues of interest to the local community or to international relations. These groups are discussed elsewhere in this study (see Chapter 7).

As we have pointed out more extensively above, the USSR has used local communist parties in different ways at different times. The essential point in the contrast of the present period with the almost four decades before 1955 is that there was no other important Soviet presence in the Middle East in the latter, whereas Moscow is now extremely active in the region. It is as a result of this change and its implications for the diversity and flexibility required of Soviet–Middle Eastern intergovernmental relations that the role of indigenous communist parties in Soviet policy has undergone a pronounced decline in importance. The new approach to communist party participation in countries ruled by nationalist regimes whose international position is sufficiently anti–Western has been to act less as opposition elements and more as in the "national front" era, except that under current circumstances the party cooperates with the ruling group (while in the 1930s the Middle East "national fronts" opposed the colonial administration).[9]

Two innovations constitute the *ne plus ultra* of this new approach by which "virtual self-effacement of the party was accepted in order to attain ultimate communist goals at some future date."[10] The first is dissolution of the party; the second, official recognition of the nationalist ruling party by the Communist Party of the Soviet Union.

. . . In many former colonies and semi-colonies, socialist development is both possible and necessary before class stratification has become sufficiently pronounced. Under such conditions, when . . . the proletariat has not yet developed into a leading force in social development, the intermediate strata, namely the peasantry, the lower urban classes and the democratic intelligentsia, acquire political independence and thus assume a particularly active role. The revolutionary democracy becomes their spokesman.

So wrote Soviet ideologist Karen Brutents in *Kommunist* in 1964.[11] Soon thereafter, the Egyptian Communist Party dissolved to enable its members as individuals to join the Arab Socialist Union. Soviet policy has justified along these lines working closely with some Arab nationalist regimes and has in those cases usually supported the regimes or strictly limited its support of local communist parties when conflicts have arisen.

The other innovation is direct collaboration between ruling non-communist parties and the CPSU or similar institutions. This approach has been followed with Algeria, Iraq, and other ruling parties,[d] but has often resulted in friction with local communists on substantive problems.

---

[d]Interparty visits, organizational (and sometimes doctrinal) cooperation, and participation in conferences—such as the types of activity most typical of this collaboration. Such contacts have been very numerous.

5 Economic Activities

Introduction

Although Soviet economic activities in the Middle East could also be studied in the functional framework we have suggested above, we feel that all Soviet economic relations with the Third World serve essentially to support political objectives; all are designed with cooperative and penetrative goals—primarily the latter. The evidence that penetration is most important is that Soviet aid and trade with the Third World are costly to the Soviet economic system (relatively more costly than the equivalent amount would be to the United States); that the Soviet Union could easily continue to avoid economic relations with the Middle East (indeed, could function more efficiently in those circumstances); that the nature of and trends in Soviet economic enterprises in the region tend to evince political priorities; and that the Soviet Union has made little secret of its determination to demonstrate, for politically relevant ends, "that the Soviet program of modernization [is] more effective than that of the West."[1] In view of the ultimate purpose of this sphere of activity, we have divided the subject of economic activities into sections on economic assistance and trade.

Economic Assistance

The history of Soviet foreign economic assistance might be said to go back almost to the days of the revolution, because the USSR has considered the cancellation of foreign debts to the Czarist regime as a form of aid. Certainly, the Soviet Union embarked on more typical assistance programs as early as the 1930s.[2] Yet, in terms of a systematic effort more appropriately designated as a "program," Soviet economic assistance to the Third World did not commence until well after Western programs of assistance. Trade with the developing areas began about 1951; small amounts of technical assistance, through the United Nations, began in 1953. We have already considered the changes underway in the international system that gave rise to the Soviet decision to extend itself in Middle Eastern affairs. Too, we have mentioned that the postwar reconstruction and general economic position of the USSR did not permit of significant economic assistance before the death of Stalin.

81

Table 5-1
Economic Assistance to the Middle East
($U.S. million)

	USSR (1954–72)	East European (1954–72)	U.S. Development Assistance[a]		U.S. Export–Import Bank Loans		U.S. Total	
			(1946–72)	(1953–72)	(1946–72)	(1953–72)	(1946–72)	(1953–72)
Bahrain	0	0	0	0	0	0	0	0
Egypt[b]	1,198	671	931.7	919.4	55.3	48.0	987.0	967.4
Iran[b]	562	435	634.3	507.7	336.6	336.6	970.9	844.3
Iraq	549	419	45.3	43.9	11.7	11.7	57.0	55.6
Israel[b]	0	0	1,087.4	1,000.9	350.3	215.3	1,437.7	1,216.2
Jordan[b]	0	0	411.1	405.9	10.1	10.1	421.2	416.0
Kuwait	0	0	0	0	50.0	50.0	50.0	50.0
Lebanon	0	0	121.8	118.2	4.8	4.8	126.6	123.0
Oman	0	0	0	0	0	0	0	0
Qatar	0	0	0	0	0	0	0	0
Saudi Arabia	0	0	31.8	27.1	40.2	25.4	72.0	52.5
Syria	317	287	60.9	60.5	0	0	60.9	60.5
Turkey[b]	534	14	1,880.2	1,642.9	123.5	91.2	2,003.7	1,734.1
U.A.E.	0	0	0	0	0	0	0	0
Y.A.R.[b]	92	17	17.6	17.6	0	0	17.6	17.6
P.D.R.Y.	14	16	2.7	2.7	0	0	2.7	2.7

CENTO	0	0	29.8	29.8	0	0	29.8	29.8
Algeria[b]	421	246	178.9	178.9	34.0	34.0	212.9	212.9
Libya[b]	0	0	184.7	182.9	0	0	184.7	182.9
Morocco[b]	88	40	747.3	747.0	33.2	33.2	780.5	780.2
Sudan	64	153	104.4	104.4	1.3	1.3	105.7	105.7
Tunisia[b]	34	73	727.9	727.7	7.6	7.6	735.5	735.3
Middle East Total	3,266	1,859	5,254.6	4,776.6	982.5	793.1	6,237.1	5,569.7
North Africa Total	607	512	1,943.2	1,940.9	76.1	76.1	2,019.3	2,017.0
Total	3,873	2,371	7,197.8	6,717.5	1,058.6	869.2	8,256.4	7,586.7

Source: U.S. Department of State, *Communist States and Developing Countries: Aid and Trade in 1972*, RECS–10 (1973), U.S. Agency for International Development, *U.S. Overseas Loans and Grants and Assistance from International Organizations: Obligations and Loan Authorizations, July 1, 1945–June 30, 1972* (May 1973). Figures may not add due to rounding.

Note: The purpose of this table is to provide a frame of reference for Soviet assistance to the countries of the Middle East and North Africa. It should not, of course, be assumed that these are the only countries providing aid. Australia, Austria, Belgium, Canada, Denmark, France, the Federal Republic of Germany, Italy, Japan, the Netherlands, Norway, Sweden, Switzerland, the United Kindom (i.e., all the members of the Development Assistance Committee except Portugal) and China are among the other donors. International organizations have also provided significant sums. For DAC government aid, see the *Middle East Economic Digest*, Vol. 16, No. 44 (November 3, 1972), p. 1261; for Chinese aid, see U.S. Department of State, *Communist States and Developing Countries: Aid and Trade in 1972*; for the figures on international organizations assistance, see U.S. AID, *U.S. Overseas Loans and Grants* (1972).

[a]U.S. Development Assistance includes economic assistance granted under the Agency for International Development and predecessor agencies (loans, grants, and supporting assistance); Food for Peace (sales and donations, including emergency relief); and other official economic assistance (including Peace Corps, capital subscriptions and contributions to international lending organizations, UNRRA, etc.).

[b]Economic assistance figures do not include security supporting assistance that has been included in military assistance (see Table 6–4).

In 1954, then, the Soviet Union undertook its own aid program. From that time to 1972, Soviet economic assistance to the Middle East and North Africa amounted to almost $4 billion and comprised about half of all Soviet economic aid worldwide.[3] (In view of the close relationship between Soviet policy and East European political and economic decisions, especially in the 1950s, it may be worth noting that East European aid to the Middle East and North Africa over the same period totalled about $2.5 billion, or well over half of all economic aid extended worldwide from that source.[4])

Cost

The figures in Tables 5-1 and 5-2 may be viewed from a number of perspec-

Table 5–2
U.S. and Soviet Economic Assistance to the Middle East
($U.S. million)

	Soviet Economic Assistance 1954–1972	U.S. Economic Assistance 1953–1972	U.S. Economic Assistance 1946–1972
Egypt	1,198	967	987
Iran	562	844	971
Iraq	549	56	57
Israel		1,216	1,438
Jordan		416	421
Kuwait		50	50
Lebanon		123	126
Saudi Arabia		53	72
Syria	317	61	61
Turkey	534	1,734	2,004
Y.A.R.	92	18	18
P.D.R.Y.	14	3	3
CENTO		30	30
Algeria	421	213	213
Libya		183	185
Morocco	88	780	781
Sudan	64	106	106
Tunisia	34	735	736
Total Middle East	3,266	5,570	6,237
Total North Africa	607	2,017	2,019
Regional Total	3,873	7,587	8,256

Source: U.S. Aid, *U.S. Overseas Loans and Grants*; U.S. Department of State, *Communist Aid–1972*, Table 1.

tives. It is important to recall, however, that Soviet economic assistance is more expensive to the USSR than is American aid to the U.S. economy—that is, the real cost to the Soviet economy for a given amount of economic assistance is greater than the costs to Western economies for the same amount of aid. This is so for several reasons.

First, and most apparent, *the Soviet economy is not as highly developed* as that of the United States. Therefore, expenditure of the same resources for economic assistance would naturally involve greater proportionate diversion of resources for the Soviet Union.

Second, because *the Soviet economy is an over-full employment economy*, there is no way foreign assistance can avoid bringing about a reduction in consumption, investment, or military expenditures.

Third, as we have already noted, *foreign assistance projects are the least rational* approach to *expenditures of resources* in an economy structured like that of the Soviet Union.[5]

Characteristics

Soviet aid is generally provided in the form of credits. Probably because of the ubiquitous planning requirements, aid and trade have been closely linked. Although aid can be offered more quickly than in other systems (since it is not subject to domestic debate), project planning and implementation have been slower and worse, and product quality has generally been lower.[6] The planning hand can also be seen in the overall assistance profile with its greatly varying totals from one year to the next. Since credit once extended has taken some time to be drawn, if it is drawn at all, two or three consecutive barren years of aid would leave the effectiveness of the central plan open to great outside influences—speed of drawing on extended credits—if the assistance remained at a high level. Instead, the aid has been very uneven. For example, economic assistance to the Middle East and North Africa for the five-year period of 1967 to 1971 has varied as shown in Table 5–3.[7]

Table 5–3
Five-Year Pattern of Soviet Aid

($U.S. million)

	1968	1969	1970	1971	1972
Middle East	178	487	76	418	66
North Africa	0	42	44	189	0
Total	178	529	120	607	66

Soviet economic assistance programs aim at the state sector of the recipient country's economy (although in several cases the benefits to the private sector are great).[8] The common impression that a premium is placed on high-visibility (or "impact") projects is misleading.[9] Such projects have been relatively few (though more numerous, and perhaps more grandiose, than in Western aid programs). Similarly misleading is the fact that most Soviet credits support the development of industry.[10] The overall figures do indeed validate that statement, since about half of Soviet economic aid to the Middle East has been for industrial development. But 40 percent of all Soviet industrial assistance has been in India, so that much less resource emphasis on industrialization is evident in other areas such as the Middle East.[11] Similarly, while it is true that the USSR has concentrated upon a few states in the Middle East rather than dispersing aid resources throughout the area,[12] this is also a reflection of the political relations between the donor and recipient. As Soviet relations with Iran and Turkey have improved, a considerable amount of aid has been sent to both states, and as new states with governments well-disposed to the USSR have come to the international scene (e.g., the People's Republic of South Yemen now known as the People's Democratic Republic of Yemen), Soviet aid has been tendered. "Selectivity and receptivity in this context are two sides of the same coin."[13]

The USSR has always stressed that Soviet assistance is offered with no strings and irrespective of the nature and foreign policy of recipient countries. It may be worth considering however that of all countries receiving $50 million or more in Soviet assistance, only a half dozen did not follow a foreign policy line sympathetic to the USSR or were not neighbors. Even if India and Pakistan are not counted as neighbors, the number is well under ten, about half in Latin America.[14]

Another key characteristic of Soviet foreign aid has been its relationship to the wishes of indigenous elites, to their "psychological needs." "If their development plans called for major infrastructural projects, Moscow was ready . . . ,"[15] irrespective in many cases of sound, objective economic planning.

A further advantage of Soviet aid over Western loans has been that repayment is generally in barter or local currency rather than in convertible currencies. In some cases, this has enabled recipients to use products difficult to sell in the West and that are needed domestically to repay Soviet loans (for example, the $200 million loan to Turkey).[16]

The administrative organization of Soviet foreign assistance has been much more stable than that of the United States. Constant restructuring and reorganization have characterized the latter, while the administrative framework of the former has remained virtually untouched almost since its inception. Within the recipient countries, such a comparison cannot be made, because only in very few host countries has the Soviet program employed any permanent economic mission. Since Soviet programs are project oriented, they are usually uncoordinated. Each project constitutes its own administration.[17]

Usually, Soviet aid is extended in a line of credit to be expended on specific projects mutually agreed upon at a later date.[a] These credits are almost always a loan—very little of Soviet aid is grant—repayable in kind or in local currency with a low interest rate but no grace period. The credits are generally to purchase equipment. The technicians and trainees' services are also covered. However, local costs incurred by the technicians are the host country's responsibility (which often delays a project).[18]

Since almost all (95 percent) Soviet aid is in the form of loans usually with a twelve-year repayment period, and since the program began in the 1950s, actual new expenditures over repayments are small. Grant aid, most frequently of a medical nature, is considered an expression of Soviet friendship. This is distinct from loans, which are viewed as contributions to development.[19]

In recent years, the economic assistance program has undergone some important changes. The ineffectiveness of the past assistance in making a substantial contribution to development; the very limited political leverage gained by substantial investment of resources; the growing demands on Soviet resources for other purposes; and the determination to increase the commercial benefits to the Soviet Union are among the more important reasons for the new approach. The changes have resulted in greater consideration of the rates of return on project aid, in terms both of the Soviet investment and the recipients'; more frequent and careful cost surveys; greater attention to comparative long-range Soviet commercial benefits as between various project possibilities; and modifications in loan terms.[20]

General Development Assistance

Soviet economic aid has emphasized primarily (1) industrialization, (2) electrification and the exploitation of major rivers, (3) mineral exploration and exploitation, but there have been (4) other specialized areas of assistance in specific countries. Technical assistance and other education and training have been further fields of aid activity.

Industrialization

Major undertakings such as steel plants and other important industries

---

[a]In such cases as the Aswan Dam, a major agreement is concluded dealing exclusively with the project.

have been the hallmarks of Russian aid in many developing countries. This sector of aid fits, but undermines, current trade patterns (see below). Industrialization aid often involves considerable technical aid and training, which increases contact between the industrial cadres of the Soviet Union and the developing countries. To the extent the newly developed industries rely on Soviet-built parts and other supplies and require Soviet training, or Soviet maintenance, these projects increase the dependency factor in relations with the USSR.

Moreover, the training in and implementation of Soviet industrial theory and practices are thought to increase the respect for Soviet society and for the historical development approach employed there, adding to the prestige of the Soviet Union and perhaps to its commercial products' acceptability as well.

Rivers and Electrification

The single, best-known Soviet assistance project anywhere in the developing world has undoubtedly been the construction of the Aswan Dam in the Arab Republic of Egypt. Aswan is by no means the only major example of this type of assistance provided nor is it merely a show piece. Aswan is an integral part of Egypt's electrification program, and the USSR has assisted in other projects within this program as well. At the same time, Aswan is a good example of a high-visibility project with high pay-off. Similar, though smaller, dams are being constructed elsewhere with Soviet aid.

Mineral Exploration and Exploitation

A more recent aid activity that has been pursued with increasing vigor is the exploration for and exploitation of mineral resources, including petroleum. For example, Soviet geologists have been exploring for natural gas, gold, ferrous and non-ferrous metals (platinum and tungsten) in diverse areas in Algeria.[21] Most of this activity in the Middle East either is commercial in nature or takes the form of technical assistance. Some, however, takes the form of financial aid. Soviet assistance to oil prospecting in Egypt's Sinai area, for example, was "stupendous" financial aid.[22]

Specialized Assistance

As in the case of other aid donors, a number of Soviet projects are innovative responses to the circumstances of individual developing countries. Among the most important of these has been an entire field of development assistance in the maritime sector. Port development at Hodeida and Berbera, shipyard construction at Alexandria and Basra, harbor and dock improvement at Aden, maritime surveys and studies for Iraq, and assistance to marine industries and navigation have each figured in the overall program.[23]

Education, Training, and Technical Assistance

Educational and training aid, and technical assistance, generally constitute one of the most important aspects of the aid effort. The rationale for emphasis upon this segment is the theory that individuals trained by the Soviet Union, either in their own country or especially in the USSR, will be more sympathetic to the Soviet Union and its allies than to others in their attitudes, perceptions, and actions, private and official. In some training and education areas, the self-selective process ensures that it is the elites of the country who are being exposed to this experience, which suggests the approach is affecting those who "make a difference." As in the case of aid to industrialization projects (to many of which technical assistance is related), training may induce trainees (who are potential decision makers) to use Soviet methods, products, or personnel.

Soviet education has generally been considered inferior to its Western counterpart by the Arabs. Trainees, however, develop a vested interest in doing their best to alter these views. To the extent Soviet education and training are viewed favorably in relation to Western education and training, the qualifications of the trainees are enhanced.

Technical assistance personnel in the Middle East constitute one of the Soviet Union's major endeavors. Having long decried the lack of technically competent workers in engineering, science, education, and labor as "one of the most pernicious legacies of long colonialist rule,"[24] Moscow took advantage of this vacuum to stress training of indigenous personnel in all its projects, primarily in an on-the-job context but in many cases through scholarships to the USSR.[25]

Perhaps with a view to avoiding some of the frictions that often develop between host country nationals and technical personnel from the donor state, technical training reduces the overall Soviet personnel commitment to individual countries. As a result, a larger number of technical experts may be sent at first,[b] but these personnel are generally sent for shorter

---

[b]This increases the difficulty recipient countries have in finding the resources to pay local costs and therefore often results in further delays in beginning the project. See Karel Holbik *The United States, The Soviet Union and the Third World* (Hamburg: Verlag Weltarchiv GMBH, 1968), p. 54.

periods. There is less long-term contact between recipient and donor nationals, and the latter endeavor to restrict participation in projects to a minimum once local personnel are trained.

Soviet technical aid personnel are highly competent. As often as possible, bachelors are sent, but with the growth of the program this objective has been less and less practicable. Many of the experts have a working knowledge of Arabic. The linguistic problem is, in any event, minimized as increasing numbers of trainees return from the Soviet Union with understanding of at least rudimentary Russian.[26]

In 1972, over half of all Soviet technical assistance personnel were working in the Middle East and North Africa (see Tables 7–5 and 7–6). Over 90 percent of the technical trainees from developing countries in the Soviet Union came from the Middle East. Approximately 40 percent of the 22,000 technical personnel from the Third World trained in the USSR since the inception of the programs in 1956 has come from Middle Eastern and North African countries. (Academic and technical exchanges are further discussed in Chapter 7; military advisory personnel, in Chapter 6.)

These programs have made real contributions to the development of Third World countries. Whether they have been of major benefit to the Soviet Union is dubious. While the size of the technical assistance program is minimal compared with the Western programs as a whole, the effect and even the figures in individual countries do not allow of this generalization. Soviet technical assistance, training in the USSR, or experts, constitute a major segment of that type of aid to Egypt, Iraq, Syria, and the two Yemens.

Summary

Soviet economic assistance, like its Western counterpart, has not yet given the USSR significant influence over the actions of the recipients in matters they consider important. It has been an expensive—and from the economic as well as the political viewpoint, not dramatically effective—technique. It does provide a certain degree of influence with respect to local governments in non-regional matters; the contact between Soviet and indigenous personnel has already provided through intelligence[c] and acquaintance occasional benefits to the USSR;[d] and the development assistance program continues to hold considerable potential gains for the Soviet Union, commercially and politically.

---

[c]The USSR has, however, made a distinct effort to keep intelligence operations separate from economic assistance. Holbik, *The United States*, p. 24.

[d]As, for example, in the case of Yemen, where Abdullah as-Sallal, later president, was befriended by Soviet technical assistance personnel while he was still a harbormaster at Hodeida.

Trade

The Soviet Union is not a great trading country, participating less in trade (relative to the size of its economy) than almost any other state.[27] International commerce entails problems for the centrally planned economy, since if carried on as in free economies, it would introduce perturbations for planning. (To overcome this difficulty, Soviet foreign trade is effected in large measure on the basis of long-term agreements.[28]) Second, the irrational pricing structure enables foreigners to purchase goods at prices below the true production cost. Because of controls instituted for this and other reasons, the Soviet Union and Eastern European governments generally balance trade bilaterally.[29]

Because developing countries' economies are usually characterized by balance of payments problems, those governments, too, prefer bilateral balancing. Moreover, they are willing to accept goods of lower quality than are required when they deal with the West.[30]

Thus, while Soviet trade with the Middle East has always been modest, it has increased noticeably as Soviet relations with the region grew. For example, trade with Egypt increased in size well over 1,000 percent between 1954 (before the arms agreement) and 1961. Economic relations with Iran and Turkey grew markedly in the 1960s, and the former is now the Soviet Union's second major trading partner in the Middle East (after Egypt). (See Tables 5–4 and 5–5.)

Only one Middle East state's exports to the Soviet Union surpass one fifth (20 percent) of its total exports, and that is Egypt, 38 percent of the exports of which went to the USSR in 1970 and over half the exports of which went to the Soviet Union and Eastern Europe. (See Table 5–6.)

Eastern Europe also takes an active part in Middle East trade, however, and while the Eastern European countries do not necessarily act at Soviet instigation, neither do they act in contravention of Soviet policy. It will be seen from Table 5–7 that in 1970 Eastern European trade with the Middle East surpassed Soviet trade in over half the countries of the area and was only slightly less than Soviet trade in another three cases. Indeed, if Algeria, Egypt, and Iran are excepted, Eastern European regional trade considerably exceeds that of the Soviet Union. (Even with Algeria included, the two figures are about the same.)

As we have pointed out, Soviet trade and aid programs are closely related, since assistance is generally given in terms of credits. As a result, Soviet exports to the Middle East are often industrial and other equipment for the carrying out of aid projects.[31] Indeed, despite innumerable Soviet statements over the years deprecating the terms of trade and the nature of trade between the West and the Middle East, Soviet commerce with the Middle East follows a similar model of exchanging industrial goods and

Table 5-4
Soviet Trade with the Middle East
(Million rubles)

	1961		1965		1971		Total Trade % Change 1961–1971
	Imports	Exports	Imports	Exports	Imports	Exports	
Algeria		1.3	3.4	13.9	69.3	52.6	9277
Egypt	86.0	97.8	147.1	187.8	300.7	343.2	250
Iran	16.5	16.3	16.3	13.8	100.1	139.3	630
Iraq	4.2	33.6	3.3	26.6	5.5	99.1	177
Jordan				2.6		5.9	∞
Kuwait				6.0		17.4	∞
Lebanon	3.4	4.2	2.2	5.0	0.7	18.4	189
Libya	0.5	1.3	0.4	2.5	3.6	8.9	394
Morocco	4.7	3.0	9.9	7.6	18.9	28.2	512
Saudi Arabia				3.2		5.4	∞
Sudan	9.4	8.4	11.2	6.5	47.0	20.1	277
Syria	3.9	15.3	16.7	11.4	26.4	51.9	308
Tunisia	2.5	2.1	3.2	5.9	6.3	3.6	115
Turkey	4.4	5.2	17.0	15.0	33.6	68.4	952
Y.A.R.	1.3	1.9	0.9	7.2	0.3	7.2	134
P.D.R.Y.						2.2	∞
Total Middle East	136.8	190.4	231.6	315.0	612.4	871.8	354
Total World	5,249.1	5,398.4	7,252.5	7,357.2	11,230.9	12,425.6	122
Middle East % of World	2.6	3.5	3.2	4.3	5.5	7.0	

Table 5–5
Recent Soviet Trade with the Middle East
(U.S. million)

	1967		1968		1969		1970		1971	
	Imports	Exports	Imports	Exports	Imports	Exports	Imports	Exports	Imports	Exports
Algeria	16.2	31.6	27.7	31.9	61.6	57.7	62.0	69.4	77.8	58.4
Egypt	145.1	281.3	170.7	198.0	228.1	238.2	310.6	363.2	334.1	381.3
Iran	30.6	63.0	40.1	88.1	56.4	161.6	69.1	187.8	111.2	154.8
Iraq	5.1	36.7	4.1	50.8	4.7	67.7	4.6	66.0	6.1	110.1
Israel	0.2	0.6				0.3				
Jordan		3.1		3.4	0	4.3	0	7.1		6.6
Kuwait		10.8		15.0	0	15.3	0.3	10.8	0.8	19.3
Lebanon	3.9	9.1	3.4	13.6	3.0	11.6	4.2	15.2	4.0	20.4
Libya	0.1	3.1		6.1		10.8		14.3		9.9
Morocco	20.3	20.0	18.3	19.2	17.9	37.1	19.6	36.1	21.0	31.3
Saudi Arabia		1.8		3.9	0.2	4.6	0	6.0		6.0
Sudan	8.3	4.6	12.1	16.0	13.7	16.0	49.9	36.1	52.2	22.3
Syria	18.2	34.2	20.9	42.1	37.3	47.8	19.2	46.4	29.3	57.7
Tunisia	4.3	6.1	5.4	3.3	3.4	4.2	2.9	3.4	7.0	4.0
Turkey	27.9	28.1	30.0	30.8	29.9	57.9	30.1	62.4	37.3	76.0
Y.A.R.	0.7	10.1	1.6	6.4	1.4	9.7	1.1	11.1	0.3	8.0
P.D.R.Y.	0.1	1.2		1.4	1.0	6.9	0.2	4.8		2.4

Table 5–6
Soviet Shares of Middle East Trade, 1970

Country	% Exports to USSR	% Imports from USSR
Algeria	5	5
Egypt	38	22
Iran	3	8
Iraq	0	12
Israel	—	0
Jordan	—	4
Kuwait	NA	2
Lebanon	2	2
Libya	—	2
Morocco	4	6
Saudi Arabia	0	1
Sudan	17	9
Syria	9	11
Tunisia	2	1
Turkey	5	7

finished products for agricultural supplies. Moreover, Soviet–Middle East trade has conformed to the prevailing world price structure.[32]

Soviet trade with the Middle East was very limited before 1955 and consisted primarily of small exchanges with such countries as Egypt and Lebanon. After the arms agreement, Soviet trade with Egypt increased greatly. It increased from $15 million in 1954 to $184 million in 1961, then to $426 million in 1967, and to over two-thirds of a billion dollars ($673.8 million) by 1970.[33] However, whereas earlier exchange had seen the USSR trade wheat for cotton (as the essential components of commerce), after 1955 the Soviet Union increasingly sent industrial materials to complete factories.[34] In return, Egypt pledged to Moscow even greater amounts of its cotton crop, some of which—given the fact that the Soviet Union was already a cotton exporter[e]—was reexported. Egypt became a microcosm of the difficulties encountered in trade with the Soviet Union: Soviet dumping and reexportation led to lower prices; diversion from Western markets to Moscow meant loss of convertible currencies and threatened potential loss of traditional markets; and Soviet goods were of inferior quality.

Unlike most other countries trading with the Middle East, the USSR has maintained a trade surplus with the area. (Only with the Sudan has there been a significantly negative balance.) This anomaly is due to the nature of the commerce, due, that is, to the fact that Soviet–Middle East

---

[e]This is not to suggest the USSR could not use Egyptian cotton. On the contrary, much of it was of high quality and was used in the textile industry. Some was not, however.

Table 5–7
Soviet and East European Trade with the Middle East
($U.S. million)

Country	1971 Trade w/ USSR	1971 Trade w/ E. Europe	1966 Trade w/ USSR	1966 Trade w/ E. Europe
Algeria	136.2	38.5	24.7	16.9
Egypt	715.4	278.0	348.7	273.5
Iran	266.0	127.4	50.4	50.8
Iraq	116.2	111.8	39.1	44.9
Israel	0	48.4	3.0	37.4
Jordan	6.6	6.8	3.7	11.2
Kuwait	20.1	22.5	7.8	13.8
Lebanon	24.4	28.2	9.4	41.3
Libya	9.9	40.7	4.1	19.2
Morocco	52.3	44.0	20.2	50.1
Saudi Arabia	6.0	15.0	2.9	—
Sudan	74.5	51.7	14.7	28.9
Syria	87.0	60.0	43.0	66.7
Tunisia	11.0	36.0	12.5	23.5
Turkey	113.3	96.4	46.2	114.3
Y.A.R.	8.3	0	13.4	—
P.D.R.Y.	2.4	0	1.3	4.3

trade has not involved oil to any important extent.[f] However, as Soviet imports from the Middle East are a proportionately growing aspect of worldwide Soviet imports (see Table 5–4), and as the Soviet petroleum demand/production ratio increases, the oil sector of Middle East trade may well grow.[g] Certainly, Eastern Europe and the Soviet Union are very much involved in Middle East petroleum commerce today, as they were not only a few years ago.

The most advanced stage of trade between the Soviet Union and Arab countries may be seen in Egypt. If this is a model for Soviet international commerce with developing countries, it suggests that the USSR, far from demonstrating reluctance to become more heavily involved in the Middle East, is anxious to do so. For under the new economic agreements signed between Egypt and the USSR, factories geared specifically to the Soviet market are being constructed in Egypt. This technique should support Egyptian economic development, improve Egypt's chances of repaying its

[f]About 1 percent of Middle East oil went to the Soviet Union in 1971; See "Soviet Treaties Should Boost Middle East Trade," *Middle East Economic Digest*, vol. 16, no. 29 (July 21, 1972), p. 812.

[g]Oil exported to the USSR from Algeria, Iraq, and Libya increased in 1971 by 125 percent over the previous years; see "Soviet Treaties."

debt to Moscow, and create a strong link between the Egyptian economy and the Soviet Union.

Yet, Egypt appears to have not only the greatest economic exchange with the Soviet Union but also a history of far more extensive economic interaction with the USSR than other Arab states that began even before, but noticeable especially after, World War II. Throughout the late 1950s and early 1960s, over half of Soviet trade with the Middle East was with Egypt. Only in 1968, after Iran's economic relations with the Soviet Union began to increase, did Soviet–Egyptian trade fall below 50 percent of the regional total. And as late as 1971, Egypt and the USSR carried on 43 percent of the Soviet trade with the Middle East as a whole. Thus, it is misleading to use Egypt as a paradigm for Soviet economic methods in the entire region.

Moreover, the facile conclusion that economic dependence does prejudice political decisions is fallacious. Even Egypt's heavy trade with the USSR is not the decisive factor in their relations. True, close economic ties may increase the cost of specific political options, "but . . . it seems questionable that any arbitrarily selected share in the total trade turnover of a less developed country is a valid indicator of the influence of the USSR or any other country over the affairs of the LDCs. In the vast majority of cases even a poor nation would sever crucial economic relations rather than sacrifice its political independence beyond a point deemed by itself to be acceptable."[35]

6

Military Activities

Introduction

Military activities primarily support two types of state objectives—foreign political and military policy. These activities can be considered to fall into five categories: (1) facilities and forces, (2) arms tranfers, (3) training, (4) exercises, and (5) visits. The more important of these activities from the military point of view also tend to have more important political ramifications, positive or adverse. Before 1955, there was no Soviet activity of these types in the Middle East at all. Currently, the USSR is engaged in each of these activities.

Facilities and Forces

Facilities

There are no permanent Soviet military installations in the Middle East. It has long been Soviet policy to denounce "foreign bases" as a threat to international peace and security and to deny that the USSR seeks any. Military bases in the traditional sense need not be established in the Middle East to accomplish most Soviet objectives.[1] And the political costs of establishing formal Soviet bases overseas—overturning consistent Soviet policy in this regard—might be great. Instead, informal basing arrangements may be concluded when necessary.

In any event, the USSR has relied primarily upon self-sufficiency at sea—that is, by carrying out much of its own refueling, repair, and supply and by using several areas in international waters for anchorages.[2]

These international anchorages are not the only facilities of which the Soviet Navy makes use, however. From 1958 to 1961, berthing privileges for Soviet submarines were extended by Albania, but the aggravation of the Sino–Soviet conflict led to the termination of that activity.[3] Since then, despite innumerable reports of Soviet bases in one or more countries of the Middle East,[a] the closest the USSR has come to a formal basing arrange-

---

[a]The most widely circulated report was one concerning Mers-el-Kebir in Algeria, but a typical report is illustrated in Francis Ofner, "Soviet's [sic] Stalk West's Oil Supply," *Christian Science Monitor*, April 11, 1972, in which an Israeli analysis is said to conclude that Soviet bases exist or may exist or are being requested in Egypt, Yemen, South Yemen and Socotra, and Iraq.

ment were the extensive facilities used in Egypt until the summer of 1972.

There is some disagreement as to the nature and scope of military facilities in Egypt utilized by the USSR. Several airfields were either reserved for exclusively Soviet use, or were otherwise Soviet controlled, but sources disagree on the number of such installations. There were about six airfields in Egypt under varying degrees of Soviet control. In any event, the decision by President Anwar Sadat to exclude most of the Soviet advisors from Egypt has removed these Egyptian installations from foreign control.[4]

Ports used extensively by the Soviet fleet included Latakia in Syria; Alexandria, Port Said, and Mersa Matruh, in Egypt; and, secondarily, Tartus, also in Syria.

A final type of facility to be considered is the missile base. Soviet-operated and controlled surface-to-air missile bases in Egypt were numerous before the summer of 1972. Although some even more advanced SAM missiles have been sent to Egypt since the large-scale removal of Soviet advisors from that country, the new effort is much more limited in scope.[5]

Forces

As we have pointed out, the Soviet Union did not deploy ships to the Mediterranean on anything like a permanent basis until the submarine base at Valona (Albania) was established. However, the withdrawal of the submarines from Valona left no local defense against the Sixth Fleet, which from the early 1960s added a significant threat to Soviet defense: submarines carrying the Polaris missile. It is unnecessary to go into the chronology in detail here[6]—much of which would of necessity be highly speculative, in any event—but it is important to consider the presumed motivations and objectives of Soviet planners in expanding the area of Soviet fleet operations. It appears that deployments to the Mediterranean, and then to the Indian Ocean were initiated to enhance the strategic defense capabilities of the USSR as later versions of the Polaris missile became operational. A major consideration was to prevent the withholding of U.S. strategic forces on the Mediterranean from the initial strikes of a general war. It is clear, however that flag-showing purposes were also considered a function of the new deployments. Indeed, in view of the relative probability of peaceful competition and outright war between the United States and the Soviet Union, political purposes are the more important from an everyday point of view, even if they are not uppermost in the eyes of defense planners. It is much more likely—and certainly more desirable—that the political functions of the Mediterranean Squadron will be served than it is that its military functions will be.

The military purpose of the Soviet naval forces deployed in the Middle East area has been discussed in Chapter 2. In terms of the strategic objectives, the *cause célèbre* of the growth of Soviet strength in the Mediterranean and Indian Ocean waters is highly exaggerated. These forces, despite their rapid growth and modernization, in no way portend an effective offensive naval establishment in either location. The Soviet Mediterranean squadron, established in 1964 as a subordinate command of the Soviet Black Sea Fleet, is a balanced force of modern surface-craft, submarines, intelligence and ASW vessels, and logistics auxiliaries, many of the ships equipped with the latest versions of Soviet missiles. It includes elements of Northern and Baltic fleets, as well, however, for training and interfleet coordination. Since 1968, the Mediterranean Squadron has usually boasted at least one helicopter carrier for anti-submarine warfare (ASW) operations.[7]

Soviet military planners, like their American counterparts, must consider the aggregate of forces likely to be aligned against their own local forces in the event of a major war. Hostile forces, in this context, then, must include not only those of the United States, but, in addition, the Mediterranean contingents of at least several other Western navies. Mediterranean naval power is demonstrated in Table 6–1. However, numbers alone cannot adequately establish the relative power of these fleets. The Italian fleet is the most important of those belonging to countries on the Mediterranean littoral. It is a modern, highly trained, well-fitted naval force. The Spanish navy is modernizing, as well, but much of its strength (including its only helicopter carrier) is deployed in the Atlantic. French forces concentrate more heavily on the Atlantic, too, although an intervention force of 2 carriers, 1 missile carrier, 2 missile frigates, 4 missile escorts and some additional escort vessels can be rapidly formed and added to the Mediterranean elements already on station. Review of the Soviet squadron's composition and of the politico-military environment to which it is a response suggests strongly that the Soviet Mediterranean naval forces have a defensive mission in the event of war, a mission stressing destruction of as much of the Sixth Fleet and its organic firepower (including carriers and missile-carrying submarines) as possible.[8]

The Soviet Union has had no significant land presence in the Mediterranean region until the increase in Soviet advisors in Egypt reached the point where many were involved in missions designed to support Soviet, rather than Egyptian, strategic objectives. Even then, most of that effort was centered in reconnaissance missions regarding the Sixth Fleet and potential air support for the Mediterranean Squadron.[9] At the same time, the large number of Soviet air personnel flying in Egypt provided useful training in desert flying.[10]

A further—and very important—politico-military objective has been to

Table 6-1
Middle East Military, Air, and Naval Forces

	Army/Land Forces (in thousands)	Combat Aircraft	SAM	A/C Carriers	Helo Carriers	Cruisers & Missile Cruisers
U.S.	—	180	—	3	—	2
U.S.S.R	—	—	—	—	1	2
U.K.	10	45	4	—	—	1
Spain	100	215	16	—	1	—
France	76	420	40	—	1	3
Italy	307	320	112	—	1	—
Yugoslavia	190	342	48	—	—	—
Albania	28	72	"several"	—	—	—
Greece	118	202	30	—	—	—
Turkey	360	311	30	—	—	—
Syria	100	210	8	—	—	—
Iran	160	160	batteries 30	—	—	—
Iraq	90	189		—	—	—
Lebanon	13	18		—	—	—
Jordan	65	50		—	—	—
Saudi Arabia	36	71	10 Bns	—	—	—
Kuwait	7	30		—	—	—
Bahrain	1	—		—	—	—
Qatar	2	4		—	—	—
U.A.E.	6	12	on order	—	—	—
Oman	6	15		—	—	—
Yemen	10	c.100		—	—	—
DPRY	10	22		—	—	—
Israel	62	432	48	—	—	—
Egypt	255	768	600	—	—	—
Sudan	35	40		—	—	—
Libya	20	22		—	—	—
Tunisia	20	12		—	—	—
Algeria	53	181	1 Bn	—	—	—
Morocco	48	48		—	—	—

	Destroyers Escorts, Corvettes	Intell. and Oceanographic Vessels	Patrol, Missile Patrol, Coastal Patrol, Torpedo Boats, etc.	Landing Craft	Submarines	Minesweepers, Minelayers
U.S.	21	2	2	3	6	4
U.S.S.R	10	6	3	3	12	2
U.K.	2	—	—	10	—	19
Spain	13	—	20	5	4	10
France	14	2	11	4	11	61
Italy	28	—	12	30	9	30
Yugoslavia	20	—	75	—	5	8
Albania	4	—	40	23	4	22
Greece	12	2	20	?	2	26
Turkey	16	—	31	—	10	2
Syria	—		20		—	
Iran	7		—	4	—	6
Iraq	3		16	—	—	—
Lebanon	—		8	1	—	—
Jordan	—		11	—	—	—
Saudi Arabia	—		23	—	—	—
Kuwait	—		8	2	—	—
Bahrain	—		"several" (4 on order)	—	—	—
Qatar	—		12	—	—	—
U.A.E.	—		1	—	—	—
Oman	—		—	—	—	—
Yemen	—		—	—	—	—
DPRY	1		—	—	—	1
Israel	19		28	10	2	11
Egypt	—		32	12	12	—
Sudan	—		6	2	—	—
Libya	2		12	—	—	2
Tunisia	3		6	—	—	—
Algeria	7		44	12	12	11
Morocco	3		12	1	—	—

Sources for this Table are on page 102.

impede the accessibility of Mediterranean ports to the U.S. Navy, especially in the eastern Mediterranean. In order to create potentially troublesome domestic conditions in the local countries, agitators and international communications techniques have been employed. These methods, together with the evolution of international conditions, have resulted in a sharp cutback in the ports in which American vessels may call.

With regard to the realization of Soviet political goals, the Mediterranean squadron is of symbolic importance. First, it demonstrates the fact that the Mediterranean is no longer an American—or even a purely Western—lake. Second, and similarly, the naval force symbolizes the Soviet presence; its size and modernization—considering the USSR is not a riparian state—show this is a great power presence. Third, probably more important than the degree to which the Squadron has degraded the strategic capabilities of the Sixth Fleet[b] is the degree to which indigenous peoples perceive this to be the case. Fourth, the Squadron has clearly placed additional constraints on American freedom of action. Additionally, the possibility of Soviet military intervention in local affairs has been made more credible, perhaps directly or indirectly influencing internal Arab politico-military events. This and other considerations already mentioned are particularly relevant in Greece, Turkey, and Iran, where a certain sense of isolation may have been created by the new Soviet naval presence coupled with the more enduring geopolitical realities. Finally, the existence of Soviet personnel and materiel in Arab countries can be considered a "trigger" similar to U.S. forces in Europe, a tool for deterrence of Israeli military operations.[11]

Arms Transfers

Certainly the most widely reported Soviet activity in the Middle East has been the transfer of large numbers of arms to certain Arab states. (See Table 6–2.) The military aid provided by the USSR to Middle East coun-

---

[b]It should be noted that non-aligned local states do not necessarily relish the prospect of a superpower competition on their riparian borders. This may be partial explanation for the Soviet reliance on the USSR's proximity to the Mediterranean as a justification for both its growing naval presence there and its opposition to the powerful presence of the American Sixth Fleet. From Algeria to Yugoslavia have come statements objecting to the presence of both Soviet and U.S. naval forces in the Mediterranean.

Sources: International Institute for Strategic Studies, *Strategic Survey 1971* and *The Military Balance 1972–1973*; Louis Legendre, "Méditerranée et problèmes de défense," *Revue de défense nationale*, Vol. 28 (October 1972), p. 1483; Stanford Research Institute, *Area Handbook for the Peripheral States of the Arabian Peninsula* (Washington, D.C.: Foreign Area Studies, American University, 1971), p. ix; Stockholm International Peace Research Institute, *The Arms Trade with the Third World* (Stockholm: Almquist and Wiksell, 1971). Figures relating to France, the United Kingdom, the United States, the USSR, and Spain refer only to those forces destined for Mediterranean use.

Table 6–2
Major Arms Suppliers to the Middle East and North Africa

	United States				United Kingdom				France				USSR			
	1950–55	1956–60	1961–65	1966–71	1950–55	1956–60	1961–65	1966–71	1950–55	1956–60	1961–65	1966–71	1950–55	1956–60	1961–65	1966–71
Bahrain								X								
Egypt	X				X			X				X	X	X	X	X
Iran	X	X	X	X		X	X	X			X	X		X	X	X
Iraq	X	X			X	X	X	X		X	X	X		X	X	X
Israel	X	X	X		X	X	X	X	X	X	X					
Jordan		X	X		X	X	X	X		X	X	X				
Kuwait					X	X	X				X	X				
Lebanon		X			X			X	X	X	X	X				
Oman								X								
Qatar								X								
Saudi Arabia	X	X	X	X	X	X	X	X	X		X	X				
Syria	X	X			X				X		X	X	X	X	X	X
Turkey	X	X	X	X		X					X					
U.A.E.			X					X								
Y.A.R.								X						X	X	X
P.D.R.Y.																X
Algeria											X	X		X	X	X
Libya		X	X	X		X	X	X			X	X			X	X
Morocco		X	X	X		X	X			X	X	X		X	X	
Sudan			X			X	X	X		X	X	X			X	
Tunisia				X			X	X		X	X	X				X

tries with good Soviet relations has, in fact, been a key element in the growth of Soviet regional involvement and influence. That arms transfers were designed to build influence rather than build effective military establishments is clear: large amounts of weapons were supplied for some years to Algeria, Egypt, Iraq and Syria without adequate training or support.[12] This approach has been modified since 1967 Arab–Israeli hostilities, however.[13]

Many observers have concluded that the Soviet arms supply was designed to exacerbate local tensions and cause greater disenchantment with the West; that the USSR did not feel itself bound by any restraint in arms supply; and that it was an irresponsible policy with dangerous potential and disastrous consequences.[14] On the other hand, until 1958, the USSR was willing to join in supplier restraints to the Middle East;[15] consistently refrained from introducing technologically decisive weapons systems or from providing certain types of offensive systems desired by the Arabs until 1974;[16] and has sought to use its own influence throughout the Arab military staffs to prevent the outbreak of renewed hostilities between Israeli and Arab forces. There are several reasons for the restraint that was in evidence: the desire to discourage an attack on Israeli-held lands; disquiet over the possibility of a Soviet–American confrontation; determination to prevent disclosure of technological advances.[17] Moreover, Soviet restrictions on spare parts have been relatively strict in order to preclude major wars of long duration.[18]

Scope

The size of the Soviet Middle Eastern military assistance program has, in fact, been quite large. In comparative terms, it has represented over 40 percent of Soviet military aid worldwide[19] and, excepting Turkey, nearly equals combined Western arms transfers. (See Table 6–3.)

The total figures, including Turkey and all military equipment (rather than just major weapons) show that Soviet military assistance and sales to the Middle East and North Africa until 1971 amounted to almost $5 billion. (This may be compared with the U.S. figure of $6.7 billion.[c])

From Table 6–4 it is evident that U.S. military transfers even before 1973 have considerably exceeded those of the Soviet Union. If, however, Turkey is excluded, the regional totals are very similar. Still, some major differences are in evidence. First, virtually all Soviet weapons transfers are

---

[c]The United States figure is misleadingly low because sales in Table 6–4 are given in terms of deliveries through 1969 rather than commitments. Commitments to general Middle East countries, particularly Iran, portend sizeable future deliveries over the next few years. Moreover, commitments and deliveries to Israel and Iran since the compilation of these data total several billions of dollars.

Table 6-3
Arms Transfers to the Middle East and North Africa:
Major Weapons, 1950–1969
($U.S. million in 1968 dollars)

	Recipient		
Donor	Middle East	North Africa	Middle East/ North Africa
U.S.A.	1,009	54	1,063
U.K.	538	27	565
France	500	42	542
Germany	51	6	57
Italy	51	6	57
U.S.S.R.	1,971	153	2,524

Note: The Sudan and Turkey are excluded. It is not the intent of this table to suggest that the countries listed have been the sole providers of military equipment to the Middle East. Other suppliers of major equipment items have included Canada, the People's Republic of China, Czechoslovakia, the Netherlands, Pakistan, South Africa, Sweden, Switzerland and Yugoslavia. Middle Eastern countries that have transferred such equipment under sales, grant, or different agreements to other Middle East states include Egypt, Iraq, Morocco, Saudi Arabia, and Turkey.
Source: SIPRI, *The Arms Trade with the Third World.*

loans and sales, while two-thirds of the U.S. figure represent grants. Second, as in economic assistance—and to a large extent for the same reason—most Soviet military aid has been concentrated on a few recipients: five countries have received 96 percent of the regional Soviet-supplied arms. Indeed, 70 percent has gone to Egypt (50 percent) and Iraq (20 percent). While it may be shown that Turkey (51 percent) and Iran (23 percent) have taken an even higher proportion of American military aid and sales (74 percent)—a proportion that will have grown markedly by 1975[d]—transfers to other countries have been more widely and evenly dispersed. Moreover, U.S. figures cover the period from 1946 to 1954 when no Soviet military aid was provided to the Middle East.

It is also frequently maintained that the Soviet Union has aggravated regional tensions by supplying large quantities of military equipment to the parties to local conflicts. To some extent it is undoubtedly true that Soviet arms supplies have contributed to arms races both in the Maghreb and in the Arab east. At the same time, Western policies—certainly including those of the United States—have been far from exemplary in this regard. In the Iraqi–Iranian controversy, Iraq, at odds with Tehran for much of the last decade, has felt compelled to acquire additional weaponry to counteract the sizeable and rapidly growing Iranian inventory. Similarly, with respect to the countries most directly involved in the Arab–Israeli

[d]Sales to both countries—but especially to Iran—have been large since 1970.

Table 6–4
U.S. and Soviet Military Assistance and Sales to the Middle East and North Africa, 1946–1972.

	Military Assistance: Grants[a]	Military Assistance: Loans[b]	Security Supporting Assistance (Grant and Loan)	Military Sales[c] (1950–72)	Commercial Military Sales (1963–72)	Total Government	Total U.S.	($U.S. million) USSR Total
Bahrain	0	0	0	0	0.1	0	0.1	
Egypt	0	0	30.0	0.4	1.6	30.4	32.0	2,700
Iran	870.0	469.4	210.5	1,801.9	99.7	3,351.8	3,451.5	500
Iraq	47.8	0	0	13.2	5.6	61.0	66.6	1,000
Israel	0	97.1	50.0	1,716.8	132.6	1,863.9	1,996.5	
Jordan	126.0	9.0	259.2	201.7	4.6	595.9	600.5	
Kuwait	0	—	0	—	1.2	0	1.2	
Lebanon	14.4	0	0	15.1	2.6	29.5	32.1	
Oman	0	0	0	0	0.8	0	0.8	
Qatar	0	0	0	0	0	0	0	
Saudi Arabia	36.7	147.8	0	693.5	117.5	878.0	995.5	
Syria	0.1	0	0	—	3.8	0.1	3.9	715
Turkey	3,560.4	0	852.7	29.9	18.9	4,443.0	4,461.9	
U.A.E.	0	0	0	0	0.4	0	0.4	
Y.A.R.	—	0	27.2	0	0	27.2	27.2	75
P.D.R.Y.	0	0	0	0	0	0	0	25
CENTO	0	0	25.8	0	0	25.8	25.8	

Algeria	0	0	1.4	0	0.3	1.4	1.7	400
Libya	16.1	0	27.8	30.9	37.8	74.8	112.6	
Morocco	42.8	3.6	76.7	63.7	1.7	186.8	188.5	15
Sudan	0.7	0	0	1.5	2.1	2.2	4.3	65
Tunisia	40.0	0	17.3	5.2	0.2	62.5	62.7	
Total Middle East	4,655.4	723.3	1,455.4	4,472.5	389.4	11,306.6	11,696.0	5,018
Total North Africa	99.6	3.6	123.2	101.3	42.1	327.7	369.8	480
Total ME/NA	4,755.0	726.9	1,578.6	4,593.8	431.5	11,634.3	12,065.8	5,498

[a]Military Assistance Program, Excess grants at legal value (1/3 of acquisition value), service-funded foreign assistance program grants, and the Turkish portion of Greek–Turkish aid grants.

[b]Export–Import bank and other military assistance loans. Does *not* include value of ship loans and leases.

[c]Cash and credit sales both included. Government transactions only.

Sources: U.S. A.I.D., *U.S. Overseas Loans and Grants*; Defense Security Assistance Agency, *Military Assistance and Foreign Military Sales Facts April 1973* and backup data; U.S. Department of State, *Communist States and Developing Countries: Aid and Trade in 1972*.

conflict, it is problematic indeed to suggest the USSR and Israel's hostile neighbors have been the main culpable parties in the local arms race when Israel purchases additional highly sophisticated weaponry from the West while already in a position of clearcut military superiority.

On the other hand, relative to the absorptive capacity of the recipients, there can be no question that several Arab states—notably Algeria, Egypt, Iraq, and Syria, have at various times been "oversupplied." However, these supplies have been provided less for military than for political reasons and have less important military than political ramifications. They were sent in response to the requests of Arab leaders, to satisfy their prestige or similar needs. In some cases they were sent specifically for reexport to other environments (e.g., the Congo, Nigeria, the Yemen), or storage outside the immediate field of Arab–Israeli battle.[20]

Another difference in the Soviet and American ledgers is that Soviet interests were served by breaking through the barriers of containment. To the extent that meant being responsive to governments whose felt need for arms was spurred by the then principal suppliers, the Soviet Union was willing to undertake the role. As in economic aid, military agreements have been determined more by the recipients' willingness to accept Soviet arms than by the conscious effort of Moscow to build up the inventories of some states over against those of their neighbors. Nevertheless, where the Soviet Union became a significant supplier in the Middle East, there the Soviet Union became the virtually sole supplier at least of major weapons systems. (See Table 6–5.) For that reason, there was a certain additional requirement on Soviet policy as against that of the United States, which until 1967 avoided becoming the major arms supplier to any country except the so-called "Northern Tier" breakfront of containment, Iran and Turkey. (Pakistan is not considered in this study.) Soviet supplies, that is, were of necessity larger than they might have been had the recipients received arms from other suppliers.[e]

Economic Implications

Soviet prices for military equipment have been usually relatively low, and their attraction has been enhanced by repayment terms—barter. However, as Uri Ra'anan has pointed out:

Even if Soviet prices were relatively reasonable, massive arms deals involving increasingly valuable, sophisticated items were likely to prove very costly to marginal economies; crops would have to be mortgaged for years ahead.[21]

---

[e]As Table 6–5 demonstrates, Iraq did receive substantial amounts of some arms from the United Kingdom and France even after the 1958 coup. In this case, Soviet supplies were still large, but proportionately smaller (relative to Syria, for example), than after the June 1967 war when the USSR became the sole supplier there.

Table 6–5
Arms Suppliers in Selected Middle East Countries, 1950–1970

	U.S.				U.K.			
	A/C	Msl	Nav	Arm	A/C	Msl	Nav	Arm
Egypt (to 1955) from 1955	(13Tspt) (3H) (1R)			(150T)	(67F) (11T) (6T) (10S) 1Tspt		(1E) (2MTB) (2C) (3L)	57T
Iraq to 1958 from 1958	(5F)			(40T)	(52F) (12T)(2H) (2Tspt) 50F 31T 12		8PB	(115T) (20AC) (10T) 100A
Syria (to 1956) from 1956	(5T) (1Tspt)				(63F) (10T) (1Tspt)			
Algeria	2T							
Iran	237F 29T 26Tspt 16H	100+SA 768AA	6PB 4LC 6M 1T 4C 1Tnk	365T 50A	2H	420SA	2SDV	
Turkey	59T 700F 21Tspt 30R 5H	600AA 300AS 150AS 24SS	4L 7S 1SR 1R 11M 5PB 2D 1B	330T 430A 25D	25F		4D	
Israel	50F 73B 26T 6Tspt 47H 2S	416SA ?AA ?AS	1CT 1PB 14LC	50T	20F 20B 5T		2LC 2PB 2D 5S	465T
Morocco	20F 79T 20Tspt 5H			15AC				

Key and Source for this table appear on page 113.

Table 6–5 (continued)

	France				Italy			
	A/C	Msl	Nav	Arm	A/C	Msl	Nav	Arm
Egypt (to 1955) from 1955				(20T) (20SPG)				
Iraq (to 1958) from 1958	8Tspt 12H			70T 70AC				
Syria (to 1956) from 1956	(13Tspt)		3PB		(50F) (26T)			
Algeria	28T 10H			15AC				
Iran	16H				162H	?SS	1CT 1O	
Turkey			1B		90H			
Israel	265F 60B 100T 6Tspt 18H	100+AA 300AS 352SS	6MTB 12G	300T 30AC	20H			
Morocco	1F 14T 1Tspt		3PB 15C 1C 1LC 1F	45T 15AC	11H			

Table 6–5 (continued)

	Germany				Canada		Other	
	A/C	Msl	Nav	Arm	A/C	Nav	A/C	Nav
Egypt (to 1955) from 1955					(15T)		Yugo-slavia	(6MTB)
Iraq (to 1958) from 1958					(21T)			
Syria (to 1956) from 1956								
Algeria							Cuba (4F) Egypt (23T)	(2M) (2MTB)
Iran	90F				70F 6Tspt			
Turkey	84F 18T	300AT	9L 11MTB 1S	79T 69AV	24T 120F	9E 4M	Nether-lands (65F) Denmark	(1MI)
Israel	25T			200+T			Sweden (25F) Nether-lands (40T)	
Morocco	24T						Iraq (4F)	

Table 6–5 (continued)

| | U.S.S.R | | | | Czechoslovakia | |
	A/C	Msl	Nav	Arm	A/C	Arm
Egypt (to 1955) from 1955	711F 85B 30T 17Tspt 52H	100AA 150AS 320SA 500AT	33MTB 8M 2D 14S 8SC 20PB 18LC 1RA 5T 7A	161OT 600A 150D	86F 39B 36T 10Tspt	150T
Iraq (to 1958) from 1958	159F 17B 26T 20Tspt 11H	192AA 30SA	12MTB 3SC 14PB	220T 200A		
Syria (to 1956) from 1956	251F 7B 26T 8Tspt 25H	200AA 60SA 60SS	15MTB 10PB 2M	535T 400A 100D	7T	50T
Algeria	59F 18B 21T 10H	40SA 24SS	6MTB 2SC 3PB 1TR	150T 150A 50D		
Iran				100A		
Turkey						
Israel						
Morocco	16F 2B 2T			35T 10D		80T

The additional dangers are (1) that these major changes in commodity exports, by involving the loss of traditional Western markets and thereby forcing these markets into procurement elsewhere or reduction of utilization of the commodity, will result in the rigid linking of the Arab commodity exports to the Soviet economy;[f] and (2) that the growing repayment requirements will prejudice the industrialization effort by increasing rather than decreasing the demand for agricultural production to meet the payment schedule.[22]

At the same time, until the 1967 conflict, most of the military equipment sent by the USSR to the Middle Eastern regimes was obsolete or obsolescent. In recent years, however, the Middle East (particularly Egypt and Syria) has received more modern arms, which in some cases comprise weapons systems that have not even been provided to the Soviet Union's Eastern European allies. Provision of advanced equipment has deepened Soviet involvement also by necessitating the dispatch of Soviet advisors and technical experts to train locals for, and to maintain, the equipment.

Training

Advisory assistance and training in the military sciences are of two types: (1) local training, requiring the presence of Soviet advisors in the Middle Eastern country and (2) training within the USSR.

In-Country Soviet Military Training
and Advisory Assistance

The overwhelming majority of all Soviet military personnel stationed in the Third World are in Middle Eastern states. Before most Soviet advisors

---

[f]Of course, in theory there is nothing inherently more dangerous in this link than in the tie with the West. But the Soviet economy's use of Middle East goods is in many cases not based on economic demand. Thus, there is always the possibility of reexport and a worsening of the price structure for the specific commodities involved.

A/C	Missiles	Naval Vessels		Armor
B Bomber	AA Air-to-air	A Amphibious vessel	MI Minelayer	A Armored Personnel Carrier
F Fighter	AS Air-to-Surface	B Boom Defense Vessel	MTB Motor Torpedo Boat	AC Armored Car
H Helicopter	AT Anti-tank	C Corvette	O Other	AV Armored Recovery Vehicle
R Reconnaissance	R Rocket	CT Cutter	PB Patrol Boat	D Tank Destroyer
S Seaplane	SA Surface-to-air	D Destroyer	R Repair Ship	SPG Self-Propelled Gun
T Trainer	SS Surface-to-surface	E Escort	RA Rocket Assault	T Tank
Tspt Transport		F Frigate	S Submarine	
		G Gunboat	SC Submarine Chaser	
		H Hovercraft	SDV Seaward Defense Vessel	
		L Motor Launch	SR Submarine Reserve Ship	
		LC Landing craft	T Tug	
		M Minesweeper	Tnk Tanker	
			Tr Trawler	

Source: Based on SIPRI, *The Arms Trade with the Third World.*

were withdrawn from Egypt in 1972, Egypt alone held well over three-fourths of the total. Since August 1972, although some Soviet personnel remained in Egypt, a small number have returned and the numbers in Iraq and Syria have grown markedly. (See Table 6–6).

The theory behind assignment of military advisory and training personnel is that apart from training and assistance, their presence symbolizes the highly developed situation of the sending state; that interaction between local and foreign personnel will contribute to admiration, affection, and a positive orientation toward the latter and their country of origin; that in-country personnel will be more likely to have a direct influence on policy and performance of host nationals and will establish potentially useful contacts among host country nationals; and that information useful to the sending state may be procured through this technique.

There is evidence to support all of these assumptions; but there is also evidence to suggest the situation is considerably more complex. Unequal relationships often breed bad feelings, especially between individuals of two very different cultures. Foreign personnel may be a source of irritation and jealousy; they may be unable to establish relationships in which useful intelligence is easily obtained. Even if they influence decisions—and there is substantial evidence they usually do not in the absence of special working relationships at high levels—the difference between "low" and "high" politics is relevant. Moreover, presence of sizeable numbers of foreign military personnel in an environment characterized by international conflict threatens to involve the foreign personnel in these delicate problems and may find the sending state in a particularly sensitive political position.

Table 6–6
Soviet Military Personnel in the Middle East and North Africa, 1971

Egypt	5,500
Iran	*
Iraq	500
Syria	1,100
Y.A.R.	100
P.D.R.Y.	200
Algeria	1,000
Morocco	*
Sudan	100
Middle East	7,400+
North Africa	1,100+
Middle East/North Africa	8,500+
Worldwide Total	9,450

*Small numbers (probably not more than 25–50 in each case) of Soviet military personnel were known to be in Iran and Morocco.

Source: U.S. Department of State, *Communist States and Developing Countries: Aid and Trade in 1972*, p. 13.

Table 6-7
Western Military Personnel in the Middle East and Middle Eastern Military Trainees in the United States

Middle East Country	Military Personnel: Deploying Countries				Military Trainees in the United States (1972)
	United States (1972)	United Kingdom (1972)	Spain (1971)	France[b]	
Bahrain	<250				
Iran	1000				1524
Israel					44
Jordan					144
Lebanon					32
Oman		<250			
Qatar					
Saudi Arabia	<250				82
Turkey	7000				148
U.A.E.		>125			
Morocco	1000		17,000[a]		105
Tunisia	24				58
	c9520	c400	17,000	unknown	2137

[a]Spanish forces located at Ceuta and Melilla (Spanish sovereignty).

[b]French military training personnel were stationed in Algeria and Morocco in 1971.

Source: SIPRI, *Yearbook of World Armaments and Disarmament 1971–1972;* Office of the Assistant Secretary of Defense (Comptroller); Office of the Assistant Secretary of Defense (International Security Affairs); Defense Security Assistance Agency; International Institute for Strategic Studies.

Military Training Within the USSR

Of the thirteen developing countries sending military personnel to the Soviet Union for training,[23] eight are in the Middle East and North Africa;[g] but the total number of foreign military trainees in the USSR is substantially lower than the number of Soviet military personnel in the developing countries (2,500 to 16,500 in 1971). The observations concerning this type of training are similar to those presented below under cultural activities.

Excercises

Excercises are not a major tool of great power influence in the region. Although both the United States and the Soviet Union have occasionally conducted joint exercises with local states, this is not a widespread custom, and its "influence-spreading" is more or less limited to the military of the local states. Since, however, such exercises are generally only conducted between states already enjoying close relations, the potential pay-off is further limited.

Visits

The fifth military activity is widely believed to have a greater potential impact on local citizenry than many of the others, although its effect is long term, unmeasurable, and of little inherent military value. This category includes all visits, and it is a broad area embracing naval visits, which are generally of a relatively high visibility, and other military visits that have a public relations aspect.

Since the beginnings of the growth of the Mediterranean squadron and the increasing Soviet presence in the Indian Ocean, Soviet ships have been very active by making numerous visits to many port countries of the Middle East and North Africa. Similarly, Soviet support for local Arab military establishments has resulted in trips to the Middle East by a number of Soviet military delegations.

While the United States appears to have been about as active as the Soviet Union in visiting the local states, the major difference is in trend. The United States has had increasing numbers of ports and countries

---

[g]Egypt, Iran, Iraq, Syria, Yemen A.R., P.D.R. Yemen, Algeria, and the Sudan. See U.S. Congress, House of Representatives, *U.S. Interests in and Policy toward the Persian Gulf,* 92nd Cong., 2nd Sess., February 2, 1972, p. 10, and the Stanford Research Institute, *Area Handbook for the Peripheral States of the Arabian Peninsula* (Washington, D.C.: Foreign Area Studies, American University, 1971) for the various countries.

closed to naval and military visits, and an ever larger number welcome the Soviet contingents. This phenomenon is primarily a function of the prevailing state of political relations between governments, but in some cases, local governments enjoying good relations with the United States have requested the United States to defer or cancel visits in order to defuse potential civil disturbances planned to protest the U.S. presence.

We have organized Table 6–8 to show naval visits distinct from other military visits because the former tend to have, except in cases where visits take the place of basing arrangements (as in Latakia for the Soviet Union), more of a "flag-showing" purpose, while visits by military delegations seem more often to reflect joint planning and consultation—that is, on the one hand, a greater military purpose and, on the other, a greater effect on the elites than on the public as a whole (relative to naval ship visits).

If ship visits have any public relations purpose, their impact should be in countries with which the visitor is not on friendly terms. Curiously, however, both Soviet naval visits and their U.S. counterparts are overwhelmingly to countries with which relations are already cordial. The only exception to this pattern in 1971, so far as Soviet visits are concerned, was the visit of a *Kotlin* class ASW Destroyer to Bahrain in late June. So long as

Table 6–8
Soviet and U.S. Naval Visits, 1971

Country	Soviet Naval Visit	U.S. Naval Visit
Bahrain	X	X
Egypt	X	
Iran		X
Iraq	X	
Israel		X
Jordan		X
Kuwait		X
Lebanon		
Oman		X
Qatar		X
Saudi Arabia		X
Syria	X	
Turkey		
U.A.E.		X
Y.A.R.		
P.D.R.Y.	X	
Algeria		
Libya		
Morocco		
Sudan	X	
Tunisia		

the pattern persists, the incremental pay-off of visits beyond a bare minimum or of any visits at all if the political cost is high appears to be marginal. This does not seem to have slowed the visiting schedule of either the U.S. or the Soviet naval visits in the Middle East, however.

Conclusion

In conclusion, it is clear that the military activities of the Soviet Union serve a primarily political purpose, even though some serve the strategic military interests of the USSR. Both countries are relatively active in most of the military activity categories, but the trend suggests strongly a growing role for the Soviet Union and a declining one for the United States. (See Table 6–9)

American facilities have been eliminated in Libya, and reduced in Morocco and Turkey. The Bahrain facility is on an unsure footing following the 1973 hostilities. Soviet arms sales have increased in number of recipients and quantity. American weapons transfers, on the other hand, while increasing in volume, are no longer undertaken with a number of foreign clients. (Table 6–10).

Arms transfers, moreover, can be among the most important means of gaining influence, since in time of conflict spare parts and other materiel are critical. On the other hand, periods of actual military conflict are the exception not the rule; as a result, the supplier, driven by the goal of securing influence, may be more dominated by the recipient than vice versa.

In every type of military activity in the Middle East the Soviet Union

Table 6–9
U.S. and Soviet Military Activities in the Middle East and North Africa, 1945–1971

| | 1945–54 | | 1955–64 | | 1965–72 | |
	U.S.	*USSR*	*U.S.*	*USSR*	*U.S.*	*USSR*
Facilities	X		X		X	
Permanent forces	X		X	X	X	X
Arms transfers	X		X	X	X	X
Training	X		X	X	X	X
Exercises	X		X		X	X
Visits	X		X	X	X	X

Table 6–10
U.S. and Soviet Weapons Transfers Countries, 1950–1971

Supplier Country	Recipient Area	1950–55		1956–60		1961–65		1966–71	
		No. of Countries	% of Total	No. of Countries	% of Total	No. of Countries	% of Total	No. of Countries	% of Total
U.S.	Middle East	7	(70%)	7	(70%)	6	(55%)	5	(31%)
	North Africa	0	(0%)	1	(25%)	3	(60%)	3	(60%)
	Total Middle East/North Africa	7	(64%)	8	(57%)	9	(56%)	8	(38%)
USSR	Middle East	2	(20%)	4	(40%)	4	(36%)	6	(38%)
	North Africa	0	(0%)	0	(0%)	2	(40%)	3	(60%)
	Total Middle East/North Africa	2	(18%)	4	(29%)	6	(38%)	9	(43%)

has become a participant—with one exception. Officially, no Soviet military installations are established in any non-aligned countries. That the USSR has abnegated traditional basing agreements for more expediential arrangements only demonstrates both its major power role in the area and its political sagacity acquiring base functions without base responsibilities or opprobrium.

7 Cultural Activities

Introduction

For planning purposes, Soviet political, economic, military, and cultural activities all look to primarily political ends. However, only Soviet cultural activities are undertaken as a group exclusively for political objectives. That is not to say individuals and groups participating in these programs invariably look upon their roles in this light, for such is not the case; nor should it be inferred that even at the governmental planning level, national pride is not a key factor of impetus in cultural exchange. Yet, to the extent cultural programs involve rational allocations of resources towards the achievement of specified ends, the conclusion is inescapable that the long-run goal is political—evolution towards a global environment that will accommodate and support Soviet domestic and foreign policy objectives.[a]

In the Third World, generally, and in the Middle East, particularly, the path toward the ultimate objective has been the short-run goal of creating the image of the USSR as a "model state"—that is, a country to be emulated. Additionally, in supporting this and other goals, it has been sought to cast Western motives and methods in an unfavorable light. However, increasingly in recent years, the emergence of China as a developing state—a superpower in embryo—has evoked Soviet concern that the Chinese "model" might be or become more attractive or easier for the developing peoples to identify with. As a result, China, too, has been an object of opprobrium in Soviet cultural diplomacy.

The tools and techniques employed to support the goals of the USSR's cultural activities are unusually diverse, including these essential areas: (1) domestic and international interest groups, (2) communications, and (3) exchange.

Interest Groups

A wide range of groups may be counted as quasi-automatic instruments of Soviet policy. These associations are based on professional or avocational

---

[a]This objective is not dissimilar from its American counterpart. However, the degree of national control over cultural resources and their nature vary considerably between the two countries.

interests and are related to the USSR in different ways. Nevertheless, the common feature of all is the relatively consistent support each provides for what its leadership believes to be Soviet policy.

We have already discussed the most obvious example of these interest groups: communist political groups, especially local communist parties. The occasions on which communist parties dissent from announced (as distinguished from real) Soviet policy are rare, indeed, although some local Marxist–Leninist groups do subscribe to policies quite distinct from the CPSU line.

Associations closely related to political parties are groups like the "friendship societies," for example, the Soviet–Egyptian Friendship Society. These organizations, as groups of like-minded individuals freely associating to further agreed objectives—eternal friendship between local and Soviet peoples—often undertake to explicate and justify Moscow's policies to their compatriots and to apotheosize the peoples, policies, and way of life of the USSR. On the transnational front, the best-known organization of this nature is the World Council of Peace among whose members are many prominent Arabs.[1]

Vocational interest groups have been an effective instrument of Soviet policy for many years. As the vanguard of the proletarian classes, the CPSU has long organized, subsidized, and controlled a variety of labor groups through the World Federation of Trade Unions (WFTU) and other such institutions. In the Arab Middle East, the Arab Federation of Petroleum Workers and the International Confederation of Arab Trade Unions of which it is a part have made a concerted effort to become the Arab League trade unions. Both are affiliated with the WFTU. Yet, by 1972, the WFTU was more counterproductive than helpful for Soviet policy in the Arab world.[2]

Vocational interest groups in which the USSR has been active have not been limited to labor unions, however. Several scientific and technical organizations and others, such as the International Association of Democratic Lawyers, have been tools of Soviet policy in large measure.[3]

Other cultural interest groups had different target audiences: sports, art, youth, and students. From the early years of the USSR, the regime essayed to organize and control sports organizations; the Red Sport International's noted World War II battle to take over the Socialist Workers' Sport International is the prime example.[4] This conflict is no longer exemplary of the Soviet use of sport, however. Currently, the USSR's sports success has been well established: "Soviet athletes are crack troops in the . . . cultural offensive" and reach a total audience larger than several other cultural fields (e.g., dance, theater) combined.[5] This facet of the Soviet cultural program is discussed below.

Artistic and religious interest groups have not generally been responsive to Soviet policy, although, again, considerable effort has been exerted on behalf of Soviet political objectives in these areas through communications and exchange.

Communications: Channels and Messages

Communications Channels

The Soviet Union employs a panoply of media in its international communications. The most significant of these, in terms of the Middle East, are radio, newspapers, books, political tracts, and face-to-face (word-of-mouth) communication.

As we have already pointed out, a number of radio stations broadcast from USSR territory in Arabic, Hebrew, Kurdish, Persian, and Turkish, and some broadcasts in English and French are specifically targeted for the Middle East. In addition to these overt communications, there are several clandestine sources broadcasting to the Middle East. These stations, such as Radio Iran Courier and Voice of the Iraqi People, tend to take a stronger position than those previously cited and often support views different from the positions officially espoused by the Soviet government.

Several newspapers of the Middle East also reinforce Soviet policy. For example, *Al-Akhbar* (weekly) and *An-Nida* (daily) in Beirut reflect the views (and benefit by the subsidies) of the local communist party, which itself follows CPSU policy very closely. Even among the newspapers not financed by communist groups there are many whose owners' or editors' views are such that reportorial interpretation and description tend to further Soviet interests. Moreover, there is increasing reliance on Soviet, East European, and Chinese news agencies. TASS, for example, is now used more than Western press services in Iraq and Syria. In terms of shaping the everyday perceptions of the peoples of the Middle East, use of Soviet press agencies may well be among the most important tools of Soviet policy.

Magazines are much less effective instruments. Magazines in Russian suffer from the obvious linguistic impediment of a relatively minute Middle East population literate in Russian. Local censorship further reduces the potential impact (and readership) of magazines, even those in Arabic.

Like magazines, Soviet books have not scored a major success in the Middle East. Apart from technical and scientific tracts, where the low price has often made up for the difference in printing quality, Soviet books have not been able to compete with those from the West. This medium, too, then, has not been productive.

Political tracts, on the other hand, have often flourished, particularly in countries where official views do not correspond with those of Moscow. Even though incarceration and death may be the risks, there has not usually been a dearth of those willing to circulate such material among their trusted peers. However, tracts of this nature appeal by definition to views not shared by the ruling elite. They are limited to audiences with a relatively high degree of political consciousness, and they tend to concentrate on issues of high short-term salience—issues that are in many cases somewhat ephemeral.

Face-to-face communications also operate under distinct and important constraints. First, the opportunities for interacting on a substantive basis with Middle East elites, while rapidly increasing, has only in the last few years developed on a meaningful scale as the Soviet presence has grown. Second, these opportunities are limited by sensitivity involved in undertaking politically oriented discussions with indigenous persons. Third, the nationality of the source in persuasive communications is of material importance in the effectiveness of the communication.[6]

It is a reasonable assumption that official Soviet representatives would be particularly subject to this limitation;[7] it is also a reasonable assumption that most local nationals would be considerably more effective, especially if their ties (such as, in this case, communist party membership) to the position advocated were loose, secret, or non-existent.

Face-to-face communications are also impeded by the relatively secluded life of the Soviet community in the Middle East countries. For the most part, the Soviets live isolated from the indigenous peoples and follow a policy of non-fraternization off the job, and although they live closer to local living standards than many Americans, their interaction with host country nationals apart from their work is minimal. This isolation probably reduces some of the frictions and resentment that result from the intrusion of foreign communities into the lives of the host nationals, but it also underscores the *foreign* element of that presence, which aggravates other potential and real problems.

Communications Messages

What are the essential messages the USSR tries to transmit to the peoples of the Middle East? What perceptions does the Soviet Union try to evoke on the part of the elites and peoples of the region? The most important of these Soviet messages revolve around the following themes.

1. The capitalist economies of the West exploit the Middle East and its resources.

2. The West wishes to keep the countries and peoples of the Middle East in a state of dependency and subordination.
3. To accomplish the above, the West uses all means at its disposal—political, economic, military, and cultural.
4. Therefore, all Western activities are designed to further ends prejudicial to the true interest of the countries and peoples of the Middle East.
5. The USSR, as a socialist country with long, recent, and demonstrably effective experience in rapid socioeconomic development, is a good model for development and is able and willing to put its experience at the disposal of developing countries.
6. The USSR is a neighbor justifiably interested in, and directly affected by, developments in the Middle East.
7. The USSR, a great power and one whose global role is increasing, will use its power for the defense of Soviet interests and to further the interests of the Middle East as well as of the USSR itself.
8. The interests of the countries and peoples of the Middle East and those of the USSR are very similar or identical in many areas.
9. Soviet assistance is provided to developing countries without strings and on terms of optimum benefit for the latter. It is designed to assist in casting off the chains of underdevelopment and dependence rather than to perpetuate them, as Western aid seeks to do.
10. Similarly, other forms of interaction with the USSR are based on the principles of soverign equality at the government level and mutual benefit at the human level; they demonstrate the quality of Soviet cultures and demonstrate to the peoples of the Soviet Union in turn the accomplishments of the cultures of the Middle East.

These themes are employed on an areawide basis. It should also be noted that they are couched in conceptions sufficiently general as to eclipse even the enduring questions of Israel and Palestine, although many of the short-term and specific messages employed integrate the above themes into the Israel-Palestine issues.

Cultural Exchange

Cultural exchange has several faces and serves several purposes for Soviet policy. Under the rubric of "exchange," we include cultural agreements; culturally related visits; the cultural output of the USSR to the extent it is an input to the Middle East; education and training other than military; and diverse honors bestowed on individuals from the Middle East.

Cultural exchange between the USSR and the Middle East has been growing in recent years, and noteworthy has been the increase in exchanges involving mass organizations (youth, unions, and women's organizations, for example). Among those states of the Middle East and North Africa that have been independent for more than a few years, only Israel, Saudi Arabia, and Libya have not been involved in recent Soviet cultural exchange.

Agreements

Cultural agreements represent the formal side of cultural exchange. While little may take place even with such institutional sanction, virtually no exchange is carried on in the absence of some kind of agreement. By January of 1972, thirteen Middle Eastern and North African states had signed cultural agreements with the Soviet Union. (See Table 7–1.)

Visits

Exchange visits represent one of the most common and varied forms of international activities, and the Soviet Union, like the United States, boasts considerable resources for this field. Visits relating to political, artistic, vocational, sporting, religious, youth, and educational exchange are only some of the wide range witnessed. While East European governments, like the USSR, have many agreements with the governments of the Middle East and North Africa, the visits differ markedly: in countries enjoying close relations with the Soviet Union and Eastern Europe, the USSR engages in a much higher proportion of non-governmental visits. This difference may suggest a greater Soviet interest in social penetration rather than merely the elaboration and perpetuation of good relations. (See Table 7–2.)

Education and Training

Probably the most important aspect of cultural activities we shall discuss is education and training. In a sense, the importance derives from the fact that this operation is only slightly cultural in nature. Much of it is technical assistance or some other form of aid. However, because of the difficulty in separating the figures for the respective components of the educational exchange program, we consider three discrete categories—Middle Eastern academic students educated in the USSR, technical personnel being trained there, and Soviet academic and technical personnel working in the Middle East.

Table 7-1
Soviet Cultural Agreements with Middle East and North African Countries, 1971

	Cultural Agreement (formal)	Cultural Agreement (informal)	Economic Agreement (general)	Coop. & Technical Agreement (general)	Friendship Treaty (with Tech. Coop. Trainee Exchange)	Information Agreement	Telecommunications (or radio/television) Agreement	Scientific Coop. Agreement and Tech. Exchange	Tourism Coop. Agreement	Technical Coop. Agreement	Total
Egypt		X	X		X	X	X				5
Iran		X	X								2
Iraq		X	X					X			3
Israel											0
Jordan		X	X		X	X					4
Kuwait	X	X									2
Lebanon		X						X			2
Persian Gulf											0
Saudi Arabia											0
Syria		X	X		X	X	X				5
Turkey		X	X								2
Y.A.R.		X	X								2
P.D.R.Y.											0
Algeria		X			X		X			X	4
Libya											0
Morocco		X	X								2
Sudan		X	X							X	3
Tunisia		X	X		X	X					4
Middle East	1	9	7		3	3	2	2		0	27
North Africa	0	4	3		2	1	1	0		2	13

Table 7–2
Soviet Visits to the Middle East, 1971

	Bahrain	Egypt	Iran	Iraq	Israel	Jordan	Kuwait	Lebanon	Oman	Qatar	Saudi Arabia	Syria	Turkey	U.A.E.	Y.A.R.	P.D.R.Y.	Algeria	Libya	Morocco	Sudan	Tunisia	Middle East	North Africa	ME/NA
Governmental		5	5	4	2	0	1	1	0	0	0	3	1	0	1	3	2	2	3	1	1	26	9	35
Political		X	X	X	X		X	X				X			X	X	X		X		X	9	3	12
Agriculture																						0	0	0
Culture		X																				1	0	1
Communication																						0	0	0
Economy		X	X	X								X	X			X	X	X	X	X		6	4	10
Education																						0	0	0
Finance																						0	0	0
Health																X						1	0	1
Labor				X																		1	0	1
Local Gvt.																			X			0	1	1
Religion																						0	0	0
Science/Tech.		X	X																			2	0	2
Social			X	X																		2	0	2
Sports																						0	0	0
Technical Experts		X		X								X						X				3	1	4
Transportation			X																			1	0	1

Non-governmental	20	9	29
Political Parties	2	1	3
Friendship Societies	0	1	1
Other Groups (AAPSO etc.)	2	0	2
Agricultural	2	0	2
Communication	1	0	1
Economy	2	1	3
Education	1	1	2
Finance	0	0	0
Health	0	1	1
Labor	2	1	3
Religion	1	0	1
Science/Tech.	2	0	2
Social Groups (women, youth)	2	1	2
Sports	1	1	2
Technical Experts	3	1	4
Transportation	0	0	0
	46	18	64

Table 7–3
Middle East Academic Students in Selected Developed Countries, 1969

Country of Study

Country of Origin	Canada	France	Germany	Italy	Spain	Switzerland	United Kingdom	Western Europe (exc. Sweden)	United States	USSR (1972)	Eastern Europe (exc. Germ. Dem. Rep.)	Yugoslavia	Other Arab States
Bahrain	0	0	0	0	2	0	36	1	6	0	0	0	573
Egypt	271	136	601	71	10	57	178	264	1,015	455	32	7	1,548
Iran	77	503	2,735	378	4	201	501	1,115	5,175	15	30	5	195
Iraq	21	79	375	54	13	0	502	100	512	225	211	140	1,317
Israel	122	158	201	1,105	16	168	182	216	2,288	0	24	3	0
Jordan	11	41	450	419	910	0	148	338	909	500	160	1,135	18,569
Kuwait	0	13	2	0	0	0	46	1	319	0	10	3	968
Lebanon	101	1,390	178	48	155	83	120	230	1,020	360	104	43	816
Oman	0	0	0	0	0	0	0	0	0	0	0	0	46
Qatar	0	0	0	0	0	0	1	0	17	0	0	0	155
SA	7	20	207	47	0	0	130	47	1,029	0	5	0	717

Syria	25	462	647	747	958	0	55	300	469	1,000	1,108	427	6,548
Turkey	41	306	1,376	58	0	144	429	610	1,309	0	3	1	125
U.A.E.	0	0	1	0	0	0	2	0	2	0	9	128	55
Y.A.R.	0	10	6	0	0	0	13	0	15	275	112	24	471
P.D.R.Y.	1	0	0	0	0	0	43	0	11	225	4	0	323
Algeria	7	1,002	31	0	4	66	33	46	45	840	110	14	316
Libya	4	27	120	205	0	0	109	37	286	0	4	1	417
Morocco	45	1,762	73	0	372	49	7	95	83	90	73	31	197
Sudan	5	31	54	0	0	0	367	73	135	350	580	201	1,337
Tunisia	16	1,793	160	50	1	40	8	135	114	90	70	13	231
Total Middle East	677	3,118	6,779	2,927	2,068	653	2,386	3,222	14,096	3,055	857	1,916	
Total North Africa	77	4,615	438	255	377	155	524	386	663	1,370	837	260	
Sub-total	754	7,733	7,217	3,182	2,445	808	2,910	3,608	14,759	4,425	694	2,176	
Palestine and Other	1	38	485	20	0	77	3	100	341	55	7	104	
Total	755	7,771	7,702	3,202	2,445	885	913	3,708	15,100	4,480	701	2,280	10,884

Source: United Nations, UNESCO, *Statistical Yearbook 1971*, U.S. Central Intelligence Agency.

Once again, when compared with the magnitude of the Western effort, the Soviet education and training program is relatively small. (See Table 7–3.)

An increasing proportion of the students from developing countries in the USSR are technical trainees (which will be discussed later). However, there are still a large number of Middle East academic students in the USSR as well. Although these students are very carefully selected by local communist parties or by the Soviet embassy in the student's country of origin,[8] no major aggregate attitudinal change favorable to the Soviet Union seems to have taken place as a result of this effort. On the contrary, despite the availability of political indoctrination in all courses of study,[9] most students return home with an essentially nationalistic outlook, neither strongly Soviet oriented nor firmly opposed to the USSR.[10] Many have encountered problems of a racial or family nature,[11] but it appears that the Soviet government has taken a number of decisions to reduce these frictions[12] and the possibility that unwanted political persuasion efforts may have counterproductive effects.[13]

Over the years there have been many Middle Eastern students in the USSR for academic purposes, and college students at all levels from undergraduate to postdoctoral. Scholarships were provided irrespective of language difficulties, and "stipends and amenities offered to Arab students were generally more attractive than those granted to native students of the communist host countries."[14]

We have already pointed out that Western institutions of higher learning have generally been more respected than those of the USSR. Yet, there were benefits to accepting scholarships to Soviet schools, particularly in cases where no option was present, since Soviet training is considered preferable on the whole to that available in the Middle East. Moreover, even though local "officials seem generally to be satisfied with the overall quality and character of the education the students have received,"[15] there has been some effort in recent years to improve the educational environment, particularly in areas of more obvious deficiency.

The result of Middle East perceptions of comparative educational effectiveness has been that the best students have tended to opt for Western education. In view of both the ability of the graduates, and the expectations of society at large, it is hardly surprising that few of those who have been through Soviet or East European educational programs have advanced to important positions within or outside the governments of the Middle East.[16] However, there have been increasing efforts in some Middle Eastern countries to give greater official recognition to the quality of Soviet degrees, and it clearly becomes the interest of graduates of Soviet educational programs to upgrade the official and unofficial esteem in which these programs are held.

Relatively few Soviet students have studied in the Arab world. Comparative figures show that many more Western scholars have exploited the opportunities for learning in these countries than have students from the Soviet Union. Indeed, Eastern Europeans have also been more active in this regard than those from the USSR. Interestingly, students from *other* Middle East countries have far surpassed others from external areas studying in the region. (See Table 7–4.)

Technical training has been one of the most important elements of the Soviet economic assistance program from its inception. (See above on economic activities.) Although often ideological in tone, the training's ideology is that of nationalism much more than communism.[17] That this ideological input has not been a major integral part of the selection and training process is clear: trainees have usually been sent to the USSR to prepare them for positions they are expected to occupy upon the completion of a specific Soviet assistance project; and trainees are often integrated into everyday factory or other work for on-the-job training.[18]

The technical training program in the USSR is expected to diminish in magnitude over time, because Soviet-built technical training institutions in the Middle East should effect the preparation of most trainees. Thereafter, the preponderance of training in the Soviet Union will be aimed at specialized and advanced preparation.[19]

Table 7–4
The Soviet Union, Eastern Europe, and the West:
Students in Selected Countries of the Middle East, 1968

Country of Origin	Country of Study						Totals
	Egypt	Iraq	Israel	Lebanon	Syria	Algeria	
United States	10	1	1,079	256		1	1,347
France	3		78	175	2	638	896
Germany	3		34	11		9	58
Italy	11		11	14			36
U.K.	6		60	94	4		164
Other Western Europe	73	1	143	62	5	18	302
Eastern Europe[a]	5	23	15	9	10	48	110
USSR	3					1	4
Other Middle East		1,468	100	17,724	6,499	470	26,261

[a]Excludes German Democratic Republic, but includes Yugoslavia and Albania.

Source: Based on United Nations, UNESCO, *Statistical Yearbook 1970.*

Soviet economic technicians in the Middle East are the other side of technical training exchange. Unlike the propaganda advantage Moscow seeks to derive regarding Soviet assistance overall, technicians eschew politics for the most part. Incidents of subversion, espionage, and for the most part even propaganda are virtually unknown. Poorly paid, poorly housed, and without an administrative staff, these personnel often seem less than friendly and are generally isolated from the host country's society.[20] Lower pay and amenities should not be taken to suggest a lower level of ability. Soviet technical experts conform to the high standards of the West. They are more specialized (and thus more individual technicians are required for large projects than is the case with U.S. aid)[21] and remain in host countries only long enough to complete the specific task to which they are assigned.[22] (See Tables 7–5, 7–6, and 7–7.)

Table 7–5
Technical Trainees from the Middle East in Selected Developed Countries, 1971.

	USSR (1972)	United States	United Kingdom	France	Germany (F. Rep.)	Italy	Other DAC
Bahrain			11				
Egypt	150	2	22	139	178	2	100
Iran	200	62	43	103	657	3	179
Iraq	150	0	15	7	94	0	29
Israel		24	81	5	70	4	4
Jordan		56	42	3	165	0	7
Kuwait			13		4		16
Lebanon		32	16	327	442		
Oman			1				
Qatar			1				1
Saudi Arabia		34		18	52	2	9
Syria	50			32	79	2	19
Turkey	300	282	84	100	706	2	44
U.A.E.							
Y.A.R.	30			3	36		4
P.D.R.Y.	60				2		1
Algeria	50		35	497	76	4	31
Libya		12	3	5	53	3	1
Morocco		82	6	163	90	6	165
Sudan			64	11	122		36
Tunisia		50	50	1,550	2,709	91	682
Total Middle East	940	492	329	737	2,485	15	413
Total North Africa	50	144	158	2,226	3,050	104	915
Total ME/NA	990	636	487	2,963	5,535	119	1,328

Source for DAC Countries: Organization for Economic Cooperation and Development/Development Assistance Committee. Source for the USSR: U.S. Central Intelligence Agency. Same sources for Tables 7–6 and 7–7.

Table 7-6

Educational and Technical Personnel from Selected Developed Countries in the Middle East, 1971

	USSR (1972)	United States	United Kingdom	France	Germany (F. Rep.)	Italy	Other DAC
Bahrain	0	0	33	0	0	0	0
Egypt	550	0	22	157	165	43	8
Iran	2,000	14	65	123	70	10	93
Iraq	650	0	1	8	11	10	13
Israel	0	5	0	0	0	0	1
Jordan	0	30	18	5	52	2	4
Kuwait	0	1	0	8	0	0	19
Lebanon	0	9	11	164	42	1	23
Oman	0	0	1	0	0	0	0
Qatar	0	0	0	0	0	0	12
Saudi Arabia	0	1	4	28	12	0	20
Syria	1,300	0	0	93	16	0	3
Turkey	180	110	22	167	169	48	66
U.A.E.	0	0	0	0	0	0	0
Y.A.R.	80	0	0	0	23	5	0
P.D.R.Y.	200	0	0	0	0	4	0
Other ME	15	0	0	0	0	0	0
Algeria	1,480	26	2	8,888	55	4	59
Libya	0	0	111	127	7	331	1
Morocco	330	43	12	8,298	86	115	152
Sudan	70	0	81	12	11	1	0
Tunisia	45	56	5	3,760	107	18	331
Total Middle East	4,975	170	177	753	560	123	262
Total North Africa	1,925	125	211	21,085	266	469	543
Total ME/NA	6,900	295	388	21,838	826	592	805

It would be interesting to compare the Soviet effort in education and training with that of the United States, but only in the field of education is anything approaching comparability attainable, given the nature of the differences between Soviet and American societies. Soviet education of students from developing countries has concentrated on engineering, while much larger numbers of students have enrolled in U.S. schools in a wider range of disciplines.[b] Moreover, the United States is but one of the leading countries in the West. Many additional Middle Eastern students are educated in the United Kingdom, France, the German Federal Republic, Austria, Italy, Belgium, Canada, Switzerland, and elsewhere in Europe.

---

[b]Engineering has been the largest single discipline of foreign student concentration in the United States. Moreover, it amounts to only about one-fifth of the total. (Engineering, on the other hand, probably constitutes a much greater proportion of the specialization of Middle East students.)

Table 7–7
Technical Exchange in 1971: An Overview

	USSR Technicians in	Western Technicians in (DAC only)	Western Volunteers in (DAC countries only)	Trainees in USSR	Trainees in DAC countries
Bahrain	0	33	8	0	11
Egypt	550	395	7	150	493
Iran	2,000	375	316	200	1,047
Iraq	650	43	0	150	143
Israel	0	6	34	0	188
Jordan	0	111	10	0	273
Kuwait	0	28	0	0	33
Lebanon	0	250	13	0	817
Oman	0	1	3	0	1
Qatar	0	12	0	0	2
Saudi Arabia	0	65	0	0	115
Syria	1,300	112	2	50	132
Turkey	180	582	159	300	1,218
Y.A.R.	80	28	0	30	43
P.D.R.Y.	200	4	0	60	3
Other Middle East	15	0	0	0	0
Algeria	1,480	9,034	120	50	643
Libya	0	577	13	0	77
Morocco	330	8,706	273	0	512
Sudan	70	105	39	0	233
Tunisia	45	4,277	384	0	5,132
Total Middle East	4,975	2,045	552	940	4,519
Total North Africa	1,925	22,699	829	50	6,597
Total Middle East/ North Africa	6,900	24,744	1,381	990	11,116

(In addition, some go to Australia, Japan, the Philippines, and other outposts of education styled in the manner of the West.)

More technical personnel from the Middle East have been trained under official auspices in France alone than in the Soviet Union. Once again, however, many Middle Eastern technical trainees have also been prepared in other countries of Western Europe as well as the United States. Moreover, several countries have had a sizeable program of training participants in third countries. (In 1971, 393 technical personnel from the

Middle East (332) and North Africa (61) were trained in third countries through U.S. government assistance.[23]) Moreover, some have been trained by private corporations, foundations, and the like.

The technical training programs undertaken within Middle Eastern countries by the USSR constitute an impressive effort to which large numbers of Soviet economic technicians and planning have been devoted. Establishment of technical training institutions in many developing states has been a hallmark of Soviet assistance. (See the section on economic activities above.) Official U.S. technicians are fewer than their Soviet counterparts, but these figures do not begin to address the total number of Western or even U.S. technical personnel in the region, since foundations and private institutions carry on a significant amount of technical training.[c]

Medals and Honors

Another Soviet activity in Middle East is the conferring of awards on individuals who either have achieved a noteworthy objective or, more commonly, who have, in the Soviet view, served the interests of the USSR. These honors are most often presented by "front" organizations, but in some cases the Soviet government or directly associated institutions are the sponsor. For example, in 1970 several leading Egyptians were elected to the Soviet Academy of Sciences. Nevertheless, such activities can hardly be a major incentive for support of Soviet policy at all levels. Their effect is probably rather limited and more in the nature of reinforcement than initial motivation.

Cultural Output

Among the most frequently employed exchange activities is the exchange of cultural output such as films; books; and religious, artistic, and other cultural materials. In these areas, the Soviet Union has been much less successful than the United States, and even more unsuccessful than the West as a whole, in creating an attentive audience. Soviet films are unpopular; books, largely unread (except in technical areas because of cost factors—but here, too, their Western counterparts are preferred); and popular music and dance are virtually unknown.[24] While the reason for the

---

[c]It should be noted that one reason the USSR has a heavier concentration of technicians overseas, even though Soviet economic assistance is provided to fewer countries than is American aid, is the greater project orientation of the former, which requires more planning and other technical work than does U.S. aid. Janos Horvath, "Moscow's Aid Program: The Performance so Far," *East Europe*, vol. 12, no. 11 (November 1963), p. 15.

relative disinterest in Soviet culture may be partially explained by its foreignness to the culture of the Middle East, some aspects are also partially explained by the small Russian language audience.[25] Even the growing local interest in Russian, the considerable efforts exerted to help foreign students, and the emphasis placed on teaching Russian in the Middle East,[26] portend no major reversal in the roles of English and French, on the one hand, and Russian, on the other hand. In some countries of the area, the language of instruction in most of the advanced education is French.

Effects and Effectiveness

We have seen that cultural objectives as apart from political goals are of no long-range importance to the USSR. What has been the impact of this surprisingly wide-ranging cultural program in the Middle East?

Interest groups are of uneven and transient importance. To the extent their appeals conflict with nationalism, such groups are largely impotent. It is in the interstices of demands of nationalism, on the one hand, and those of Soviet interests, on the other, that such groups may play a role. To date, this role has been of very limited import, and the situation is not likely to change.

Soviet communications channels and messages to the Middle East have enjoyed similarly limited impact. Despite a broad effort, and one of increasing sophistication, neither the channels nor the messages seem to have been very effective. The latter, to the extent they represent opinion trends of Middle East elites, have reflected rather than effected changes. The channels (or media) have been singularly unsuccessful in attracting and persuading local audiences from among the sectors whose opinions count, with one exception: the increasing acceptance and utilization of the Soviet press service is a phenomenon of considerable potential (and unknown actual) importance, especially in countries where government controls on media are effective.

A number of agreements have been concluded with most of the states of the region. In some instances domestic groups have had to bring pressure to bear on the local governments in order to achieve these agreements, a fact that suggests the agreements are of some moment. Yet, the only effect of the agreements is to facilitate rather than institutionalize cultural interaction. In most instances the activities can be terminated should the Middle East government concerned decide to do so.

Visits by touring groups and the cultural products of the Soviet Union have never had more than an ephemeral effect in the Middle East. Most of the populace is unaffected, and even among the educated elite there is a widespread tendency to look down upon Russian culture as inferior to that of the West, outside the historical tradition and inferior to the culture of the Middle East, and irrelevant to societal needs. With some exceptions (e.g., ballet), the ineffectiveness of these cultural activities is clear and does not appear to be about to change.

Emphasis has been placed upon language teaching by the Soviet Union as it has by other states desirous of maintaining or increasing their influence in the Middle East. While it would be easy to place too much stress on the approach, it is probably true that that part of the elite of the Middle East who learn Russian is more likely to be favorably disposed to the USSR than the average, as long as the individuals do not also learn a Western language. Such examples are relatively few. Middle East technical personnel who learn Russian as a function of their training are not necessarily affected in the same way, since the training is often not their choice and since the specialized ends involved usually eclipse the brief exposure to Russian.

To the extent the study of Western languages could be reduced in import, such a phenomenon might be of major benefit to the USSR. Yet, the teaching of Russian does not significantly reduce the Western cultural audience or the number of those who study and learn English, French, and German. Moreover, the heavy cultural penetration of many Middle Eastern societies by the West; the extended history of interaction with the West; and the proximity and communication of the West on the one hand and the Middle East on the other are all developments that place a heavy premium on the development of capability in at least one Western language for those who aspire to elite membership.

Soviet educational programs have been adversely affected by the Middle Eastern tendency to prefer Western education. While this factor has a self-destructive mechanism (motivating graduates of Soviet programs to endeavor to increase the esteem in which such programs are held), the extant bias has also reduced the quality of students choosing to attend Soviet institutions of higher learning. Few graduates have attained positions of importance. If the program is to have a substantial political impact, that impact is still in the future.

Technical training programs have a built-in limitation: they concentrate on groups unlikely to accede to positions of national leadership. However, the emphasis on training that has characterized Soviet assistance has been helpful in spreading the effects of assistance and therefore in communicating the usefulness of Soviet aid. It has not seemed to directly advance Soviet influence, but its long-term effect in countries where concentration has been pronounced—such as Egypt—may yet support the cultural penetration and affect the transaction patterns for years to come.

In sum, Soviet cultural activities have only been of potential significance in countries where the USSR's influence is already great. As a result, their impact will probably continue to be only one small—and likely the most dispensable—aspect of Soviet involvement.

**Part III
Conclusions**

8

Conclusions and
Implications

Background

From 1917 until 1955, the Soviet Union was virtually excluded from the Middle East. During this period the only local question that directly affected the USSR was the security of the Black Sea. Therefore, relations with Iran and Turkey constituted the bulk of Soviet interaction with the Middle East.

After World War II, there was little evident change in the activity level. Once again, border areas were the immediate concern, and international crises resulted from the Soviet attempt to secure and expand control of lands to the immediate south in Iran and Turkey. The result of these initiatives was the alliance of both countries with the United States, and, later, the establishment of a hostile multilateral military alliance, which linked with others, encircled the USSR.

Western *influence* in the Middle East was never a major defeat to the USSR. The Middle East is not vital to the Soviet Union: its products for the foreseeable future are of marginal significance, its military forces negligible (in terms of the threat they pose), and even its political roles of only intermittent importance. The most compelling Soviet interest in the Mediterranean/Gulf area involves the Unites States' strategic threat deployed in the region. Yet, the most important of these forces depend on *European*, not Middle Eastern territory and ports. The strategic threat to the USSR posed by the United States—especially Sixth Fleet carriers and SLBMs (submarine-launched ballistic missiles)—cannot be met by Soviet forces or technology at this time. The destruction capability of these forces is, literally, "assured." Apart from this strategic problem, about which nothing can be done now to significantly alter the outcome, the Middle East's proximity to the USSR and its role in energy supply to the West underline its importance to Moscow. The Middle East is important to the USSR—important, but not vital.

The early years after 1948 were a period in which the expansion of Soviet power was largely internal—economic reconstruction and military and industrial development. By the time of Stalin's death in 1953, this phase had ended. The Soviet Union had begun to undertake broader involvement in world affairs, particularly those of the Third World, including the Middle East. Economic, technical, and military assistance programs were initiated, and changes were introduced to communist doctrine to justify the developing currents of Soviet policy.

Recent Soviet Policy and
Activities

Exclusion of the Soviet Union from the Middle East had been successful only because the 1945 to 1955 period was transitional. The policy had no long-term possibility of success. A great power cannot be totally excluded from so large a region when that region is proximate. Indeed, no external power can be expected to acquire more than a modest degree of influence in the entire Mediterranean area. The states of the Middle East, North Africa, and southern Europe are too diverse in interests, level of development, and hence national objectives.

However, the Kremlin's strong suit is the Arab–Israeli conflict, for the alignment of Israel with the United States—and certainly this is the Arab perception and one the USSR seeks to perpetuate—gives the Soviet Union unusually wide latitude in its relations with Arab governments. It permits good relations with parties to different sides of many regional quarrels. The interests of both Israel and the USSR, as their leaders view those interests, are served by the identification of Israel with the United States and of the United States with Israel. The possibility that U.S. support of Israel—support at such a level that the Arabs perceive it as being largely unqualified now—may be reduced is the greatest danger to the expanding Soviet role in Middle Eastern affairs.

That the Soviet Union has become more involved in the Middle East since 1955, 1960, or even 1965 is not a revelation. In virtually every field of endeavor, Soviet–Middle East interaction has exploded in quantity and often—though less often—in quality as well. Having benefitted in the late 1950s and early 1960s from the growth of the spirit of non-alignment, Soviet relations with the Arab states of the Middle East in the next decade were abetted by the widespread association of the United States with Israel. Indeed, in many Arab states after 1967, pressure on their governments to look to the Soviet Union or Western friends rather than to the United States became a major factor in day-to-day government operations. Disenchantment with U.S. policy grew to the extent that even after a reversal of the anti–American trend following the 1973 war, no important approach to resolution of the Arab–Israeli conflict could be undertaken without Soviet support or acceptance.

Control over the Dardanelles, long a Soviet objective, probably retains some importance. However, modern technology has significantly reduced the critical nature of the Black Sea to strategic military options directed against the southern USSR. The Dardanelles' role may be greater in peacetime as a result: Soviet limitations and opportunities for countries seeking intelligence on Soviet forces reduce the latter's flexibility.

On the other hand, it is only reasonable to assume that Soviet concern over the destiny of Iran and Turkey continues at a high level. In peace or in war, geographic contiguity invites a high priority. Both Iran and Turkey, therefore, probably attract greater Soviet interest than any single Arab country. Relations with both have improved considerably over the years, and every indication suggests that Moscow will continue to build friendly ties across the spectrum of intergovernmental relations with Iran and Turkey.

In the Middle East, the most pervasive Soviet links have been constructed patiently—and sometimes at considerable cost—with Egypt. Soviet–Egyptian interaction antedates World War II and historically surpasses contacts with any other Arab country. In the context of the post–World War II era, considerable investment in Egypt may be misleading, however. The underlying reasons for the focus on Egypt have been eminently pragmatic: (1) Egypt provided the opportunity; (2) Egyptian leadership was dynamic and ignited aspirations that coincided with Soviet policy and that were felt throughout the Middle East; and (3) Egypt was more stable than the other Arab countries in which Soviet influence became noticeable—Iraq, Syria, and the Yemen.

The conditions that made Egypt a favorable area to serve as the center for the expression of Soviet involvement in the Middle East changed after 1967 and particularly after Nasser's death in 1970. As a result, the growing Soviet activities in other areas of established interest took on greater significance.

In fact, Soviet interest was never exclusively centered in Egypt. The countries of greatest importance to Moscow were Iran and Turkey. Both border on the USSR, both are traditional areas of Russian expansion, and Turkey controls the entrance to the Black Sea. Yet, from the 1940s, Iran and Turkey seemed beyond the Soviet power of attraction: each, following the postwar territorial and other disputes with its large neighbor to the north, had secured a measure of American protection. Relations improved in the 1960s, but the developing intimacy between the USSR and several Arab regimes created more than a little disquiet for both Iran and Turkey.

Within the Arab Middle East, the dramatic growth in the importance of Persian/Arab Gulf oil to the industrialized countries of the West, including the United States, has created a powerful incentive for the establishment of greater Soviet influence in the Gulf region, an incentive underscored by the economic uncertainties of the Soviet Union's own future oil production and by close relations in petroleum matters as well as political affairs with Iraq. Fragile traditional regimes built on anachronistic formulations; regional instability; an important oil producer on close terms with the Soviet Union; and the dynamic forces behind change are all factors weighted in favor of a greater Soviet role in the area.

The increased Soviet activity in the Gulf area must continue to center on Iraq. Internal stability has not been the most notable characteristic of post–1958 Iraq, but nevertheless it remains the only Soviet friend in the Gulf. Iraq is also a country rich in petroleum resources and anxious to expand its role. Not unmindful of the hazard better Soviet–Iraqi relations might pose to the evolving ties between Tehran and Moscow, the Soviet Union can be expected to put firm limits on its support of Iraq except insofar as Arab–Israeli issues are concerned.

In Iraq, Syria, and the two Yemens, Soviet Middle East fortunes have been tied to a number of unstable regimes and ephemeral personalities. Still, the growth of the Soviet presence and role across the region has been remarkably consistent over time, if very uneven in individual countries. For a time, only the Nasser regime in Egypt seemed likely to endure. That Sadat follows a set of priorities somewhat different from his predecessor's is evident, but the primary Soviet technique in dealing with Arab regimes has always been patience and self-restraint. Even in periods when vituperative polemic was directed against the USSR, only very rarely did the Soviet Union officially respond in kind.

Thus, the increasing Soviet activity level in Iraq and Syria and the reduction of the Soviet role in Egypt should not be presumed to indicate a decisive or final shift in emphasis. Rather, these phenomena reflect the erosion—perhaps only temporary, perhaps more enduring—of the conditions that led to the original focus on Egypt and new developments in the Gulf area. To "roll with the punch" requires a high quality of statesmanship and a persistent view of long-term interests that is not diverted by momentary difficulties, no matter how explosive.

Costs

Yet, it cannot be denied that Soviet influence has been costly. Although Soviet economic assistance has been almost exclusively in the form of loans, some of these debts have been retired. Second, this economic assistance is particularly expensive to the Soviet Union and comparatively more costly than equivalent amounts are to Western economies. Yet, Soviet aid is expected to continue, and because of the success of Soviet policy, the demands on it are greater than ever. Third, until 1973, the USSR could not escape being identified with a loser. Neither training, nor aid, nor weapons altered local Israeli military predominance. The October 1973 war suggests that Soviet training and weapons hold out the hope of closing the Arab–Israeli military gap, however. Fourth, the possibilities of a superpower confrontation are greater in the Middle East, than anywhere else in the world. Fifth, Soviet participation in the Middle East has cost Moscow the aura of political virginity that was maintained so long as it was excluded from the region. Because of the numerous intraregional conflicts, it has been and should be more difficult for the Soviet Union to increase its influence throughout the Middle East than in the past. Almost any significant improvement in relations with one regime tends to alienate others. Choices must now be made. Finally, the Soviet position on the Arab–Israeli problem is largely responsible for the international attention focused on the Jewish question in the USSR, because the level of attention is in large measure a function of Israeli policy.

Benefits

What is the pay-off of the investments the USSR has made? Briefly, the results are not unmixed blessings. Like the United States, the Soviet Union has found that success may sometimes result in greater risks and problems than failure does. Soviet influence in the Middle East is amorphous: it may be employed with great effect relative to international issues to the extent they are *not* regionally important, but in questions of significance to the Middle East all evidence indicates that local governments continue to make decisions on the basis of perceived self-interest. Ironically, the impact of the states of the Middle East on issues not regionally important is very slight, while these states are primary factors in regional developments.

Yet, on the whole, the most important objectives of postwar Soviet Middle East policy, those determined by security requirements and the political needs inherent in great-power status, have been met. The CENTO alliance is no longer a threat; Iran and Turkey enjoy relatively good relations with their northern neighbor; support for U.S. global initiatives from Middle East regimes is scarce; fewer and fewer ports welcome vessels of the Sixth Fleet; and other strategic forces considered hostile by the Soviet Union have diminished in size.

The continuous aim of Soviet policy in the Middle East has been to reduce Western influence. In this endeavor, the USSR has employed the panoply of Soviet resources—psychological, economic, and military, as well as political. Moscow has undertaken general communications themes remarkable for their endurance and flexibility. Yet, it has not been possible to eliminate the age-old Western influence that has penetrated Middle Eastern societies very deeply. Nor is it possible for such a power to extrude the Western official presence from the area. The diversity of the region is too great, and the interests of the West are too varied. Individual governments may pursue policies that undermine their countries' interests in selected states, or even in many, but a third country cannot affect this condition across the board.

Moreover, the USSR has not shown itself willing to court a risk in pursuit of its Middle East objectives. Indeed, Soviet policy has been characterized by a great deal of self-restraint in all aspects. Although willing to support the Arabs' and to a lesser extent the Palestinian resistance's short-run political aims, Moscow has never espoused elimination of Israel or the use of terrorism. In the supply of weapons, qualitative limitation has been a consistent element. Even when the possibility that much of the Soviet investment in Egypt might be at stake—since expulsion of Soviet advisors certainly carried the implicit threat of an effort to improve relations with the United States—these restrictions were maintained.

Thus, while the reduction of Western influence is a Soviet aim, its elimination is probably not considered feasible. The fact that Western policies are becoming increasingly distinct from U.S. policy cannot have been overlooked, since this development prevents the use of one approach to reduce the totality of Western influence.

Implications

On the other hand, fear of Arab dependence on the USSR is based upon a series of misconceptions of contemporary international politics. While it would be foolish to deny that the close relationship of two polities has important implications for the foreign policy of both, it is still quite incorrent to assume that anything short of complete independence produces a "satellite" status. All states are interdependent to some degree. Economic dependence has not, for example, been the decisive factor in the foreign policy of the new states. (It is, of course, one factor.) On matters of importance to them, Middle Eastern states will continue to act in accordance with their own interests. They will be "deliverable" for neither great power—nor for other powers—solely on the basis of political or economic interactions that surpass the norm for "friendly relations." Indeed, in many ways, the effects on local governments are more of a restraint on great powers' local initiatives than on the activities of local states.

Implications for the United States

The position of the United States in the Middle East is not one concerning which optimistic forecasts are in order. That the United States could be extruded from the area by the USSR is beyond the realm of possibility; that it may lose its most important interests through its own activities and policies is not. The Soviet Union's presence and influence have been assured as a direct result of the Arab–Israeli conflict. Moreover, they have replaced Western influence and presence in large measure.

Currently, all major Western countries are in a slow process of dissociating themselves from American Middle East policy. This development will almost certainly arrest the growth rate of Soviet influence. In some cases, in fact, the reverse process will set in. (In others, Soviet presence will continue to increase.) A more important result for the United States—one the USSR can be expected to exploit—will be the future isolation in the Arab world of Washington as Israel's sole supporter. The implications of this process of dissociation for U.S. interests in general are not difficult to imagine. Yet, the meaning for traditional American friends—such as Saudi Arabia, Jordan, and Lebanon—and their ties with the United States are even more ominous.

From a political standpoint, the Soviet Union will cease to be the major beneficiary of the U.S. Middle East policy when European countries act independently of Washington. However, it must be said that in terms of U.S. interests, such a development will be slight recompense for the cost. In fact, the USSR's presence in the Middle East represents but a marginal threat to U.S. interests there. The major threat will continue to be Arab reaction to U.S. policy in the area.

Similarly, the Soviet Union is not a threat to U.S. or other Western economic interests in the Middle East. For reasons we have discussed above, the USSR has little leverage in Middle East oil matters, and less in the countries most likely to supply U.S. oil needs. This situation may change in the future if some of the most pessimistic views of the energy problem prove to be accurate.[a] To the extent American commercial interests are threatened, the danger will not derive from Soviet policy, but, again, from the Arab reaction to U.S. policy. The latter will be judged on its own merits as perceived by the peoples and governments of the Middle East.

The effectiveness of cultural activities is very difficult to evaluate. We have employed the standard measures of cultural diplomacy, but these are measures of *output* not of effectiveness. It is the observable situation that conduces to the conclusion that cultural activities have not been very successful in achieving Soviet objectives. Even that limited success may be put to the test over the next few years, as European states increasingly opt

---

[a]If, for example, the production-consumption situation reaches the point where a cut-off of oil in one or two countries may produce an international crisis, as has been forecast by knowledgeable officials, then certainly the Soviet Union could play a key role.

for policy lines independent of the United States, for the cultural resources of the West as a whole are much greater than those of the Soviet Union, and the cultural penetration of the area by the West has already endured for centuries.

Options for the United States

The current situation in the Middle East can easily result in the further erosion of the United States image in the Arab countries. Every Israeli act of violence, but particularly those carried out within the borders of sovereign Arab countries, carries with it the appearance of U.S. approval, no matter how inaccurate that appearance. The resurgence of American influence and prestige is based upon Arab perception of the new-found U.S. determination to resolve the Arab–Israeli problem. Over time, however, if no settlement is achieved, if the United States remains Israel's almost exclusive military and political supporter, and if no serious and effective effort is implemented to address the Palestinian issue, the U.S. position in the Arab world will deteriorate beyond even its pre–October 1973 state.

If some means can be found to escape the political deadend noted above, political, economic, military, and cultural tools to begin reconstruction of the United States' position are certainly available. A reservoir of local American cultural resources exists in institutions such as the American University of Beirut and the American University of Cairo; in the arts, in the form of American literature and films; and in the English language itself. The possible economic steps are numerous. Many involve government actions, public and private, to encourage investment in the Middle East. In any event, the economic sector of United States–Middle East interactions is the area most likely to require painful readjustments for the United States over the next decade.

Overall, then, Soviet policy and activities in the Middle East do not represent a threat to U.S. interests. To the extent there are important American interests in countries long cut off from the United States, the governments will still act in accordance with their own perception of national interests. Only in Iraq may Moscow be in a position to increase the cost to decisively dissuasive levels. (This is the more possible as a result of the fact that no bureaucracy with an extant power base within such states as Iraq and the P.D.R.Y. has a vested interested in the U.S. tie.)

In what directions, then, can U.S. policy move in order to restore the American position in the Middle East? If a settlement is—as many people have concluded—impossible, then there is probably little the United States can do (except as short-term palliatives) within the framework of commitment to Israel's security. If, on the other hand, a settlement can be achieved, the American position can be salvaged.

Manifestly, the impossibility of reaching a settlement cannot be proven. Since the role of the United States with respect to the Arab countries of the Middle East is dependent upon Arab perceptions of U.S. policy, and since U.S. concern for Israeli security (not the security itself) is largely a matter for U.S. decision makers, it is evident that the United States should make every effort to facilitate—and exert pressure (where necessary) towards the realization of—a settlement of the Arab–Israeli conflict. Such a settlement must, as a minimum, address the recognition of Israel, peace treaties between Israel and her Arab neighbors, Israeli navigation and commercial rights, the Palestinian issue, Jerusalem, and the Arab territories occupied by Israel in 1967.

Less momentous initiatives may also support U.S. interests. Any action that demonstrates the American interest in Arab countries will soften the conviction that the United States seeks to put all its Middle East eggs in the Israeli basket. Arms agreements, economic and military assistance, and cultural programs are all appropriate tools in this regard. However, because of the salience of the Arab–Israeli conflict, Arabs' views of the U.S. position on that complex of issues will continue to be the chief yardstick by which U.S. policy is judged. Without progress toward a settlement, a security assistance agreement with Jordan or Lebanon, for example, is seen in one light; with progress, such agreements take on an altogether different appearance.

Movement on the central Middle East problem—that is, the Arab–Israeli conflict—is a recognized prerequisite of U.S. foreign policy for attainment of several objectives. The findings of this study serve to underscore the necessity of such progress—and above all, of *an active role* for the United States *in the pursuit* of a settlement—in order to ensure that the U.S. position in the Middle East will not be eroded by continued Soviet exploitation of the Arab–Israeli conflict.

The major problem for the United States that the Soviet presence brings to the troubled Middle East is the added flexibility that presence confers upon the states of the area. Renewed European interest in building better relations with the Arab Middle East further underwrites this flexibility. But the result is only a threat to U.S. interests so long as U.S. policy is perceived by the Arab countries and peoples of the Middle East to be hostile to their own interests. The desire to maintain cooperative, mutually productive relations with the United States and the interest in doing so are both clearly evident. Should U.S. policies change in such a way as to permit of the realization of these inclinations and interests, the potential damage to U.S. interests in the Middle East represented by the Soviet presence there will have been rendered moot.

Notes

Notes

Chapter 1
Soviet Foreign Objectives: Framework for
a Middle East Policy

1. See, for example, Alexander Dallin, "Soviet Foreign Policy and Domestic Politics: A Framework for Analysis," *Journal of International Affairs*, vol. 23, no. 2 (1969), pp. 250–65; Erik P. Hoffmann and Frederic J. Fleron, eds., *The Conduct of Soviet Foreign Policy* (Chicago: Aldine-Atherton, 1971); William Zimmerman, "The Sources of Soviet Conduct: A Reconsideration," paper delivered at the American Political Science Association Annual Meeting, September 1972.

2. X (George Kennan), "The Sources of Soviet Conduct," *Foreign Affairs*, vol. 24, no. 4 (July 1947), pp. 566–82.

3. Graham Allison, *Essence of Decision: Explaining the Cuban Missile Crisis* (Boston: Little, Brown & Co., 1971); Allison and Morton H. Halperin, "Bureaucratic Politics: A Paradigm and Some Policy Implications," in Raymond Tanter and Richard H. Ullman, eds., *Theory and Policy in International Relations* (Princeton: Princeton University Press, 1972).

4. Ivar Spector, *The Soviet Union and the Muslim World, 1917–1958* (Seattle: University of Washington Press, 1959), chapter 1.

5. See Max Beloff, *The Foreign Policy of Soviet Russia 1929–1941*, 2 vols., (London: Oxford University Press, 1949), Vol. II, chapters 3 and 9.

6. Adam B. Ulam, *Expansion and Coexistence: The History of Soviet Foreign Policy 1917–1967* (New York: Frederick A. Praeger, 1968), p. 111.

7. Stephen Page, *The USSR and Arabia: The Development of Soviet Policies and Attitudes towards the Countries of the Arabian Peninsula 1955–1970* (London: Central Asia Research Center in association with the Canadian Institute of International Affairs, 1971), pp. 16–17.

8. Adam B. Ulam, *Expansion and Coexistence*, p. 417.

9. A.A. Zhdanov, in Comintern, "Report on the International Situation," *For a Lasting Peace, for a People's Democracy* (n.p.), November 10, 1947.

10. Uri Ra'anan, "Soviet Global Policy and the Middle East," *Naval War College Review*, vol. 24, no. 1 (September 1971), pp. 19–21.

11. See Ra'anan, "Soviet Global Policy," pp. 19–22.

12. See Chapter 6 of this volume, and Geoffrey Jukes, "The Indian Ocean in Soviet Naval Policy," *Adelphi Papers*, no. 87 (May 1970), pp. 5–6.

Chapter 2
Soviet Regional Objectives
in the Middle East

1. See Max Beloff, *The Foreign Policy of Soviet Russia 1929–1941*, 2 vols., (London: Oxford University Press, 1949), Vol. II, p. 201.

2. See Chapter 1 of this volume, as well as Stephen Page, *The USSR and Arabia: The Development of Soviet Policies and Attitudes Towards the Countries of the Arabian Peninsula 1955–1970* (London: Central Asian Research Centre in association with the Canadian Institute of International Affairs, 1971), p. 15, and Beloff, *Foreign Policy*, Vol. II, p. 39.

3. "Thesis on the Eastern Question adopted by the Fourth Comintern Congress," November 1922, in Jane Degras, ed., *The Communist International, 1919–1943: Documents* (London: Oxford University Press, 1956), Vol. I, p. 385.

4. See William Eagleton, *The Kurdish Republic of 1946* (London: Oxford University Press, 1963).

5. For a particularly intriguing approach, see Uri Ra'anan, *The U.S.S.R. Arms the Third World: Case Studies in Soviet Foreign Policy* (Cambridge, Mass.: M.I.T. Press, 1969). But cf. Miles Copeland, *The Game of Nations* (London: Weidenfeld and Nicolson, 1969).

6. See Abraham S. Becker and Arnold L. Horelick, *Soviet Policy in the Middle East* (Santa Monica: Rand Corporation, 1970), p. 29; and David J. Dallin, *Soviet Foreign Policy after Stalin* (Philadelphia: J.B. Lippincott Company, 1961), p. 403.

7. See Page, *The USSR and Arabia*, for an interesting example of the consistency of this policy towards the two traditional regimes over five decades.

8. Malcolm H. Kerr, *The Arab Cold War*, 3rd ed., (London: Oxford University Press, 1972).

9. Becker and Horelick, *Soviet Policy*, p. 29.

10. See Becker and Horelick, *Soviet Foreign Policy*, p. 67; William E. Griffith, "La Coopération avec l'Union Soviétique au moyen orient et en Afrique du Nord," *Politique étrangère*, vol. 36, nos. 5–6 (1971), pp. 688–9; Arnold L. Horelick, *Soviet Policy Dilemmas in the Middle East* (Santa Monica: Rand Corporation, 1968), pp. 6–7; Philip E. Mosely, "Soviet

Search for Security," *Proceedings of the Academy of Political Science* (hereafter *Proceedings*), vol. 29, no. 3 (March 1969), pp. 220–1.

11. I. William Zartman, "Military Elements in Regional Unrest," *Proceedings*, vol. 29, no. 3 (March 1969), p. 81.

12. See, for example, Griffith, "La coopération," p. 688; Wynfred Joshua, *Soviet Penetration into the Middle East*, rev. ed. (New York: National Strategy Information Center, Inc., 1971), pp. 3–4.

13. Maxime Rodinson, "L'U.R.S.S. et les pays arabes," *Politique étrangère*, vol. 36, nos. 5–6 (1971), p. 680.

14. "Soviet Treaties Should Boost Middle East Trade," *Middle East Economic Digest*, vol. 16, no. 29 (July 21, 1972), p. 813.

15. Cf. Zartman, "Military Elements," p. 81.

16. Nadav Safran, "How Long Will Sadat last? Moscow's Not-So-Secret Wish," *The New Middle East*, nos. 42/43 (March/April 1972), p..6.

17. Ibid.

18. See the figures in John A. Berry, "Oil and Soviet Policy in the Middle East," *Middle East Journal*, vol. 26, no. 2 (Spring 1972), p. 150.

19. C. Powell Hutton, "Changing Soviet Oil Interests: Implications for the Middle East," *Naval War College Review*, vol. 24, no. 2 (October 1971), p. 82.

20. Berry, "Oil and Soviet Policy," pp. 151–2.

21. See Berry, "Oil and Soviet Policy," pp. 150–1; Hutton, "Changing Soviet Oil Interests," pp. 77–82.

22. EUROPA Publications, Ltd., *The Middle East and North Africa, 1972–1973*, 19th edition (London, 1972) p. 35. Moreover, these reserves are understated. See footnote o, above. They are also understated for tax purposes by oil companies and for political purposes by governments in large oil-reserve countries. See James E. Akins, "The Oil Crisis: This Time the Wolf is Here," *Foreign Affairs*, vol. 51, no. 3 (April 1973), p. 464.

23. Joshua, *Soviet Penetration*, pp. 3–4.

24. See the *Middle East Economic Digest*, vol. 16, no. 28 (July 14, 1972), pp. 783–6.

25. See R.N. Andreasyan and A. Ya. El'yanov, *Blizhniy Vostok: Neft': nezavisimost'* (Moscow: Iz. Vostochnoy Literatury, 1961), pp. 197–200, 288, as cited in Stephen Page, *The USSR and Arabia*, p. 57.

26. Page, *The USSR and Arabia*, p. 57, and citations.

27. See A. S. Becker, *Oil and the Persian Gulf in Soviet Policy in the 1970's* (Santa Monica: Rand Corporation, 1971), pp. 23, 25–26.

28. See Gardner Patterson, "Declining American Involvement,"

Proceedings, vol. 29, no. 3 (March 1969), pp. 97–98; Jay C. Mumford, "Soviet Motivation in the Middle East," *Military Review*, vol. 52, no. 9 (September 1972), p. 49.

29. Berry, "Oil and Soviet Policy," p. 159.

30. Joseph J. Malone, *Dynamics of Military Balance: Middle East/Mediterranean—Final Report* (research study prepared for the Advanced Research Projects Agency, Office of the Secretary of Defense, U.S. Department of Defense, 1972), p. 23.

31. See Carl H. Amme, "The Soviet Navy in the Mediterranean Sea," *Naval War College Review*, vol. 21, no. 10 (June 1969), p. 155.

32. See Geoffrey Jukes, "The Indian Ocean in Soviet Naval Policy," *Adelphi Papers*, no. 87 (May 1972), pp. 5–6; Alan C. Chase, *Soviet Military Goals in the Middle East* (Montgomery, Ala.: Air University, 1972), p. 22; C.B. Joynt and O.M. Smolansky, *Soviet Naval Policy in the Mediterranean* (Bethlehem, Pa.: Lehigh University, 1972) and sources in note 33.

33. See, generally, Michael K. MccGwire, "The Background to Russian Naval Policy," *Brassey's Annual: The Armed Forces Year-Book*, vol. 79 (1968), pp. 141–58; MccGwire, "The Background to Soviet Naval Deployments," *The World Today*, vol. 27, no. 3 (March 1971), pp. 93–103; MccGwire, "Soviet Naval Capabilities and Intentions," in Royal United Service Institution, *The Soviet Union in Europe and the Near East: Her Capabilities and Intentions*—A Report of a Seminar sponsored jointly by Southampton University and the Royal United Service Institution and held at Milford-on-Sea between Monday 23rd March and Wednesday 25th March 1970, pp. 33–51; MccGwire, "Soviet Naval Procurement," ibid., pp. 74–87; Robert W. Herrick, *Soviet Naval Strategy* (Annapolis: U.S. Naval Institute, 1968); and the sources cited in the previous note. For contrasting views, see E.M. Eller, *The Soviet Sea Challenge* (Chicago: Cowles, 1972); Georgetown University, Center for Strategic Studies, *Soviet Sea Power* (Washington, D.C., 1969); and Norman Polmar, *Soviet Naval Power* (New York: National Strategy Information Center, Inc., 1972).

34. See J.C. Hurewitz, "Origins of the Rivalry," *Proceedings*, vol. 29, no. 3 (March 1969), p. 16; cf., e.g., Brezhnev's demand that the Sixth Fleet withdraw from the Mediterranean, TASS, April 24, 1967. Widespread attacks along this line developed in the wake of this appeal.

35. Cf. Thomas W. Wolfe, *The USSR and the Arab East* (Santa Monica: Rand Corporation, 1969), p. 8.

36. See Safran, "How Long?"

37. See Becker and Horelick, *Soviet Policy in the Middle East*, p. 97; Joseph C. Harsch, "Will U.S. Escalate Mideast Arms Race?" *Christian*

Science Monitor, June 7, 1971; and Anthony Astrachan, "Kremlin Re-thinks its Mideast Stance," *The Washington Post*, March 1, 1971.

38. Lincoln P. Bloomfield and Amelia C. Leiss, "Arms Transfers and Arms Control," *Proceedings*, vol. 29, no. 3 (March 1969), p. 50. For example, Soviet use of airfields in Egypt—in some cases so exclusive as to be Soviet airfields in all but name—were used for strategic missions relating to the U.S. Sixth Fleet.

39. See Jay C. Mumford, "Soviet Motivation in the Middle East," p. 49. Cf. the ramifications of the "considerable efforts ... being made with Russian . . . technical help to improve port facilities in places commanding the narrow passages around Arabia." Laurence W. Martin, "The Changing Military Balance," *Proceedings*, vol. 29, no. 3 (March 1969), p. 66.

40. See, for example, Centre d'Etudes Politiques, "Intérêts et politiques de la France et des Etats-Unis au Moyen-Orient et en Afrique du Nord," special issue of *Politique étrangère*, vol. 36, nos. 5–6 (1971). This intimacy is especially pronounced in North Africa. Cf. David C. Gordon, *North Africa's French Legacy 1959–1962* (Cambridge: Harvard University Press, 1964).

Chapter 3
Constraints on Soviet Policy
in the Middle East

1. Thomas W. Wolfe, *Policymaking in the Soviet Union: A Statement with Supplementary Comments* (Washington, D.C.: Rand Corporation, 1969), p. 12.

2. See Vadim V. Pokshishevski, "1970 Soviet Census Results," *Britannica Book of the Year 1972*, p. 703. Aspaturian, however, disputes Jewish population figures: "Many Jews are giving Russian as their nationality, either because they don't want any trouble or the authorities are indiscriminately counting Jews as Russians to support and justify" assimilation. Vernon V. Aspaturian's comments in U.S. Congress, House of Representatives, *Soviet Involvement in the Middle East and the Western Response*, Joint hearings before the Subcommittee on Europe and the Subcommittee on the Near East, Committee on Foreign Affairs, 92nd Cong., 1st sess., 19–21 October and 2–3 November 1971, p. 76.

3. See U.S. Congress, *Soviet Involvement*, pp. 76–77.

4. Robert G. Wesson, "The Soviet Interest in the Middle East," *Current History*, vol. 59, no. 350 (October 1970), p. 217.

5. See, e.g., Aspaturian, "Internal Forces and Soviet Policy in the Eastern Mediterranean," in U.S. Congress, *Soviet Involvement*, pp.

87–88; Joseph C. Harsch, "Suez Reprieve: Did Soviets Have Second Thoughts on Israel?" *Christian Science Monitor*, February 6, 1971, p. 1.

6. Vernon V. Aspaturian, "The Soviet Military–Industrial Complex—Does it Exist?" *Journal of International Affairs*, vol. 26, no. 1 (1972), pp. 3, 13.

7. Aspaturian, "The Soviet Military–Industrial Complex," p. 14.

8. Ibid., p. 17.

9. See Aspaturian, "Internal Forces," pp. 88–89; Ilana Dimant–Kass, "The Soviet Military and Soviet Policy in the Middle East, 1970–1973," *Soviet Studies*, vol. 26, no. 4 (October 1974), pp. 502–522.

10. Aspaturian, "The Soviet Military–Industrial Complex," p. 7.

11. See Ibid.; Roman Kolkowicz, *The Soviet Military and the Communist Party* (Princeton, N.J.: Princeton University Press, 1967); Thomas Wolfe, *The Soviet Military Scene: Institutional and Defense Policy Considerations* (Santa Monica: Rand Corporation, 1966); and William T. Lee, "The 'Politico–Military–Industrial Complex' of the U.S.S.R.," *Journal of International Affairs,* vol. 26, no. 1 (1972).

12. Aspaturian, "The Soviet Military–Industrial Complex," pp. 2–3. However, this observation may reflect at least as directly on the sophistication of Western understanding of the Soviet Union as it does on the bureaucratic processes of the Soviet Union itself.

13. Arnold L. Horelick, *Soviet Middle East Policy: Origins and Prospects* (Santa Monica: Rand Corporation, 1971), p. 196.

14. See, e.g., Uri Ra'anan, *The U.S.S.R. Arms the Third World: Case Studies in Soviet Foreign Policy* (Cambridge, Mass.: M.I.T. Press, 1969).

15. Uri Ra'anan, "Soviet Global Policy and the Middle East," *Naval War College Review*, vol. 24, no. 1 (September 1971), pp. 19–22.

16. See Graham Allison, *Essence of Decision: Explaining the Cuban Missile Crisis* (Boston: Little, Brown & Co., 1971); and Wolfe, *Policymaking*, pp. 3–9.

17. See Carl J. Friedrich and Zbigniew Brzezinski, *Totalitarian Dictatorship and Autocracy*, 2nd ed., rev. (New York: Frederick A. Praeger, 1965), chapter 11, for an excellent discussion of the role of the "monopoly of mass communications" in the Soviet state and audience reaction.

18. See Ithiel de Sola Pool, "Opportunities for Change: Communications with the U.S.S.R.," paper delivered at a conference sponsored by Radio Liberty and New York University, November 20, 1965, for a stimulating discussion of this point.

19. Cf. Robert L. Tuck, "Influencing Political Change by Broadcasting to the Soviet Union," paper presented at the 1966 meeting of the American Political Science Association.

20. Cf. Maxime Rodinson, "L'U.R.S.S. et les pays arabes," *Politique étrangère*, vol. 36, nos. 5–6 (1971), p. 684.

21. See, for example, Robin Buss, "Wary Partners: The Soviet Union and Arab Socialism," *Adelphi Papers*, no. 73 (December 1970), p. 1. Ideological agility also explains the difficulty analysts have had in reaching agreement on the substance of doctrine with respect to specific problems. Cf., e.g., C. Grant Pendill, Jr., " 'Bipartisanship' in Soviet Foreign Policy-Making," in Erik P. Hoffman and Frederic J. Fleron, Jr., eds., *The Conduct of Soviet Foreign Policy-Making* (Chicago: Aldine-Atherton, Inc., 1971), p. 71, who takes the traditional assumptions regarding Soviet adherence to and the content of the "two camp" thesis, with Ra'anan, *The U.S.S.R. Arms the Third World*, p. 39.

22. See George Lenczowski, *Soviet Advances in the Middle East* (Washington, D.C.: American Enterprise Institute, 1971), p. 19; Lawrence L. Whetten, *The Soviet Presence in the Eastern Mediterranean* (New York: National Strategy Information Center, 1971), pp. 13–15; and A.A. Zhdanov, "Report on the International Situation," *For a Lasting Peace, for a People's Democracy* (n.p.), November 10, 1947.

23. Resolution of XXIV CPSU Congress, passed April 9, 1971, in *New Times*, no. 16 (April 21, 1971), pp. 24–26. See Lilita Dzirkals, "Present Soviet Policy toward Third World States," unpublished ms. (Santa Monica: Southern California Arms Control and Foreign Policy Seminar, November 1971).

24. Whetten, *The Soviet Presence*, p. 13.

25. Franklyn D. Holzman, "Soviet Trade and Aid Policies," *Proceedings of the Academy of Political Science*, vol. 29, no. 3 (March 1969), pp. 108–9.

26. Ibid., see Part II of this volume for more detail.

27. Aspaturian, "The Soviet Military–Industrial Complex," p. 3.

28. See John R. Thomas, "The Dilemmas of Soviet Policy in the Middle East," *Parameters*, vol. 1, no. 2 (Fall 1971), p. 38. Similarly, it should not be assumed that the thinking of military "hawks" is predominantly colored by military considerations. Some of the most well-known "hard-liners" in the Soviet military hierarchy are political officers. See Lee, "The 'Politico–Military–Industrial Complex' of the U.S.S.R.," p. 80.

29. See Rupert Emerson, *From Empire to Nation: The Rise to Self-Assertion of Asian and African Peoples* (Cambridge, Mass.: Harvard University Press, 1959).

30. U.S. Department of State, Bureau of Intelligence and Research, *Communist States and Developing Countries: Aid and Trade in 1971*, RECS–3, May 15, 1972, p. 2. It should not be assumed that the Soviet total

approaches the U.S. economic assistance, however. From 1956 through 1971, a roughly comparable period, U.S. economic assistance to developing countries reached almost $51 billion. U.S. Department of Commerce, *Statistical Abstract of the United States, 1972*, p. 770.

31. See Whetten, *The Soviet Presence*, p. 40.

32. Ibid., p. 13.

33. See, for example, Edward R.F. Sheehan, "Why Sadat Packed Off the Russians," *New York Times Magazine*, August 6, 1972, p. 10; and Arnold L. Horelick, *Soviet Policy Dilemmas in the Middle East* p. 2.

34. Philip E. Mosely, "Soviet Search for Security," *Proceedings*, vol. 29, no. 3 (April 1969), pp. 220–1.

35. Abraham S. Becker and Arnold L. Horelick, *Soviet Policy in the Middle East* (Santa Monica: Rand Corporation, 1970) pp. 73–74.

36. Cf. Aaron S. Klieman, *Soviet Russia and the Middle East* (Baltimore: John Hopkins Press, 1970), p. 72; Curt Gasteyger, "Moscow and the Mediterranean," *Foreign Affairs*, vol. 46, no. 4 (July 1968), p. 682.

37. Whetten, *The Soviet Presence*, p. 13.

38. Walter Z. Laqueur, *The Struggle for the Middle East* (London: Routledge and Kegan Paul, 1969), pp. 183–5.

39. See Robert O. Freedman, "The Soviet Union and the Middle East: The High Cost of Influence," *Naval War College Review*, vol. 24, no. 5 (January 1972), p. 17; and Wynfred Joshua, *Soviet Penetration into the Middle East*, rev. ed. (New York: National Strategy Information Center, Inc., 1971), pp. 25–26.

40. Horelick, *Soviet Policy Dilemmas*, p. 7.

41. Horelick, *Soviet Middle East Policy*, p. 197.

42. See Klieman, *Soviet Russia and the Middle East*, p. 77; and Thomas, "The Dilemmas of Soviet Policy," p. 41.

43. Lenczowski, *Soviet Advances*, p. 162.

44. Whetten, *The Soviet Presence*, pp. 2–3.

45. Ibid., p. 2.

46. Laurence W. Martin, "The Changing Military Balance," *Proceedings*, vol. 29, no. 3 (March 1969), pp. 72–73.

47. Klieman, *Soviet Russia and the Middle East*, p. 72.

48. See Becker and Horelick, *Soviet Policy in the Middle East*, p. 96.

49. Whetten, *The Soviet Presence*, p. 39.

50. Laqueur, *The Struggle*, p. 184.

51. Horelick, *Soviet Policy Dilemmas*, p. 7.

52. Thomas, "Dilemmas of Soviet Policy," p. 38.

163

53. Whetten, *The Soviet Presence*, pp. 2–3.

54. Ibid.

55. Nationalist governments are "satisfied with the window dressing and not overly concerned about Soviet internal policy toward Islam as long as Moscow [does] not meddle in their internal affairs," Stephen Page, *The USSR and Arabia: The Development of Soviet Policies and Attitudes towards the Countries of the Arabian Peninsula 1955–1970* (London: Central Asian Research Centre in association with the Canadian Institute of International Affairs, 1971), p. 121.

56. Joseph J. Malone, *Dynamics of Military Balance: Middle East/Mediterranean* (research study prepared for the Advanced Research Projects Agency, Office of the Secretary of Defense, U.S. Department of Defense, 1972), p. 8.

57. Lenczowski, *Soviet Advances*, p. 167.

58. See Buss, "Wary Partners," p. 1: the USSR has been "wary of identification with the revolutionary Left in the Arab World, . . ." has shown little support for radical guerrillas, and has tried to moderate the local communist parties. Cf. Frederick C. Barghoorn, "Soviet Cultural Effort," *Proceedings*, vol. 29, no. 3 (March 1969), p. 161.

Chapter 4
Political Activities

1. Stephen Page, *The USSR and Arabia: The Development of Soviet Policies and Attitudes towards the Countries of the Arabian Peninsula 1955–1970* (London: Central Asian Research Centre in association with the Canadian Institute of International Affairs, 1971), pp. 120–1; Vernon V. Aspaturian, *The Union Republics in Soviet Diplomacy: A Study of Soviet Federalism in the Service of Foreign Policy* (Geneva: Librairie E. Droz, 1970).

2. "Moscow appears to have always avoided the temptation to establish with one country relations so close that they excluded good relations with others . . .," Pierre Rondot, "L'Egypte à l'heure du choix," *Revue de défense nationale,* vol. 28 (October 1972), p. 1472.

3. Uri Ra'anan, *The U.S.S.R. Arms the Third World: Case Studies in Soviet Foreign Policy* (Cambridge, Mass., M.I.T. Press, 1969), chapter 1; George Lenczowski, *Soviet Advances in the Middle East* (Washington, D.C.: American Enterprise Institute, 1969), pp. 56–57.

4. "Nasser's brand of 'positive neutralism' had made great gains in stature at the Bandung Conference and seemed likely to spread among other Middle East countries; since this policy, by definition, meant the

expansion of relations with the communist bloc, it was obviously in the Soviet interest to support Nasser to the fullest extent . . .," Page, *The USSR and Arabia*, p. 27.

5. Lenczowski, *Soviet Advances*, p. 59.

6. Ibid., p. 57; Wolfe, *The USSR and the Arab East* (Santa Monica: Rand Corporation, 1969), p. 5; R.D. McLaurin and Mohammed Mughisuddin, *Cooperation and Conflict: Egyptian, Iraqi, and Syrian Interests and U.S. Policy* (Washington, D.C.: American Institutes for Research, 1975).

7. See L. John Martin, "Effectiveness of International Propaganda," *Annals*, vol. 398 (November 1971), pp. 61–70, for a stimulating discussion of this idea.

8. See Lenczowski, *Soviet Advances*, pp. 66–67. For examples, see the Foreign Broadcast Information Service daily reports.

9. See Lenczowski, *Soviet Advances*, p. 19–20.

10. Ibid., p. 20.

11. Quoted in Jaan Pennar, *The U.S.S.R. and the Arabs: The Ideological Dimension* (New York: Crane, Russak & Company, Inc. 1973), p. 7.

Chapter 5
Economic Activities

1. John S. Badeau, "Internal Contest in the Middle East," *Proceedings*, vol. 29, no. 3 (March 1969), p. 177, discussing Soviet Prime Minister Khrushchev's statements at the opening of the Aswan High Dam.

2. Karel Holbik, *The United States, the Soviet Union and the Third World* (Hamburg: Verlag Weltarchiv GMBH, 1968), p. 22.

3. U.S. Department of State, Bureau of Intelligence and Research, *Communist States and Developing Countries: Aid and Trade in 1972* (hereafter *Communist Aid–1972*), RECS–10, 1973, table 1.

4. Ibid.

5. See Franklyn D. Holzman, "Soviet Trade and Aid Policies," *Proceedings*, vol. 29, no. 3 (March 1969), pp. 106–7. However, Soviet foreign assistance represents the use of surplus industrial capacity. Moreover, to the extent Soviet aid has promoted trade with developing countries more rapidly than it would otherwise have eventuated there has been an additional benefit. See James Richard Carter, *The Net Cost of Soviet Foreign Aid* (New York: Frederick A. Praeger, 1969).

6. Walter Z. Laqueur, *The Struggle for the Middle East, 1958–1968* (London: Routledge and K. Paul, 1969), p. 143; and "Soviet Aid to Arab

Countries," *An-Nahar Arab Report*, vol. 1, no. 4 (March 30, 1970), Backgrounder.

7. U.S. Department of State, *Communist Aid–1972*, table 1; *Communist States and Developing Countries: Aid and Trade in 1971*, table 1; *Communist States and Developing Countries: Aid and Trade in 1970*, RECS–15, September 22, 1971, table 1; *Communist States and Developing Countries: Aid and Trade in 1969*, RECS–5, July 9, 1970, table 1; *Communist Governments and Developing Nations: Aid and Trade in 1968*, RSE–65, September 5, 1969, table 1.

8. See Robert S. Walters, *American and Soviet Aid: A Comparative Analysis* (Pittsburgh: University of Pittsburgh Press, 1970, p. 65.

9. For example, Laqueur, *The Struggle*, p. 143.

10. For example, Holbik, *The United States*, p. 27.

11. Leo Tansky, *U.S. and U.S.S.R. Aid to Developing Countries: A Comparative Study of India, Turkey, and the U.A.R.* (New York: Frederick A. Praeger, 1967), p. 30.

12. U.S. Department of State, *Communist States and Developing Countries: Aid and Trade in 1971*, p. i.

13. Tansky, *U.S. and U.S.S.R. Aid*, p. 17.

14. Cf. Laqueur, however, who seems to support the Soviet claim; see *The Struggle*, p. 181.

15. George Lenczowski, *Soviet Advances in the Middle East* (Washington, D.C.: American Enterprise Institute, 1971), pp. 59–60.

16. See Robert O. Freedman, "The Soviet Union and the Middle East: The High Cost of Influence," *Naval War College Review*, vol. 24, no. 5 (January 1972), p. 20.

17. Walters, *American and Soviet Aid*, p. 113.

18. See Tansky, *U.S. and U.S.S.R. Aid*, pp. 25–31; Walters, *American and Soviet Aid*, chapter 7; and Marshall I. Goldman, *Soviet Foreign Aid* (New York: Frederick A. Praeger, 1967).

19. Walters, *American and Soviet Aid*, chapter 8; Holbik, *The United States*, p. 53.

20. Ibid., p. 4; Holzman, "Soviet Trade and Aid Policies," p. 111 and Elizabeth Valkenier, "New Soviet Views on Economic Aid," *Survey*, no. 76 (Summer 1970), pp. 17–29. Cf. Stephen Page, *The USSR and Arabia: The Development of Soviet Policies and Attitudes towards the Countries of the Arabian Peninsular 1955–1970* (London: Central Asian Research Centre in association with the Canadian Institute of International Affairs, 1971), p. 29, who correctly points out that "in its first years, Russian aid had a tremendous impact on the international situation."

166

21. Joseph J. Malone, *Dynamics of Military Balance: Middle East/Mediterranean—Final Report* (research study prepared for the Advanced Research Projects Agency, Office of the Secretary of Defense, U.S. Department of Defense, 1972), pp. 114–5.

22. "Soviet Aid to Arab Countries," *An-Nahar Arab Report*.

23. Aaron S. Klieman, *Soviet Russia and the Middle East* (Baltimore: Johns Hopkins Press, 1970), pp. 61–62. Too, the USSR has indicated to Malta that Soviet ships might make increasing use of Maltese drydocks, welcome news to Malta's economy, depressed since British "evacuation" east of Suez. Soviet maritime assistance has often gone hand-in-hand with strategic moves in the Mediterranean. Consequently, aid recipients' bilateral relations with the United States have been complicated. See McLaurin and Mughisudden, *Cooperation and Conflict*, chapters 2–5.

24. V. Rymalov, *Economic Cooperation between the USSR and Underdeveloped Countries* (Moscow: Foreign Languages Publishing House, n.d.), p. 58.

25. K. Billerbeck, *Soviet Bloc Foreign Aid to the Underdeveloped Countries: An Analysis and a Prognosis* (Hamburg: Archives of World Economy, 1960); Page, *The USSR and Arabia*, p. 28; U.S. Department of State, Bureau of Intelligence and Research, *The Sino–Soviet Economic Offensive through 1960*, no. 8426, March 21, 1961, p. 15; Malone, *Dynamics*, p. 64.

26. See "Egypt: Soviet Way of Life," *An-Nahar Arab Report*, vol. 1, no. 3 (March 23, 1970), p. 2; "Egypt: Protection for Soviets," ibid., vol. 1, no. 1 (March 9, 1970), p. 1.

27. Holzman, "Soviet Trade and Aid Policies," p. 105.

28. Ibid., p. 106.

29. Ibid.

30. Ibid., p. 108.

31. "Soviet Treaties should boost Middle East Trade," *Middle East Economic Digest*, vol. 16, no. 29 (July 1972), p. 812.

32. Page, *The USSR and Arabia*, p. 107; and "Some Soviet Views on Trade with Developing Countries," *Mizan*, vol. 7, no. 10 (November 1965), p. 6.

33. Laqueur, *The Struggle*, p. 140; and U.S. Department of State, *Communist States and Developing Countries: Aid and Trade in 1971* and *Aid and Trade in 1968*.

34. "Soviet–Arab Economic Relations–1," *An-Nahar Arab Report*, vol. 4, no. 2 (January 8, 1973), Backgrounder.

35. Walters, *American and Soviet Aid*, p. 99.

Chapter 6
Military Activities

1. Maxime Rodinson, "L'U.R.S.S. et les pays arabes," *Politique étrangère*, vol. 36, nos. 5-6 (1971), p. 679.

2. J.C. Hurewitz, "Origins of the Rivalry," *Proceedings*, vol. 29, no. 3 (March 1969), p. 14. These anchorages include primarily Alboran (near Morocco), the Gulf of Hammamet (off Tunisia), Hurd Bank (off Malta), Kithira (off Greece), one east of Cyprus, and near Socotra (South Yemen); and secondarily, one off Rota (Spain), another near La Galite (Tunisia), and others in the Gulf of Sirte (Libya), Gulf of Sollum (Egypt), and near Manfredonia (Italy). International Institute for Strategic Studies, *Strategic Survey 1971*, p. 33; Statement of James H. Noyes, in U.S. Congress, House of Representatives, Committee on Foreign Affairs, Subcommittee on the Near East, *U.S. Interests in and Policy toward the Persian Gulf*, 92nd Cong., 2nd sess., February 2, 1972, p. 10.

3. Noyes statement, p. 13.

4. See "Soviet Military Aid to the Arab World, 1967–1972," *An-Nahar Arab Report*, vol. 4, no. 1 (January 1973), Backgrounder; Alfred W. Hansen, *The Bear in Sheik's Clothing* (Montgomery, Ala.: Air Command and Staff College, 1972), pp. 28A, 48; U.S. Department of Defense, *Air Force Policy Letter for Commanders*, 8–72 (April 15, 1972), p. 1; Institute for Strategic Studies, *Strategic Survey 1970*, p. 49. Soviet control of Khormaksar airport, South Yemen, has also been reported; see "Soviet Military Aid to the Arab World."

5. For material concerning the situation before July 1972, see Hansen, *The Bear*, chapter 4, and *Strategic Survey 1970*. The former must be used with considerable care, as the author's sources are at times far from reliable.

6. Michael K. MccGwire has already produced a series of excellent analyses of Soviet naval strategy: "The Background to Russian Naval Policy," *Brassey's Annual: The Armed Forces Year Book* (1968), vol. 79, pp. 141–58; "The Background to Soviet Naval Developments," *The World Today*, vol. 27, no. 3 (March 1971), pp. 93–103; and "Soviet Naval Capabilities and Intentions" and "Soviet Naval Procurement" in Royal United Service Institution, *The Soviet Union in Europe and the Near East: Her Capabilities and Intentions*, pp. 33–51 and 74–87, respectively. See also Geoffrey Jukes, "The Indian Ocean in Soviet Naval Policy," *Adelphi Papers*, no. 87 (May 1972), pp. 4–12, for an application of the MccGwire thesis to the Indian Ocean; and C.B. Joynt and O.M. Smolansky, *Soviet Naval Policy in the Mediterranean* (Bethlehem, Pa.:

Lehigh University, Department of International Relations, Research Monograph no. 3, 1972).

7. A good discussion of the Soviet squadron is found in some of MccGwire's articles, above, and in chapter 3 of Lawrence L. Whetten, *The Soviet Presence in the Eastern Mediterranean* (New York: National Strategy Information Center, 1971).

8. This discussion has relied upon the following sources: International Institute for Strategic Studies, *The Military Balance 1972–1973* and *Strategic Survey 1971*; Louis Legendre, "Méditerranée et problèmes de defénse," *Revue de defénse nationale*, vol. 28 (October 1972), pp. 1482–5; and Whetten, *The Soviet Presence*, chapter 3.

9. Alfred W. Hansen, *The Bear*, p. 31 and sources.

10. William Beecher, "Egypt's Noisy Silent Partner," *Army*, vol. 21, no. 11 (November 1971), p. 11.

11. See Arnold L. Horelick, *Soviet Middle East Policy: Origins and Prospects* (Santa Monica: Rand Corporation, 1971); Walter Laqueur, *The Struggle for the Middle East* (London: Routledge and K. Paul, 1969), p. 155; Laurence W. Martin, "The Changing Military Balance," *Proceedings*, vol. 29, no. 3 (March 1969), p. 63; Maxime Rodinson, "L'U.R.S.S. et les pays arabes," pp. 679–80; Carl H. Amme, "The Soviet Navy in the Mediterranean Sea," *Naval War College Review*, vol. 21, no. 10 (June 1967), p. 154. It is important to recognize, however, that the possibility of a U.S. perceived commitment to Israel constitutes an even more important deterrent to Soviet action. To the extent it is believed such a commitment might be felt and honored at a moment of threat to Israel, the power (influence) of the U.S. naval presence is great. The possibility of a Soviet perceived commitment to one or more Arab states beyond resupply, though entertained by some before 1967, is not now generally accepted.

12. Geoffrey Kemp, "Strategy and Arms Levels, 1945–1967," *Proceedings*, vol. 29, no. 3 (March 1969), p. 33.

13. Ibid.

14. For example, Wynfred Joshua, "Arms for the Love of Allah," *United States Naval Institute Proceedings*, vol. 96, no. 3 (March 1970), pp. 30–39; Ferdinand Otto Miksche, "Soviet Influence in the Mediterranean," *Military Review*, vol. 51, no. 9 (September 1971), pp. 62–65; Joseph S. Roucek, "Las implicaciones de la expansión naval soviética en el Mediterraneo," *Revista de estudios política*, nos. 169–170 (January–April 1970), pp. 123–35.

15. Abraham S. Becker and Arnold L. Horelick, *Soviet Policy in the Middle East* (Santa Monica: Rand Corporation, 1970), p. 29 and note.

16. Kemp, "Strategy and Arms Levels," p. 25.

17. George Lenczowski, *Soviet Advances in the Middle East* (Washington, D.C.: American Enterprise Institute, 1971), pp. 60–61.

18. L.P. Bloomfield and Amelia C. Leiss, "Arms Transfers and Arms Control," *Proceedings*, vol. 29, no. 3 (March 1969), p. 46.

19. SIPRI, *The Arms Trade with the Third World* (Stockholm: Almquist & Wiksell, 1971), pp. 190–1. Of the worldwide figure, 37.5 percent went to the Middle East, 3 percent to North Africa; ibid.

20. Kemp, "Strategy and Arms Levels," pp. 33–34.

21. Uri Ra'anan, *The U.S.S.R. Arms the Third World: Case Studies in Soviet Foreign Policy* (Cambridge, Mass.: M.I.T. Press, 1969), p. 161.

22. Other considerations increasing the opportunity cost of Soviet military assistance are discussed in Ra'anan, *The U.S.S.R. Arms the Third World*, pp. 162–3.

23. U.S. Department of State, *Communist States and Developing Countries: Aid and Trade in 1971*, p. 16.

Chapter 7
Cultural Activities

1. See the *International Yearbook of Communist Affairs* (published annually by the Hoover Institution, Stanford University) of any recent year for more information on this and similar organizations.

2. Joseph J. Malone, *Dynamics of Military Balance: Middle East/Mediterranean—Final Report* (research study prepared for the Advanced Research Projects Agency, Office of the Secretary of Defense, U.S. Department Defense, 1972), pp. 78–79.

3. Again, the *International Yearbook on Communist Affairs* describes these groups and their link to the USSR succinctly.

4. Henry W. Morton, *Soviet Sport: Mirror of Soviet Society* (New York: Collier Books, 1963), p. 69.

5. Ibid., p. 81.

6. See Vernon A. Stone and Harrogadde S. Eswara, "The Likability and Self-Interest of the Source in Attitude Change," *Journalism Quarterly*, vol. 46, no. 1 (Spring 1969), pp. 61–68.

7. But see Don D. Smith, "Some Effects of Radio Moscow's North American Broadcasts," *Public Opinion Quarterly*, vol. 34, no. 4 (Winter 1970–1971), pp. 539–51.

8. Karel Holbik, *The United States, the Soviet Union and the Third World* (Hamburg: Verlag Weltarchiv GMBH, 1968), p. 56.

9. Ibid.

170

10. Frederick A. Barghoorn, "Soviet Cultural Effort," *Proceedings of the American Academy of Political Science*, vol. 29, no. 3 (March 1967), p. 166.

11. Malone, *Dynamics*, pp. 60–61.

12. Holbik, *The United States, the Soviet Union*, p. 56.

13. George Lenczowski, *Soviet Advances in the Middle East* (Washington, DC.: American Enterprise Institute, 1971), p. 63.

14. Ibid., p. 62.

15. U.S. Department of State, *Educational and Cultural Exchange, 1971*, p. 18.

16. Ibid.

17. Frederick James Tickner, *Technical Cooperation* (New York: Frederick A. Praeger, 1965), p. 104.

18. Leo Tansky, *U.S. and U.S.S.R. Aid to developing Countries: A Comparative Study of India, Turkey, and the U.A.R.* (New York: Frederick A. Praeger, 1967), p. 31.

19. U.S. Department of State, *Educational and Cultural Exchanges, 1970*, p. 16.

20. Holbik, *The United States, the Soviet Union*, p. 55.

21. Leo Tansky, "Soviet Foreign Aid to the Less-Developed Countries," U.S. Congress, Joint Economic Committee, 89th Cong., 2nd sess., 1966, *New Directions in the Soviet Economy*, part 4, p. 953.

22. Robert S. Walters, *American and Soviet Aid: A Comparative Analysis* (Pittsburgh: University of Pittsburgh Press, 1970), pp. 140–1.

23. U.S. AID, *Operations Report, FY 1971*.

24. See John S. Badeau, "Internal Contest in the Middle East," *Proceedings of the Academy of Political Science*, vol. 29, no. 3 (March 1969), pp. 171–2.

25. Ibid.

26. Barghoorn, "Soviet Cultural Effort," p. 163.

Bibliography

Bibliography

Abu–Jaber, Faiz S. "The Soviets and the Arabs, 1917–1955." *Middle East Forum,* vol. 45, no. 1 (1969), pp. 13–44.

_____. "Soviet Attitudes Toward Arab Revolutions: Yemen, Egypt Algeria, Iraq and Palestine." *Middle East Forum,* vol. 46, no. 4 (1970), pp. 41–65.

Achiminow, Herman F. "Das Mittelmeer—eine Sowjetische–Arabische See? Raum, Zeit Und Soziale Prozesse." *Wehr und Wirtschaft,* vol. 11, no. 11 (November 10, 1967), p. 567.

Acimovic, Ljubivoje. "An Independent Mediterranean." *New Middle East* no. 17 (February 1970), pp. 23–36. Reprinted in *Survival,* vol. 12, no. 5 (May 1970), pp. 164–168.

Adie, W.A.C. *China, Israel and the Arabs.* London: Institute for the Study of Conflict, 1971.

Akins, James E. "The Oil Crisis: This Time the Wolf is Here." *Foreign Affairs,* vol. 51, no. 3 (April 1973), pp. 462–490.

Alkazaz, A. "Die Irakische–Sowjetischen beziehungen—eine analytische übersicht." *Orient,* vol. 13, no. 2 (June 1972), pp. 45–67.

Allison, Graham. *Essence of Decision: Explaining the Cuban Missile Crisis.* Boston: Little, Brown, 1971.

American Petroleum Institute. *Petroleum Facts and Figures.* Washington D.C.: 1972.

Amme, Carl H. "The Soviet Navy in the Mediterranean Sea." *Naval War College Review,* vol. 21, no. 10 (June 1969), pp. 154–9.

Andreasyan, R.N. "Middle Eastern Oil: Present and Future." *International Affairs* (Moscow), July 1960, pp. 26–29.

Army Institute for Advanced Russian and East European Studies. *Soviet Affairs Symposium: The 51st Year: The Jubilee Ends, The Problems Multiply.* Presented at the Second Soviet Affairs Symposium, Garmisch–Partenkirchen, Germany, June 5–7, 1968.

Aspaturian, Vernon V. "Internal Forces and Soviet Policy in the Eastern Mediterranean." In U.S. Congress, House of Representatives, Committee on Foreign Affairs, Subcommittee on Europe and Subcommittee on the Near East, 92nd Congress, 1st Session, Joint Hearings, *Soviet Involvement in the Middle East and the Western Response,* October 19–21, November 2–3, 1971, pp. 82–90.

————. "The Soviet Military–Industrial Complex—Does it Exist?" *Journal of International Affairs*, vol. 26, no. 1 (1972), pp. 1–28.

————. *The Union Republics in Soviet Diplomacy: A Study of Soviet Federalism in the Service of Foreign Policy*. Geneva: Librairie E. Droz, 1970.

Avery, Peter. "The Many Faces of Iran's Foreign Policy." *New Middle East*, no. 47 (August 1972), pp. 17–19.

Azar, Edward E. "Profiling and Predicting Patterns of Inter–Nation Interactions: A Signal Accounting Model." Paper prepared for delivery at the 66th annual meeting of American Political Science Association, Los Angeles, California, September 8–12, 1970.

Badeau, John S. *The American Approach to the Arab World*. New York: Harper and Row, 1968.

————. "Internal Contest in the Middle East." *Proceedings of the Academy of Political Science*, vol. 29, no. 3 (March 1969), pp. 170–86.

Baldwin, Hanson R. *Strategy for Tomorrow*. New York: Harper and Row, 1970.

————. "The Stakes Are Oil." *Army*, vol. 21, no. 8 (August 1971), pp. 10–15.

Ballis, William B. "Soviet Foreign Policy toward Developing States: The Case of Egypt." *Studies on the Soviet Union*, vol. 7, no. 3 (1968), pp. 84–113.

Barger, Thomas C. "Middle East Oil since the Second World War." *Annals of the American Academy of Political and Social Science*, vol. 401 (May 1972), pp. 31–44.

Barghoorn, Frederick C. "Soviet Cultural Effort." *Proceedings of the Academy of Political Science*, vol. 29, no. 3 (March 1969), pp. 156–69.

Becker, Abraham S. *Oil and the Persian Gulf in Soviet Policy in the 1970s*. Santa Monica: Rand Corporation. 1971.

————. and Arnold L. Horelick. *Soviet Policy in the Middle East*. Santa Monica: Rand Corporation, 1970.

Beecher, William. "The Soviet Push in the Mideast." *Army*, vol. 18, no. 4 (April 1968), pp. 20–26.

Beloff, Max. *The Foreign Policy of Soviet Russia, 1929–1941*. 2 volumes. London: Oxford University Press, 1949.

Beltrametti, E. "Unirsi è necessario per lo marine d'Europa." *Politica estera*, vol. 8, no. 3 (March 15–April 15, 1970), pp. 20–25.

Belyayev, Igor and Evgeny Primakov. "The Situation in the Arab World." *New Times*, no. 39 (September 27, 1967), pp. 38.

Benson, Charles. "A Strategic Alternative." *National Review*, vol. 22 (November 17, 1970), pp. 1206–10.

Berner, Wolfgang. "Die Sowjetunion und die Entstehung des Nahost-Konflikts." *Europa-Archiv*, vol. 22, no. 14 (July 25, 1967), pp. 493–504.

Berreby, Jean-Jacques. "Le pétrole, enjeu stratégique autour de la Méditerranée." *Politique étrangère*, vol. 36, no. 5–6 (1971), pp. 519–32.

Berry, John A. "Oil and Soviet Policy in the Middle East." *Middle East Journal*, vol. 26, no. 2 (Spring 1972), pp. 149–60.

_____. "The Growing Importance of Oil." *Military Review*, vol. 52, no. 10 (October 1972), pp. 2–16.

Binder, Leonard. "Les Etats-Unis, la France et le conflit israélo–arabe." *Politique étrangère*, vol. 36, no. 5–6 (1971), pp. 629–46.

Blixt, Melvin D. "Soviet Objectives in the Eastern Mediterranean." *Naval War College Review*, vol. 21, no. 7 (March 1969), pp. 4–27.

Bloomfield, Lincoln P. and Amelia C. Leiss. "Arms Transfers and Arms Control." *Proceedings of the Academy of Political Science*, vol. 29, no. 3 (March 1969), pp. 37–54.

Burrell, R.M. "Opportunity Knocks for the Kremlin's Drive East." *New Middle East*, no. 46 (July 1972), pp. 9–13.

Burrowes, Robert and Douglas Muzzio. "The Road to War: An Enumerative History of the External Politics of Israel, Jordan, Saudi Arabia, Syria and the U.A.R., 1965–1967." Paper prepared for delivery at 66th annual meeting of American Political Science Association, Los Angeles, California, September 8–12, 1970.

Buss, Robin. "Wary Partners: The Soviet Union and Arab Socialism." *Adelphi Papers*, no. 73 (December 1970).

Cabiaux, M.P. "La Turquie et ses relations avec l'Union Soviétique: antécédents historiques et incidence sur l'engagement dans l'affrontement Est–Ouest." *Chronique de politique étrangère*, vol. 19. no. 6 (November 1966) pp. 619–730.

Cable, James. *Gunboat Diplomacy: Political Applications for Limited Naval Force*. New York: Frederick A. Praeger, 1971.

Calchinovati, G. "Italy and the Arab World." *Africa Quarterly*. vol. 9, no. 4 (January–March 1970), pp. 331–337.

_____. "La bonifica del lago mediterraneo." *Astrolabio*, vol. 8, no. (May 31, 1971), pp. 6–8.

Campbell, John C. *The Middle East in the Muted Cold War*. (Denver, Colorado: University of Colorado, 1964).

_____. "American Search for Partners." *Proceedings of the Academy of Political Science*, vol. 29, no. 3 (March 1969), pp. 198–215.

_____. "Les transformations de l'environnement régional dans la prochaine décennie." *Politique étrangère*, vol. 36, no. 5–6 (1971), pp. 473–88.

_____. "The Soviet Union and the United States in the Middle East." *Annals*, vol. 401 (May 1972), pp. 126–35.

_____. and Helen Caruso. *The West and the Middle East*. New York: Council on Foreign Relations, 1972.

Carder, M., "Le Kremlin déboussolé." *Esope*, vol. 17, no. 342 (October 1970), pp. 1–6.

Carlson, Sevinc. "Japan's Inroads into the Middle East and North Africa." *New Middle East*, no. 22 (July 1970), pp. 14–17.

Carmichael, Joel. "The Nationalist–Communist Symbiosis." *Problems of Communism*, vol. 8, no. 3 (1959), pp. 35–41.

Carrère d'Encausse, H. "L'URSS et le Moyen Orient." *Orient*, vol. 10, no. 37 (ler trimestre 1966), pp. 7–25.

Carter, James Richard. *The Net Cost of Soviet Foreign Aid*. New York: Frederick A. Praeger, 1969.

Cass, William F. "Middle East Oil: The Subsurface Weapon." *United States Naval Institute Proceedings*, vol. 99, no. 1/839 (January 1973), pp. 18–25.

Cattan, Henry. *The Evolution of Oil Concessions in the Middle East and North Africa*. Dobbs Ferry, New York: Oceana Publications, 1967.

Ceccarini, E. "Le isocrisie coranico-conciliari." *Nord è Sud*, vol. 17, no. 131 (November 1970), pp. 7–16.

Chambre, Henri. *Union Soviétique et développement économique*. Paris: Aubier-Montaigne, 1967.

Chase, Alan C. *Soviet Military Goals in the Middle East*. Montgomery, Ala.: Air University, Report #0555-72, 1972.

Chauvel, Jean. "Les puissances et la Méditerranée." *Politique étrangère*, vol. 36, no. 5–6 (1971), pp. 463–72.

Churba, Joseph. *Soviet Penetration into the Middle East*. Maxwell Air Force Base, Ala., Documentary Research Division, Aerospace Studies Institute, 1968.

_____. *Perceiving Options in the Middle East*. Maxwell Air Force Base, Ala., Documentary Research Division, Aerospace Studies Institute, Air University, 1970.

Clemens, Walter C. "How the USSR Brought Peace to the Middle East in 1972." *War/Peace Report*, vol. 10 (June/July 1970), pp. 14–22.

Connolly, V. *Soviet Economic Policy in the East*. London: Oxford University Press, 1933.

Copeland, Miles. *The Game of Nations*. London: Weidenfeld and Nicolson, 1969.

Cottrell, Alvin J. "Russia Nears Domination of Middle East—from

Morocco to Indian Subcontinent." *Navy,* vol. 13, no. 11 (November 1970), pp. 10–17.

———. "The Soviet Union in the Middle East." *Orbis,* vol. 14, no. 3 (Fall 1970), pp. 588–98.

———. "Conflict in the Persian Gulf." *Military Review,* vol. 51, no. 2 (February 1971), pp. 33–41.

———. "The Soviet Union as a Major Power in the Middle East: A Review of Recent Literature." *World Affairs,* vol. 133, no. 3 (March 1971), pp. 315–20.

Cox, Frederick J. "The Russian Presence in Egypt." *Naval War College Review,* vol. 22, no. 6 (February 1970), pp. 44–53.

Crozier, Brian. "Communist Tactics in Europe and the Middle East." *RUSI: Journal of the Royal United Services Institution for Defense Studies,* vol. 117, no. 3 (September 1972), pp. 13–19.

Curtis, Michael. "Soviet–American Relations and the Middle East Crisis." *Orbis,* vol. 15, no. 1 (Spring 1971), pp. 403–27.

Dadant, P.M. *American and Soviet Defense Systems vis-à-vis the Middle East.* Santa Monica: Rand Corporation, 1970.

Dallin, David J. *Soviet Foreign Policy After Stalin.* Philadelphia: J.B. Lippincott Company, 1961.

Dann, Uriel. *Iraq under Qassem: A Political History, 1958–1963.* New York: Frederick A. Praeger, 1969.

Decalo, Samuel. "Israeli Foreign Policy and the Third World."*Orbis,* vol. 11, no. 3 (Fall 1967), pp. 724–45.

DeNezza, Eugene J. "Soviet Need for Middle East Oil." *Air University Review,* vol. 22. no. 4 (May–June 1971), pp. 52–57.

Devillers, P. "Européens et Maghrébins: Que peut-on faire ensemble en Méditerranée occidentale?" *Jeune Afrique,* vol. 515 (17 Novembre 1970), pp. 44–50.

Dimant–Kass, Ilana. "The Soviet Military and Soviet Policy in the Middle East, 1970–1973," *Soviet Studies,* vol. 26, no. 4 (October 1974), pp 502–522.

Dmitriev, E. "Soviet–Arab Friendship: A New Stage." *International Affairs* (Moscow), August 1971, pp. 66–68.

Drachkovitch, Milorad M., Editor. *Yearbook on International Communist Affairs.* Stanford: Hoover Institution Press, 1967.

Drambiantz, G. "The Persian Gulf: Twixt the Past and the Future." *International Affairs* (Moscow), October 1970, pp. 66–71.

Draper, Theodore. *Israel and World Politics: Roots of the Third Arab–Israeli War.* New York: Viking Press, 1967.

"Early Soviet Contacts with Arab and African Countries." *Mizan*, vol. 8, no. 2 (March/April 1966), pp. 87–91.

Edelsberg, Herman. *Whose Fight in the Middle East? An Analysis of America's National Interest*. Washington, D.C.: B'nai B'rith International Council, 1970.

Eller, E.M. *The Soviet Sea Challenge*. Chicago: Cowles, 1972.

Ellingworth, Richard. "Japanese Economic Policies and Security." *Adelphi Papers*, no. 90 (October 1972).

End, Heinrich. "Das Mittelmeer als politisches Spanningsfeld." *Europa-Archiv*, vol. 26, no. 10 (1971), pp. 741–50.

Eran, Oded and Jerome E. Singer. "Soviet Policy towards the Arab World 1955–1971." *Survey*, vol. 17 (Autumn 1971), pp. 10–29.

EUROPA Publications, Ltd. *The Middle East and North Africa*, 3rd–19th editions, 1955–1972/3.

"Everybody Out," *The Economist*, vol. 244, no. 6732 (September 2, 1972), pp.34.

Evron, Yair. "Moscow Moves Closer to Delhi: What Will It Mean for Egypt?" *New Middle East*, no. 40 (January 1972), pp. 15–17.

Forsythe, David P. "The Soviets and the Arab–Israeli Conflict." *World Affairs*, vol. 134, no. 2 (Fall 1971), pp. 132–142.

Frank, Lewis A. "Nasser's Missile Program." *Orbis*, vol. 2, no. 3 (Fall 1967), pp. 746–57.

Frankel, Charles. "L'avenir des relations franco-américaines dans le domaine de la politique culturelle au Moyen-Orient." *Politique étrangère*, vol. 36, no. 5–6 (1971), pp. 617–26.

_____. "The Cultural Contest,' " *Proceedings of the Academy of Political Science*, vol. 29, no. 3 (March 1969), pp. 139–55.

Freedman, Robert O. "The Soviet Union and the Middle East: The High Cost of Influence." *Naval War College Review*, vol. 24, no. 5 (January 1972), pp. 15–34.

Fritsch, R. "La politique de l'Union soviétique." *Revue française de science politique*, vol. 19, no. 2 (April 1969) pp. 402–13.

Gache, Paul. "La Russie et la Méditerranée." *Revue militaire générale*, vol. 9, (November 1969), pp. 505–22.

Gallagher, Charles F. "Le monde arabe et la culture occidentale." *Politique étrangère*, vol. 36, no. 5–6 (1971), pp. 587–02.

Gallois, Pierre M. "Power and Paralysis." *Orbis*, vol. 11, no. 3 (Fall 1967), pp. 664–76.

Galtung, Johan. "The Middle East and the Theory of Conflict." *Journal of Peace Research*, vol. 8 no. 3–4 (1971), pp. 173–206.

Gaspard, J. "The Kremlin without Abdul Nasser: The Soviet Union and Egypt, a New Relationship?" *New Middle East,* no. 26 (November 1970) pp. 17–19.

Gasteyger, Curt. "Moscow and the Mediterranean." *Foreign Affairs,* vol. 46, no. 4 (July 1968), pp. 676–87.

Georgetown University. Center for Strategic Studies. *Soviet Sea Power.* Washington, D.C., 1969.

Geyer, Georgie A. "Love and Hate in the Middle East." *Progressive,* vol. 36, (April 1972), pp. 27–30.

Gil Benumeya, R. "El Cercano Oriente, ante los acontecimientos de Egipto." *Revista de Política internacional,* no. 116 (July–August 1971), pp. 75–84.

Gil Benumeya, R. "Arabismo, petróleo y grandes potencias en la tensión actual de Arabia." *Revista de Política internacional* (Madrid), no. 90 (March/April 1967), pp. 259–67.

Glubb, John. "The Arabs and the West." *Army Quarterly and Defense Journal* (London), vol. 95, no. 2 (January 1968), pp. 179–80.

Goldman, Marshall I. *Soviet Foreign Aid.* New York: Frederick A. Praeger, 1967.

Gouré, Leon. *Soviet Limited War Doctrine.* Santa Monica: Rand Corporation, May 1963.

Graham, Robert. "Iraq and Iran: Gulf Power Struggle Sharpens." *New Middle East,* no. 45 (June 1972), pp. 14–16.

Griffith, William E. "La coopération avec l'Union Soviétique au Moyen-Orient et en Afrique du Nord." *Politique étrangère,* vol. 36, no. 5–6 (1971), pp. 687–703.

Gumpel, Werner. "Sowjetunion: Erdol und Nahostpolitik." *Aussenpolitik,* vol. 22 (November 1971), pp. 670–81.

Halpern, Manfred. *The Politics of Social Change in the Middle East and North Africa.* Princeton, New Jersey: Princeton University Press, 1963.

Hansen, Alfred W. *The Bear in Sheik's Clothing.* Maxwell Air Force Base: Air Command and Staff College, Research Study, May 1972.

Hartshorn, J.E. "Oil and the Middle East War." *The World Today,* vol. 24, no. 4 (April 1968), pp. 151–7.

Hatfield, Mark O. "Middle Eastern Oil and the United States: Hard Realities for U.S. Policy Guidelines." Statement before the Senate Committee on Interior and Insular Affairs, January 22, 1973.

Haykal, Muhammad Hasanayn. "Arab–Soviet Friendship." *Survival,* vol. 9, no. 11 (November 1967), pp. 358–63.

180

Hazard, J.N. "The Residue of Marxist Influence in Algeria." *Columbia Journal of Transnational Law*, vol. 9, no. 2 (Fall 1970), pp. 194–225.

Heiman, Leo. "In the Soviet Arsenal." *Ordnance*, vol. 52, no. 286 (January–February 1968), pp. 366–73.

Herrick, Robert W. *Soviet Naval Strategy*. Annapolis: U.S. Naval Institute, 1968.

Hitchcock, David I., Jr. "Joint Development of Siberia: Decision-Making in Japanese–Soviet Relations." *Asian Survey*, vol. 11, no. 3 (March 1971), pp. 279–300.

Hoffmann, Stanley. "La France, les Etats-Unis et le conflit israélo–arabe: différences et asymétries." *Politique étrangère*, vol. 36, no. 5–6 (1971), pp. 657–72.

Holbik, Karel. *The United States, The Soviet Union and the Third World*. Hamburg: Verlag Weltarchiv GMBH, 1968.

Holzman, Franklyn D. "Soviet Trade and Aid Policies." *Proceedings of the Academy of Political Science*, vol. 29, no. 3 (March 1969), pp. 104–20.

Horelick, Arnold L. *Soviet Policy Dilemmas in the Middle East*. Santa Monica: Rand Corporation, 1968.

_____. *Soviet Middle East Policy: Origins and Prospects*. Santa Monica: Rand Corporation, February 1971.

Horton, Alan W. "The Arab–Israeli Conflict of June 1967. Part I: Some Immediate Issues." *American Universities Field Staff Reports Sevice*, Northeast Africa Series, vol. 13, no. 2 (September 1967).

Hunter, R.E. "Der sowietische Dilemna im Nahen Osten." *Europa-Archiv*, vol. 25, no. 19 (October 10, 1970), pp. 723–32.

_____. "In the Middle in the Middle East." *Foreign Policy*, no. 5 (Winter 1971–1972), pp. 137–50.

Hurewitz, Jacob C. "Origins of the Rivalry." *Proceedings of the Academy of Political Science*, vol. 29, no. 3 (March 1969), pp. 1–17.

_____. *Changing Military Perspectives in the Middle East*. Santa Monica: Rand Corporation, 1970.

_____. "Le dialogue reprend." *Politique étrangère*, vol. 36. no. 5–6 (1971), pp. 723–41.

_____. ed. *Soviet–American Rivalry in the Middle East*. New York: The Academy of Political Science, 1969.

Hutton, C. Powell. "Changing Soviet Oil Interests: Implications for the Middle East." *Naval War College Review*, vol. 24, no. 2 (October 1971), pp. 76–93.

Ignatius, Paul R. "Soviet Sea Power shifts to Strategic Offensive." *Navy*, vol. 11, no. 7 (July 1968), pp. 23–27.

Imhoff, Christoph von. *Duell im Miettelmeer: Moskau greift mach dem Nahen und dem Mittlere Osten.* Freiburg, West Germany: Verlag Rombach, 1968.

International Institute for Strategic Studies. *Strategic Survey 1970.* London, 1971.

_____. *Strategic Survey 1971.* London, 1972.

_____. *The Military Balance, 1972-1973.* London, 1972.

"Islam and Communism in the Middle East." *Contemporary Review,* February 1953.

Issawi, Charles. "Regional Economies in the 1970's." *Proceedings of the Academy of Political Science,* vol. 29, no. 3 (March 1969), pp. 121-36.

Jackson, Henry M. *The Middle East and American Security Policy.* Report of Senator Henry M. Jackson to the Committee on Armed Services, United States Senate, 91st Cong., 2nd sess., Committee Print, December 1970.

Jaecques, Robert E. *Soviet Middle East Policy.* Montgomery, Ala.: Air University, Report #1435-72, 1972.

Jordan, Amos A. "Les Etats-Unis à la recherche d'une politique méditerranéenne." *Politique étrangère,* vol. 36, no. 5-6 (1971), pp. 50-17.

Joshua, Wynfred. "Arms for the Love of Allah." *United States Naval Institute Proceedings,* vol. 96, no. 3 (March 1970), pp. 30-39.

_____. *Soviet Penetration into the Middle East.* Revised ed. New York: National Strategy Information Center, Inc., 1971.

_____. and Stephen P. Gilbert. *Arms for the Third World: Soviet Military Aid Diplomacy.* Baltimore: The Johns Hopkins Press, 1969.

Joyaux, F. "La politique chinoise au Moyen-Orient." *Orient,* vol. 10, no. 40, (4e trimestre 1966), pp. 25-46.

Joynt, C.B. and O.M. Smolansky. *Soviet Naval Policy in the Mediterranean.* Bethlehem, Pa: Lehigh University, Dept. of International Relations, Research Monograph #3, 1972.

Jukes, Geoffrey. "The Indian Ocean in Soviet Naval Policy." *Adelphi Papers,* no. 87 (May 1972).

Kanet, Roger E. "The Recent Soviet Reassessment of Developments in the Third World." In Erik P. Hoffmann and Frederic J. Flevon, Jr., eds., *The Conduct of Soviet Foreign Policy.* Chicago: Aldine-Atherton, Inc., 1971, pp. 398-408.

Katin, Vladimir. "The Soviet Union and the Arab World; Defining a New Relationship." *New Middle East,* no. 39 (December 1971), pp. 16-18.

Kedourie, Elie. "Britain, France, and the Last Phase of the Eastern

Question." *Proceedings of the Academy of Political Science,* vol. 29, no. 3 (March 1969), pp. 189–97.

Kedourie, Elie, P.E.L. Fellowes, M. Mackintosh, Jon Kimche, B. Beedham, and T. Little. "The Arab–Israeli Dispute.." *Conflict Studies,* April 1971, pp. 1–42.

Kemp, Geoffrey. "Strategy and Arms Levels, 1945–1967," *Proceedings of the Academy of Political Science,* vol. 29, no. 3 (March 1969), pp. 21–36.

Kennedy, William V. "A Query on the Middle East." *America,* vol. 11 (June 29, 1968), p. 814.

Kerr, Malcolm. "The Convenient Marriage of Egypt and Libya." *New Middle East,* no. 48 (September 1972), pp. 4–7.

Khadduri, Majid. *Political Trends in the Arab World: The Role of Ideas and Ideals in Politics.* Baltimore: The John Hopkins Press, 1970.

_____. *Arab Contemporaries: The Role of Personalities in Politics.* Baltimore: The Johns Hopkins Press, 1973.

Khan, R.A. "Israel and the Soviet Union: A Review of Postwar Relations." *Orbis,* vol. 9, no. 4 (Winter 1966), pp. 999–1012.

Kilmarx, Robert A., and Alvin J. Cottrell. "The USSR in the Middle East." *Air Force and Space Digest,* vol. 53 (August 1970), pp. 40–46.

Kimche, Jon. "New Soviet Moves in the Middle East." *Midstream,* vol. 18, no. 4 (April 1972), pp. 3–11.

Kirkpatrick, Lyman B. "Cold War Operations: The Politics of Communist Confrontation." *Naval War College Review,* vol. 21, no. 2 (October 1968), pp. 110–5.

Klieman, Aaron S. *Soviet Russia and the Middle East.* Baltimore: The Johns Hopkins Press (1970).

Klinghoffer, Arthur Jay. "Pretext and Context: Evaluating the Soviet Role in the Middle East." *Mizan,* vol. 10, no. 3 (May/June 1968), pp. 86–93.

Kolkowicz, Roman. *The Soviet Military and the Communist Party.* Princeton: Princeton University Press, 1967.

Kolodziej, Edward A. "French Mediterranean Policy: The Politics of Weakness." *International Affairs* (London), vol. 47, no. 3 pp. 503–17.

Koury, Enver M. *The Super Powers and the Balance of Power in the Arab World.* Beirut: Catholic Press, 1970.

Kozicki, R.J. "Indian Policy toward the Middle East." *Orbis,* vol. 11, no. 3 (Fall 1967), pp. 786–97.

Kreker, Hans-Justus. "The Soviet Union and the Mediterranean." *Military Review,* vol. 50, no. 8 (August 1970), pp. 21–26.

183

Kruzhin, Petr. "The Soviet Fleet in the Mediterranean." *Bulletin of the Institute for the Study of the U.S.S.R.*, vol. 16, no. 2 (February 1969), pp. 35–41.

Kulski, W.W. *The Soviet Union in World Affairs: A Documentary Analysis, 1964–1972.* Syracuse: Syracuse University Press, 1973.

Labouret, Vincent. "Politique méditerranéenne de la France." *Politique étrangère*, vol. 36, no. 5–6 (1971), pp. 489–500.

Landes, David S. "Western European Relations with the Middle East." In U.S., Congress, House of Representatives, Committee on Foreign Affairs, Subcommittee on Europe and Subcommittee on the Near East, 92nd Congress, 1st Session, Joint Hearings, *Soviet Involvement in the Middle East and the Western Response*, October 19–21, November 2–3, 1971, pp. 122–5.

Landis, L. "Der Suezkanal in der politischen Strategie des Sowjetunion." *Europa-Archiv*, vol. 24, no. 3 (February 1969), pp. 107–114.

Lang, Nicolas. "L'U.R.S.S., le Proche Orient et le pétrole." *Est et Ouest*, vol. 22, no. 439 (16-31 January 1970), pp. 1–4.

_____. "L'U.R.S.S., les Palestiniens et la Jordanie." *Est et Ouest*, vol. 22, no. 443 (16–31 March 1970), pp. 1–5.

_____. "L'U.R.S.S. et le plan Rogers." *Est et Ouest*, vol. 22, no. 453 (1–15 October 1970), pp. 1–5.

Laqueur, Walter Z. *Communism and Nationalism in the Middle East.* New York: Frederick A. Praeger, 1957.

_____. "Arab Unity vs. Soviet Expansion." *Problems of Communism*, vol. 8, no. 3 (1959), pp. 42-51.

_____. Russia Enters the Middle East." *Foreign Affairs*, vol. 47, no. 2 (January 1969) pp. 298–308.

_____. *The Struggle for the Middle East: The Soviet Union and the Middle East, 1958–1968.* London: Routledge and K. Paul, 1969.

_____. "Soviet Dilemmas in the Middle East." In U.S., Congress, House of Representatives, Committee on Foreign Affairs, Subcommittee on Europe and Subcommittee on the Near East, 92nd Congress, 1st Session, Joint Hearings, *Soviet Involvement in the Middle East and the Western Response*, October 19–21, November 2–3, 1971, pp. 26–31.

_____. "On the Soviet Departure from Egypt." *Commentary*, vol. 54, no. 6 (December 1972), pp. 61–68.

_____, ed. *The Middle East in Transition.* New York: Frederick A. Praeger, 1958.

Lee, Christopher D. "Russian Trade with Seven Countries of Central Asia and the Middle East, 1945–1953." *Mizan*, vol. 10, no. 4 (July/August 1968), pp. 129–40.

_____. "Soviet and China Interest in Southern Arabia." *Mizan*, vol. 13, (August 1971), pp. 35–47.

Lee, William T. "The 'Politico–Military–Industrial Complex' of the U.S.S.R." *Journal of International Affairs*, vol. 26, no. 1 (1972), pp. 73–86.

Lefevre, J. "L'escalade soviétique au Moyen Orient—Israel sur le passage des éléphants." *L'Arche*, vol. 159 (26 May–25 June 1970), pp. 35–38, 55.

Legendre, Louis. "Méditerranée et problèmes de défense." *Revue de défense nationale*, vol. 28 (October 1972), pp. 1475–88.

Lenczowski, George. *Russia and the West in Iran, 1918–1948: A Study in Big Power Rivalry*. Ithaca: Cornell University Press, 1949.

_____. "Soviet Policy in the Middle East." *Current History*, vol. 55, no. 327 (November 1968), pp. 268–74, 303–4.

_____. *Soviet Advances in the Middle East*. Washington, D.C.: American Enterprise Institute, 1971.

_____. ed. *United States Interests in the Middle East*. Washington, D.C.: American Enterprise Institute, 1969.

Leva, A.E. "Il panarabismo, oggi." *Relazioni*, vol. 7, no. 3 (March 1970), pp. 19–30.

Lewis, Bernard. "Russia in the Middle East." *Survival*, vol. 12 (October 1970), pp. 332–6.

Linder, R. "Die Sowjetunion im Nahost." *Ost-Europa*, vol. 21, no. 5 (May 1971), pp. 305–15.

Lofgren, William W., Jr. *Sudanese Communism: A Blow to Soviet Military Objectives in Seeking Third World Leadership*. Maxwell Air Force Base: Air University, Research Study, May 1972.

Lovisetti, G. "La presenze dei piloti sovietici nella RAU." *Relazione internazionale*, vol. 34, no. 19 (9 May 1970), pp. 467–8.

Luttwak, Edward. "The Military Balance . . . Moscow Notwithstanding." *New Middle East*, no. 48 (September 1973), pp. 15–16.

McDermott, Anthony, "A Russian Withdrawal; or Divorce, Egyptian Style." *New Middle East*, no. 47 (August 1972), pp. 4–6.

_____. "Sadat and the Soviet Union." *The World Today*, vol. 28, no. 9 (September 1972), pp. 404–10.

_____. "Egypt and Europe: Strong Links May Yet Be Forged." *New Middle East*, no. 40 (October 1972), pp. 14–16.

MccGwire, Michael K. "The Background to Russian Naval Policy." *Brassey's Annual: The Armed Forces Year-Book (1968)*, pp. 141–58.

_____. "Soviet Naval Capabilities and Intentions." In Royal United

Service Institution, *The Soviet Union in Europe and the Near East: Her Capabilities and Intentions.* A Report of a Seminar sponsored jointly by Southampton University and the Royal United Service Institution and held at Milford-On-Sea between Monday 23rd March and Wednesday 25th March 1970, pp. 33–51.

_____. "Soviet Naval Procurement." In Royal United Service Institution, *The Soviet Union in Europe and the Near East: Her capabilities and Intentions.* A Report of a Seminar sponsored jointly by Southampton University and the Royal United Service Institution and held at Milford-On-Sea between Monday 23rd March and Wednesday 25th March 1970, pp. 74–87.

_____. "The Background to Soviet Naval Developments." *The World Today*, vol. 27, no. 3 (March 1971), pp. 93–103.

Mackintosh, Malcolm. "Soviet Foreign Policy." *The World Today*, vol. 21, no. 4 (April 1968), pp. 145–50.

McLane, Charles B. "Foreign Aid in Soviet Third World Policies." *Mizan*, vol. 10, no. 6 (November/December 1968), pp. 210–50.

McLaurin, R.D. and Mohammed Mughisuddin, *The Soviet Union and the Middle East*, Washington, D.C.: The American Institutes for Research, 1974.

_____. *Cooperation and Conflict: Egyptian, Iraqi, and Syrian Interests, and U.S. Policy.* Washington, D.C.: The American Institutes for Research, 1975.

McLean, John G. and Warren B. Davis. *Guide to National Petroleum Council Report on United States Energy Outlook.* Washington, D.C.: National Petroleum Council, 1972.

Malone, Joseph J. *Dynamics of Military Balance: Middle East/Mediterranean Final Report.* Research Study, Advanced Research, Projects Agency, Office of the Secretary of Defense, U.S. Department of Defense, 1 April 1972.

Mansfield, Peter. "France is Bold, Germany is Cautious, While Britain Merely Dithers." *Middle East International*, no. 14 (July 1972), pp. 9–10, 12.

Marshall, Charles Burton, "Reflections on the Middle East." *Orbis*, vol. 11, no. 2 (Summer 1967) pp. 343–59.

Martin, Laurence W. "The Changing Military Balance." *Proceedings of the Academy of Political Science*, vol. 29, no. 3 (March 1969), pp. 61–74.

"Marxist Champions of Islam." *Mizan*, vol. 8, no. 5 (September/October 1966), pp. 209–214.

Masmoudi, Mohammed. "Mediterraneo: presenza sovietica è miopia europea," *Relazione internazionale.* Vol. 34, no. 41 (10 October 1970) pp. 940–1.

Medzini, M. "Japan's Vested Interest in Middle Eastern Stability." *New Middle East,* 42/43 (March/April 1972), pp. 51–54.

Meim, P. "L'U.R.S.S., Israël et les Arabes." *Eurafrica et Tribune du Tiers Monde,* vol. 14, nos. 3–4 (March–April 1970), pp. 18–20.

"The Middle East: Soviet Anxieties." *Mizan,* vol. 9, no. 4 (July/August 1967), pp. 145–53.

"Middle East: The Soviet Stance." *Mizan,* vol. 10, no. 4 (July/August 1968), pp. 141–50.

Miksche, Ferdinand Otto. "Soviet Influence in the Mediterranean." *Military Review,* vol. 51, no. 9 (September 1971), pp. 62–65.

Milenkovic, Milutin. "New Deployment in the Middle East?" *Review of International Affairs,* no. 23 (Belgrade) 538 (September 5, 1972), pp. 9–11.

Millar, T.B. "Soviet Policies South and East of Suez." *Foreign Affairs,* vol. 49, no. 1 (October 1970), pp. 70–80.

Milstein, Jeffrey S. "Soviet and American Influence on the Arab–Israeli Arms Race: A Quantitative Analysis." *Peace Research Society (International) Papers,* vol. 15, 1971.

Mirsky, G. "Arab East: Moment of Truth." *New Times,* nos. 46 and 47 (November 12 and 20, 1967), pp. 46–47.

Morison, David L. *The U.S.S.R. and Africa.* London: Oxford University Press: 1964.

———. "Russia, Israel and the Arabs." *Mizan,* vol. 9, no. 3 (May/June 1967), pp. 91–107.

———. "Middle East: Soviet Emphasis on Realism." *Mizan,* vol. 9, no. 5 (September/October 1967), pp. 215-217.

———. "Soviet Interest in Middle East Oil." *Mizan,* vol. 10, no. 3 (May/June 1968), pp. 79–85.

———. "The Middle East: The Soviet Entanglement," *Mizan,* vol. 11, no. 3 (May/June 1969), pp. 165–73.

———. "Middle East: The Soviet–U.A.R. Posture." *Mizan,* vol. 12, no. 1 (October 1970), pp. 1–6.

———. "Moscow and the Problems of Third World Communists: The Lessons of Sudan." *Mizan,* vol. 13, no. 3 (December 1971), pp. 111–125.

Mosely, P.E. "Soviet Search for Security." *Proceedings of the Academy of Political Science,* vol. 29, no. 3 (March 1969), 216–27.

Mumford, Jay C. "Soviet Motivation in the Middle East." *Military Review,* vol. 52, no. 9 (September 1972), pp. 40–49.

Nahumi, Mordehai. "The U.S.A. and the U.S.S.R. in the Middle East." *New Outlook* (Tel Aviv), vol. 11, no. 7 (September 1968), pp. 9–15.

Neguib, Mohammed. *Egypt's Destiny*. London: Victor Gollancz, Ltd., 1955.

Nes, David G. "The Russians in the Middle East." *Middle East International*, vol. 12 (March 1972), pp. 12–13.

Noyes, James H. Statement. In U.S., Congress, House of Representatives, Committee on Foreign Affairs, Subcommittee on the Near East, 92nd Congress, 2nd session, Hearings, *U.S. Interests in and Policy Toward the Persian Gulf*, February 2, June 7, August 8 and 15, 1972, pp. 9–16.

Nutting, Anthony. *Nasser*. New York: E.P. Dutton, 1972.

Nyrop, Richard F. et al. *Area Handbook for Syria*. Washington, D.C.: USGPO for American University, Foreign Area Studies, 1971.

Page, Stephen. "Moscow and the Persian Gulf Countries, 1967–1970." *Mizan*, vol. 13, no. 2 (October 1971), pp. 72–88.

_____. *The USSR and Arabia: The Development of Soviet Policies and Attitudes towards the Countries of the Arabian Peninsula 1955–1970*. London: Central Asian Research Centre in association with the Canadian Institute of International Affairs, 1971.

Palmer, J.M. "NATO and the Mediterranean." *Revue militaire générale*, July 1972, pp. 52–67.

Patterson, Gardner. "Declining American Involvement." *Proceedings of the Academy of Political Science*, vol. 29, no. 3 (March 1969), pp. 99–103.

Peabody, James B. "Escalation or Detente in the Middle East." *Military Review*, vol. 52, no. 4 (April 1972), pp. 35–49.

"Peking's Nahostpolitik will die USA and USSR unterlaufen." *China-Analysen*, vol. 9 (October 1970), pp. 35–38.

Pendill, C. Grant, Jr. " 'Bipartisanship' in Soviet Foreign Policy-Making." In Erik P. Hoffmann and Frederic J. Fleron, Jr., eds., *The Conduct of Soviet Foreign Policy-Making*. Chicago: Aldine Atherton, Inc., 1971, pp. 61–75.

Pennar, Jaan. "Soviet Road to Damascus." *Mizan*, vol. 9, no. 1 (January/February 1967), pp. 23-29.

_____. "The Arabs, Marxism and Moscow: A Historical Survey." *Middle East Journal*, vol. 22, no. 4 (Autumn 1968), pp. 433–47.

Pergent, J. "L'aide militaire de l'U.R.S.S. à l'Egypte." *Est et Ouest*, vol. 22, no. 450 (1-15 July 1970), pp. 16–18.

Petrov, V. "Soviet Foreign Policy and the Collapse of Communist Unity." *Modern Age*, vol. 15, no. 4 (Fall 1971), pp. 338–49.

Polmar, Norman. *Soviet Naval Power*. New York: National Strategy Information Center, Inc., 1972.

Primakov, Yevgeny. "Why the Canal Must Be Re-opened: A Soviet View." *New Middle East,* no. 46 (July 1972), pp. 7–8.

Primakov, Yuri. "The Soviet Plan for Peace." *Middle East International,* no. 12, March 1972, pp. 10–11.

Proctor, J. Harris. ed. *Islam and International Relations.* New York: Frederick A. Praeger, 1965.

Quandt, William B. *American Policies in the Middle East: Choices and Constraints.* Santa Monica: Rand Corporation, April 1969.

———. *United States Relations with Algeria: Learning to do Business with Radical Nationalists.* Santa Monica, California: Southern California Arms Control and Foreign Policy Seminar, October 1971.

Ra'anan, Uri. *The U.S.S.R. Arms the Third World: Case Studies in Soviet Foreign Policy.* Cambridge, Mass.: M.I.T. Press, 1969.

———. "Soviet Global Policy and the Middle East." *Naval War College Review,* vol. 24, no. 1 (September 1971), 19–29.

Ramazani, R.K. "Soviet Military Assistance to the Uncommitted Countries." *Midwest Journal of Political Science,* vol. 3, no. 4 (November 1959), pp. 356–73.

"Recent Soviet articles on the U.A.R." *Mizan,* vol. 8, no. 1 (January/February 1966), pp. 33–37.

Reese, Howard C. "Search for Equilibrium in the Middle East." *Military Review,* vol. 48, no. 4 (April 1968), pp. 29–40.

Reich, Bernard. *Crisis in the Middle East, 1967: Implications for U.S. Policy.* McLean, Virginia: Research Analysis Corporation, 1968.

Reinhardt, G. Frederick. "The Middle East of the 1970's." *Air University Review,* vol. 21 (May/June 1970), pp. 41–50.

Rodinson, Maxime. "Marxism and Socialism." in Michael Adams ed., *The Middle East: A Handbook.* New York: Frederick A. Praeger, 1971, pp. 374–82.

———. "L'U.R.S.S. et les pays arabes." *Politique étrangère,* vol. 36, nos. 5–6 (1971), pp. 673–86.

———. *Marxisme et Monde Musulman.* Paris: Editions du Seuil, 1972, pp. 672.

Rondot, Pierre. "L'Egypte à l'heure du choix." *Revue de défense nationale,* vol. 28 (October 1972), pp. 1464–74.

Rostow, Eugene V. "The Middle Eastern Crisis in the Perspective of World Politics." *International Affairs* (London), vol. 47, no. 2 (April 1970), pp. 275–88.

———. "Il confronto USA–URSS nel Medio Oriente." *Affari esteri,* vol. 2, no. 8 (October 1970), pp. 28–56.

Roucek, Joseph S. "Las implicaciones de la expansión naval soviética en el Mediterraneo." *Revista de Estudios Política*, nos. 169–170 (January–April), pp. 123–35.

Rouillon, Fernand. "La politique française au Moyen-Orient et ses relations avec la politique américaine." *Politique étrangère*, vol. 36, nos. 5–6 (1971), pp. 647–56.

Royal Institute of International Affairs. *British Interests in the Mediterranean and Middle East: A Report by a Chatham House Study Group*. London, New York, and Toronto: Oxford University Press, 1958.

Royal United Service Institution. *The Soviet Union in Europe and the Near East: Her Capabilities and Intentions*. A report of the Seminar sponsored jointly by Southampton University and the Royal United Service Institution and held at Milford-on-Sea between Monday 23rd March and Wednesday 25th March 1970.

Rubinstein, Alfred Z. "Soviet Policy toward the Third World in the 1970's." *Orbis*, vol. 15, no. 1 (Spring 1971), pp. 104–17.

"Russian Jews and the Canal: Part of a New Initiative?" *New Middle East*, no. 41 (February 1972), pp. 3–4.

Rustow, Dankwart A. "The Appeal of Communism to Islamic Peoples." In Harris J. Proctor, ed, *Islam and International Relations*. New York: Frederick A. Praeger, 1965, pp. 40–60.

Rymalov, V. *Economic Cooperation Between the USSR and Underdeveloped Countries*. Moscow: Foreign Languages Publishing House, n.d.

Safran, Nadav. "The Soviets Show A Different Face and Much Else Looks Different." *New Middle East*, no. 39 (December 1971), pp. 19–20.

――――. "How Long will Sadat Last? Moscow's Not-So-Secret Wish." *New Middle East*, nos. 42/43 (March/April 1972), pp. 5–8.

Sager, P. *Kairo und Moskau in Arabien*. Bern: Verlag Schweizerisches Ost-Institut, 1967.

Salpeter, Eliahu. "Nearing Sadat's Deadline: Shadows in the Middle East." *New Leader*, vol. 54 (December 27, 1971), pp. 7–9.

"Sand on their Boots." *The Economist*, vol. 244, no. 6726 (22 July 1972), pp. 15–17.

Schick, Jack M. "Conflict and Integration in the Near East: Regionalism and the Study of Crisis." A paper prepared for delivery at the Sixth annual meeting of the American Political Science Association, Los Angeles, California, September 8–12, 1970.

Schöpflin, George. "Russia's Expendable Arab Communists." *New Middle East*, no. 45 (June 1972), pp. 20–21.

Schurr, S.H. and P.T. Homan. *Middle Eastern Oil and the Western World: Prospects and Problems*. New York: American Elsevier Publishing Company, 1971.

Schwadran, Benjamin. "The Soviet Role in the Middle East Crisis." *Current History*, vol. 60, no. 353 (June 1971), pp. 13–18, 50.

"Seapower: A Survey of the Royal Navy." *The Economist*, vol. 246, no. 6758 (3 March 1973), pp. Survey 1–26.

Segesvary, V. *Le réalisme khrouchtchévien: la politique soviétique au Proche-Orient*. Neuchatel: Editions de la Baconniere, 1968.

Shao, M. "Middle East Situation Causing Concern." *Asian Outlook*, vol. 5, no. 4 (April 1970), pp. 20–22.

Sheehan, Edward R.F. "The United States, the Soviet Union, and Strategic Considerations in the Middle East." *Naval War College Review*, vol. 23, no. 10 (June 1971), pp. 22–30.

―――. "Why Sadat Packed Off the Russians." *New York Times Magazine*, 6 August 1972, pp. 10–11, 39–43, 51, 54.

Sick, G.G. "Russia and the West in the Mediterranean: Perspectives for the 1970's." *Naval War College Review*, vol. 22, no. 10 (June 1970), pp. 48–69.

Sigler, John. "Reliability Problems in the Measurement of International Events in the Elite Press," Mimeo. Macalester College, April 1970.

Singh, K.R. "Soviet–U.A.R. Relations." *India Quarterly*, vol. 25, no. 2 (April–June 1969), pp. 139–52.

Slonim, Shlomo. "Egypt's Conflict of Alliances." *The World Today*, vol. 28, no. 3, (March 1972), pp. 124–32.

Smith, Harvey H. et al. *Area Handbook for the United Arab Republic (Egypt)*, Washington, D.C. USGPO for American University, Foreign Area Studies, 1970.

―――. *Area Handbook for Iraq*. 2nd edition. Washington, D.C.: USGPO for American University, Foreign Area Studies, 1971.

Smolansky, O.M. "Moscow and the Persian Gulf: An Analysis of Soviet Ambitions and Potential." *Orbis*, vol. 14, no. 1 (Spring 1970), pp. 92–108.

"Soviet Arms and Interests in the Middle East." *Middle East International*, no. 13, (April/May 1972), pp. 10–12.

"Soviet Interests in the Middle East." *Mizan*, vol. 8, no. 3 (May/June 1966), pp. 142–4.

"Soviet Interests in Syria." *Mizan*, vol. 8, no. 1 (January/February 1966), pp. 23–32.

"Soviet Opinions on Syria and the Ba'th." *Mizan*, vol. 8, no. 2 (March/April 1966), pp. 73–86.

191

"Soviet Thoughts on the New Regime in Iraq." *Mizan*, vol. 10, no. 5 (September/October 1968), pp. 194–8.

"Soviet Views on 'The Religious Factor.' " *Mizan*, vol. 8, no. 4 (July/August 1966), pp. 174–81.

Spector, Ivar. *The Soviet Union and the Muslim World 1917–1958*. Seattle: University of Washington Press, 1959.

Spiegel, Steven L. "The Dominant and the Subordinate System: The Patrons v. the Pygmies in the Middle East." Paper, APSA Annual Meeting, 7 September 1972.

Staar, Richard F., ed. *Yearbook on International Communist Affairs, 1972*. Stamford: Hoover Institution Press, 1973.

Stanford Research Institute. *Area Handbook for the Peripheral States of the Arabian Peninsula*. Washington, D.C.: USGPO for the American University, Foreign Area Studies, 1971.

Stockholm International Peace Research Institute. *The Arms Trade with the Third World*. Stockholm: Almquist & Wiksell, 1971.

"Sudanese Anti–Communism: Soviet and UAR Reactions." *USSR and Third World*, vol. 8, no. 7 (5 July–15 August 1971).

Sworabowski, Witold S., ed. *World Communism: a Handbook, 1918–1965*. Stamford: Hoover Institution Press, 1973.

Tansky, Leo. "Soviet Foreign Aid to the Less-Developed Countries." U.S. Congress, Joint Economics Committee. 89th Congress, 2nd session, 1966. *New Directions in the Soviet Economy*. Part 4.

_____. *U. S. and U.S.S.R. Aid to Developing Countries: A Comparative Study of India, Turkey and the U.A.R.* New York: Frederick A. Praeger, 1967.

Tekiner, Suleyman. "Soviet Policy Toward the Arab East." *Bulletin of the Institute for the Study of the USSR*, vol. 15, no. 3 (March 1968), pp. 29–37.

Thomas, John R. "The Dilemmas of the Soviet Policy in the Middle East." *Parameters: The Journal of the Army War College*, vol. 2 (Fall 1971), pp. 34–42.

Tickner, Frederick James. *Technical Cooperation*. New York: Frederick A. Praeger, 1965.

Tolley, Kemp. "The Bear that Swims Like a Fish." *United States Naval Institute Proceedings*, vol. 97, no. 2/820 (June 1971), pp. 41–46.

Toole, (CAPT.) Wycliffe D., Jr. "Soviet Interest in Arabia." *Military Review*, vol. 48, no. 5 (May 1968), pp. 91–97.

"The UAR and 'Proletarian Dictatorship.' " *Mizan*, vol. 8, no. 2 (March/April 1966), pp. 67–72.

"UAR and USSR: The Dialogue on Socialism." *Mizan*, vol. 10, no. 1 (January/February 1968), pp. 38–43.

Ulam, Adam B. *Expansion and Coexistence: The History of Soviet Foreign Policy 1917–1947*. New York: Praeger, 1968.

United Nations. United Nations Educational, Scientific, and Cultural Organisation. *Statistical Yearbook 1970*, 1972.

_____. *Statistical Yearbook 1971*, 1973.

U.S., Agency for International Development. *Operations Report FY 1971*, W–129, December 1971.

_____. *U. S. Overseas Loans and Grants and Assistance from International Organizations: Obligations and Loan Authorizations, July 1, 1945–June 30, 1971* (May 24, 1972).

U.S., Congress, House of Representatives, Committee on Foreign Affairs, Subcommittee on Europe and Subcommittee on the Near East, 92nd Congress, 1st Session, Joint Hearings. *Soviet Involvement in the Middle East and the Western Response*, October 19–21, November 2–3 1971.

U.S., Congress, House of Representatives, Committee on Foreign Affairs, Subcommittee on the Near East, 92nd Congress, 2nd Session, Hearings. *U. S. Interests in and Policy Toward the Persian Gulf*, February 2, June 7, August 8 and 15, 1972.

U.S., Department of Commerce. *Statistical Abstract of the United States 1972*.

U.S., Department of Defense. Defense Security Assistance Agency. *Military Assistance and Foreign Military Sales Facts*, April 1972.

U.S., Department of State. Bureau of Educational and Cultural Affairs. *International Exchange: People's Diplomacy in Action*, 1972.

_____. *A Statistical Profile of the U. S. Exchange Program 1971*.

U.S., Department of State. Bureau of Intelligence and Research. *Communist Governments and Developing Nations: Aid and Trade in 1968*, RSE–65, September 5, 1969.

_____. *Communist States and Developing Countries: Aid and Trade in 1969*, RECS–5, July 9, 1970.

_____. *Communist States and Developing Countries: Aid and Trade in 1970*, RECS–15, September 22, 1971.

_____. *Communist States and Developing Countries: Aid and Trade in 1971*, RECS–3, May 15, 1972.

_____. *Communist States and Developing Countries: Aid and Trade in 1972*. RECS–10 (1973).

_____. *Educational and Cultural Exchanges Between Communist and Noncommunist Countries in 1969*, RSES–35, August 12, 1970.

_____. *Educational and Cultural Exchanges Between Communist and*

Noncommunist Countries in 1970, RSES–34, August 30, 1971.

———. *Educational and Cultural Exchanges Between Communist and Noncommunist Countries in 1971*, RESS–57, August 31, 1972.

United States Information Agency, Washington, D. C. Research and Reference Service. *Communist Propaganda Activities in the Near East and South Asia: 1963*, October 2, 1964.

———. *Communist Propaganda Activities in the Near East and South Asia, 1964*, R–184–65, December 1965.

———. *Selected Communist Propaganda Activities in the Near East and South Asia: 1962*, April 8, 1963.

"The USSR and the Persian Gulf." *Mizan*, vol. 10, no. 2 (March/April 1968), pp. 51–59.

"The USSR and the Sudan." *Mizan*, vol. 10, no. 5 (September/October 1968), pp. 185–93.

Valkenier, Elizabeth. "New Soviet Views on Economic Aid." *Survey*, no. 76 (Summer 1970), pp. 17–29.

Vernant, Jacques. "Un espoir au Proche-Orient." *Revue de défense nationale*, vol. 27 (March 1971), pp. 454–9.

———. "Les Limites d'une coopération franco-américaine." *Politique étrangère*, vol. 36, nos. 5–6 (1971), pp. 707–22.

Vucimch, Wayne S., ed. *Russia and Asia: Essays on the Influence of Russia on the Asian Peoples*. Stamford: Hoover Institution Press, 1973.

Walters, Robert S. *American and Soviet Aid: A Comparative Analysis*. Pittsburgh: University of Pittsburgh Press, 1970.

Watt, D. C. "Persian Gulf—Cradle of Conflict?" *Problems of Communism*, vol. 21, nos. 32–40 (May/June 1972).

Welch, William. "Soviet Expansionism and Its Assessment." *Journal of Conflict Resolution*, vol. 15, (Sept. 1971) pp. 317–27.

Wesson, Robert G. "The Soviet Interest in the Middle East." *Current History*, vol. 59, no. 350 (October 1970), pp. 212–19, 242.

Wheeler, G. E. "Russia and the Middle East." *International Affairs* (London), vol. 35, no. 3 (July 1959), pp. 295–304.

———. "Soviet and Chinese Policies in the Middle East." *World Today*, vol. 22, no. 2 (February 1966), pp. 64–78.

———. "Soviet Interests in Iran, Iraq and Turkey." *World Today*, vol. 24, no. 5 (May 1968), pp. 197–203.

Whetten, Lawrence L. "Changing Arab Attitudes toward Arab Radical Movements." *New Middle East*, no. 18 (March 1970), pp. 20–27.

———. "Strategic Parity in the Middle East." *Military review*, vol. 50, no. 9 (September 1970), pp. 24–31.

_____. *The Soviet Presence in the Eastern Mediterranean*. New York: National Strategy Information Center, 1971.

_____. "Sadat's Strategic Options in the Canal War." *The World Today*, vol. 29, no. 2 (February 1973), pp. 58–67.

Wolfe, Thomas W. *Soviet Strategic Thought in Transition*. Santa Monica: Rand Corporation, 1964.

_____. *The Soviet Military Scene: Institutional and Defense Policy Considerations*. Santa Monica: Rand Corporation, 1966.

_____. *USSR and the Arab East*. Santa Monica: Rand Corporation. September, 1969.

_____. *Soviet Goals and Policies in the Middle East*. Santa Monica: Rand Corporation, 1970.

_____. *Policymaking in the Soviet Union: A Statement with Supplementary Comments*. Washington, D. C.: Rand Corporation, 1969.

Wright, Gordon. "La présence culturelle des Etats-Unis au Moyen-Orient et en Afrique du Nord: problèmes et perspectives." *Politique étrangère*, vol. 36, nos. 5–6 (1971) pp. 565–79.

Wylie, J. C. "The Sixth Fleet and American Diplomacy." *Proceedings of the Academy of Political Science*, vol. 29, no. 3 (March 1969), pp. 55–60.

Yakoylev, D. "Soviet–Iraqi Cooperation Grows and Develops." *International Affairs* (Moscow), June 1972, pp. 65–67.

Yamak, Labib Luwiyya. *The Syrian Social Nationalist Party: An Ideological Analysis*. Cambridge, Mass: Harvard University Press, 1966.

Yodfat, A. Y. "Arms and Influence in Egypt—The Record of Soviet Military Assistance Since June 1967." *New Middle East*, no. 10 (July 1969), pp. 27–32.

_____. "The USSR and the Palestine Guerrillas." *Mizan*, vol. 11, no. 1 (January/February 1969), pp. 8–17.

_____. "The USSR, Jordan and Syria." *Mizan*. vol. 11, no. 2 (April 1969), pp. 73–93.

Zador, Heinrich. "Das Gleichgewicht der Krafte im Nahen Osten." *Wehrkunde*, vol. 20 (December 1971), pp. 633–5.

_____. "Staatsbesuche im Nahen Osten." *Wherkunde*, vol. 20 (July 1971), pp. 337–40.

Zartman, I. William. "Military Elements in Regional Unrest." *Proceedings of the Academy of Political Science*, vol. 29, no. 3 (March 1969), pp. 75–87.

Zimmerman, William. "The Sources of Soviet Conduct: A Reconsideration." Paper delivered at APSA Annual Meeting, September 1972, Washington, D.C.

Zoppo, Ciro, E. "Soviet Ships in the Mediterranean and the U.S.–Soviet Confrontation in the Middle East." *Orbis*, vol. 14 (Spring 1970), pp. 109–28.

Newspaper Articles

"Algeria and France: Oil and Politics." *An-Nahar Arab Report*, vol. 2, no. 5 (February 1, 1971), Backgrounder.

"An Analysis of the Soviet Egyptian Treaty." *An-Nahar Arab Report*, vol. 2, no. 24 (June 14, 1971), Backgrounder.

"The Arab Socialist Union." *An-Nahar Arab Report*, vol. 2, no. 21 (May 24, 1971), Backgrounder.

"The Arabian Gulf: Where the Left Lies." *An-Nahar Arab Report*, vol. 2, no. 4 (January 25, 1971), pp. 3–4.

Astrachan, Anthony. "Gromyko, at U.N., Calls Arab Terrorists 'Criminal,' " *The Washington Post*, September 27, 1972, p. A21.

———. "Kremlin Rethinks Its Mideast Stance." *The Washington Post*, March 1, 1971.

"The Ba'ath: Allergic to Advice." *An-Nahar Arab Report*, vol. 1, no. 27 (September 7, 1970), p. 4.

Beecher, William. "Egypt is Reported to Get Advanced Soviet Missile." *New York Times*, November 12, 1972, p. 2.

———. "Egypt Reported to Have Received Swing-Wing Plane from Soviet and to Have Been Disappointed." *New York Times*, September 29, 1972, p. 19.

Berger, Marilyn. "Moscow Sends Syria Latest Tanks, Mig–21s." *The Washington Post*, September 28, 1972, p. A29.

Cohen, Sam. "Soviets Build Up Aid Flow to Turkey." *Christian Science Monitor*, November 18, 1970, p. 16.

"The Commandos: 'Snows of Moscow,' " *An-Nahar Arab Report*, vol. 1, no. 4 (March 30, 1970), pp. 1–2.

Cooley, John K. "Cairo Delegation to Russia to Test Future of Relations." *Christian Science Monitor*, October 14, 1972, p. 7.

———. "Cairo's Anti–Soviet Ire Heats Up." *Christian Science Monitor*, August 19, 1972, pp. 1, 3.

———. "Egyptian and Iraqi Compasses Swing toward Moscow." *Christian Science Monitor*, May 17, 1972, p. 6.

———. "France to Drop Mideast Arms Embargo?" *Christian Science Monitor*, November 25, 1972, p. 3.

_____. "Iran's Shah in Moscow to Gain Leverage." *Christian Science Monitor*, October 12, 1972, pp. 1, 6.

_____. "Israeli–Syrian Sparks Alert Arabs." *Christian Science Monitor*, November 2, 1972, p. 5.

_____. "Libya, Egypt Look North to Europe for Arms, Aid." *Christian Science Monitor*, August 7, 1972, p. 3.

_____. "Moscow Mideast Steps Assessed." *Christian Science Monitor*, April 17, 1972, p. 12.

_____. "A Navally Neutral Mediterranean." *Christian Science Monitor*, August 8, 1972, pp. 1, 5.

_____. "Sadat, in Trouble at Home, Looks toward Moscow." *Christian Science Monitor*, October 17, 1972, pp. 1, 3.

_____. "Sadat Packs for Moscow as Arab–Soviet Ties Cool." *Christian Science Monitor*, February 2, 1972, p. 3.

_____. "Soviet–Arab Relations at Key Turn." *Christian Science Monitor*, August 9, 1972, p. 4.

_____. "Soviet Naval Gains Forecast if British Forces Leave Cyprus." *Christian Science Monitor*, December 31, 1971.

_____. "Soviet Navy Sails Back into Egyptian Ports." *Christian Science Monitor*, September 25, 1972, pp. 1, 2.

_____. "Soviets, Arabs, and Palestinians Move to Protect Interests." *Christian Science Monitor*, September 2, 1972, p. 5.

_____. "Soviets, Arabs Play Out Shadowy Drama in Secret." *Christian Science Monitor*, August 15, 1972, p. 3.

_____. "Soviets Curb Arms to Egypt." *Christian Science Monitor*, December 8, 1971, pp. 1, 15.

_____. "Soviets in Arabland: Ceasefire Deadline Spotlights Mideast Intentions." *Christian Science Monitor*, November 5, 1970, p. 3.

_____. "Soviets in Syria: Welcome but Warned." *Christian Science Monitor*, August 11, 1972, p. 2.

_____. "Tabqa Dam to Transform Syrian Desert Back into Garden." *Christian Science Monitor*, December 8, 1971, p. 6.

"Egypt and the Ceasefire." *An-Nahar Arab Report*, vol. 2, no. 11 (March 15, 1971), Backgrounder.

"Egypt and the Soviet Union: Economic Cooperation." *An-Nahar Arab Report*, vol. 2, no. 13 (March 29, 1971), pp. 1–2.

"Egypt: the Dangerous Right." *An-Nahar Arab Report*, vol. 1, no. 35 (November 2, 1970), p. 1.

"Egypt: Protection for the Soviets." *An-Nahar Arab Report*, vol. 1, no. 1 (March 9, 1970), p. 1.

"Egypt: Soviet Way of Life." *An-Nahar Arab Report*, vol. 1, no. 3 (March 23, 1970), pp. 2–3.

"Egypt's Premier Ends Soviet Talk." *New York Times*, October 19, 1972, p. 7.

Godsell, Geoffrey. "Egypt's Lost Lands: UN Vote in Vain?" *Christian Science Monitor*, December 12, 1972, pp. 1–2.

_____. "Middle East Peace Impasse Tops Soviet–Egyptian Agenda." *Christian Science Monitor*, October 12, 1971, pp. 1, 5.

_____. "Podgorny to Test New Egyptian Tide." *Christian Science Monitor*, May 25, 1971, pp. 1, 3.

"Hard Times for Lebanese Communists." *An-Nahar Arab Report*, vol. 1, no. 12 (May 25, 1970), Backgrounder.

Harsch, Joseph C. "Will U.S. Escalate Mideast Arms Race?" *Christian Science Monitor*, June 7, 1971.

Hijazi, Ihsan A. "Domestic Pressure on Sadat Reported." *New York Times*, July 19, 1972, p. 1.

Hirst, David. "Soviet Arms Airlift to Syria Seen as Bid to Recoup Loss." *The Washington Post*, September 25, 1972, p. A16.

Hoagland, Jim. "150 More Soviet Advisers Reported in Syria, Airlift Ends." *The Washington Post*, October 6, 1972, p. A25.

_____. "Soviets Said to Play Up Arms Airlift to Syria." *The Washington Post*, September 28, 1972, p. A28.

Howe, Marvine. "Trip Around Persian Gulf Shows Iran's Chief Power." *The New York Times*, January 25, 1972.

"Iraq: Communist Party: Power of Survival." *An-Nahar Arab Report*, vol. 1, no. 9 (May 4, 1970), Backgrounder.

"Iraq: 'Silent Deterioration,' " *An-Nahar Arab Report*, vol. 1, no. 16 (June 22, 1970), pp. 3–4.

"Jordan-Commandos: Jedda Talks." *An-Nahar Arab Report*, vol. 2, no. 45 (November 8, 1971), pp. 2–3.

"Jordan: The Ears of Fateh." *An-Nahar Arab Report*, vol. 1, no. 19 (July 13, 1970), pp. 1–2.

Kaiser, Robert G. "Egypt Fails to Get Promise of Aid from Soviet Talks." *The Washington Post*, October 19, 1972, p. A27.

"The Kurds: A Settlement Forever!" *An-Nahar Arab Report*, vol. 1, no. 15 (June 15, 1970), Backgrounder.

"Lebanon: The Kremlin Man." *An-Nahar Arab Report*, vol. 1, no. 35 (November 2, 1970), p. 2.

"Lebanon: Soviet Temptations." *An-Nahar Arab Report*, vol. 2, no. 12 (March 22, 1971), pp. 3–4.

"Lebanon–USSR: Embargo Broken." *An-Nahar Arab Report*, vol. 2, no. 46 (November 15, 1971), pp. 1–2.

"Moscow Must Decide Course with Arabs." *Christian Science Monitor*, August 21, 1972, p. 5.

Norton-Taylor, Richard. "Common Market Plans Joint Policy in Mediterranean." *The Washington Post*, November 10, 1972, p. A10.

Ofner, Francis. "Italians Press for Reopening of Suez Canal in Jerusalem Talks," *Christian Science Monitor*, March 30, 1973, p.2.

_____. "Soviet Trio—Icebreakers in Israel." *Christian Science Monitor*, February 2, 1972, p. 9.

Pace, Eric. "Arab Guerrillas Are Reported to Get Direct Shipments of Soviet Weapons." *New York Times*, September 18, 1972, pp. 1, 2.

_____. "Soviet Union Reported to Ship Only Small Arms to Al Fatah." *New York Times*, September 22, 1972, p. 6.

"Podgorny-Sadat: Mutual Dependence." *An-Nahar Arab Report*, vol. 2, no. 22 (May 31, 1971), pp. 2–3.

Saikowski, Charlotte. "Soviet Union Gestures Cautiously to Israel." *Christian Science Monitor*, September 2, 1971, p. 4.

_____. "Soviets Try to Identify with Arab Nations." *Christian Science Monitor*, March 6, 1972, p. 2.

_____. "Soviet's [sic] Stalk West's Oil Supply." *Christian Science Monitor*, April 11, 1972.

"The Sisco Visit: Fiery Reaction." *An-Nahar Arab Report*, vol. 1, no. 7 (April 20, 1970), pp. 2–3.

"Soviet Aid to Arab Countries." *An-Nahar Arab Report*, vol. 1, no. 4 (March 30, 1970), Backgrounder.

"Soviet–Arab Economic Relations–1." *An-Nahar Arab Report*, vol. 4, no. 2 (January 8, 1973). Backgrounder.

"Soviet–Egyptian Relations." *An-Nahar Arab Report*, vol. 2, no. 23 (June 7, 1971), Backgrounder.

"Soviet–Egyptian Relations: Assurances Needed." *An-Nahar Arab Report*, vol. 2, no. 33 (August 16, 1971), pp. 1–2.

"Soviet Military Aid to the Arab World, 1967–1972." *An-Nahar Arab Report*, vol. 4, no. 1 (January 1973). Backgrounder.

"Soviet Strength in Egypt Said to Be Lowest Since '55." *The Washington Post*, August 20, 1972, p. A17.

"Soviet–Yemen Relations: Coming out of Cold." *An-Nahar Arab Report*, vol. 2, no. 47 (November 22, 1971), p. 4.

"Sudan: A Moscow Visit." *An-Nahar Arab Report*, vol. 2, no. 17 (April 26, 1971), pp. 3–4.

"Sudan Coup: Major Blunders." *An-Nahar Arab Report*, vol. 2, no. 31 (August 2, 1971), pp. 1–2.

"Sudanese Communist Party: Difficult Survival." *An-Nahar Arab Report*, vol. 1, no. 27 (September 7, 1970), Backgrounder.

"Sudanese Communist Party: Growing Tension." *An-Nahar Arab Report*, vol. 2, no. 14 (April 5, 1971), pp. 1–2.

"Syria and the Soviet Union: Another Treaty?" *An-Nahar Arab Report*, vol. 2, no. 25 (June 21, 1971), pp. 3–4.

"Syria: Moscow's Feelings." *An-Nahar Arab Report*, vol. 1, no. 21 (July 27, 1970), pp. 3–4.

"Syrian Arms—More Political than Military." *Christian Science Monitor*, October 3, 1972, p. 2.

"Syrian Communist Party: Little Influence." *An-Nahar Arab Report*, vol. 1, no. 16 (June 22, 1970), Backgrounder.

Tanner, Henry. "Egypt and Soviet Seek Better Tie." *New York Times*, October 2, 1972, p. 9.

———. "Soviet Pledge to Resume Aid to Egypt is Reported." *New York Times*, October 20, 1972, p. 2.

———. "Soviet–Egypt Rift Persists, Causing Strains in Cairo." *New York Times*, December 4, 1972, pp. 1, 23.

———. "Tough Talks Due, Egyptians Told." *New York Times*, October 8, 1972, p. 5.

"Tigris–Euphrates Linkup." *Christian Science Monitor*, December 9, 1971, p. 4.

"The Two Yemens: Tension on the Borders." *An-Nahar Arab Report*, vol. 2, no. 50 (December 13, 1971), pp. 1–2.

"U.S. Peace Plan: Nasser's Motives." *An-Nahar Arab Report*, vol. 1, no. 24 (August 17, 1970), pp. 1–2.

"Whither go the Palestinians." *An-Nahar Arab Report*, vol. 2, no. 8 (February 22, 1971), Backgrounder.

Wohl, Paul. "New Soviet Strategy in the Middle East." *Christian Science Monitor*, October 2, 1972, pp. 1, 4.

———. "Soviets Vow Support for Palestinians." *Christian Science Monitor*, September 26, 1972, pp. 1, 14.

———. "What Soviet Aims Are in Mideast." *Christian Science Monitor*, August 21, 1972, p. 9.

Sources Regularly Consulted

Al-Ahram. Cairo daily newspaper (Arabic).

An-Nahar. Beirut daily newspaper (Arabic).

Christian Science Monitor. Boston daily newspaper (English).

Foreign Broadcast Information Service.

Jeune Afrique. Paris weekly magazine (French).

Middle East Economic Digest. Weekly journal (English).

New York Times. New York daily newspaper (English).

Washington Post. Washington, D.C. daily newspaper (English).

Index

Index

About the Author

R.D. McLaurin is a research scientist at The American Institutes for Research. Following his undergraduate education at the University of Southern California and the Université de Tunis, he received the Ph.D. from the Fletcher School of Law and Diplomacy, Tufts University. Dr. McLaurin taught international relations at Merrimack College in 1966–1967, and was on the staff of the Office of the Assistant Secretary of Defense (International Security Affairs) before joining A.I.R. in 1969.

**The Middle East in
Soviet Policy**